수능 고난도 어휘까지 해결하는 진정한 어휘력

어휘끝

블랙

영단어 암기장

BLACK

words & phrases

□□ amendment	몡 (법의) 개정; 수정(안)	□□ ingest	통 삼키다, 먹다
□□ asset	몡 자산; 이점	□□ inject	통 주사하다, 주입하다; (자금을) 투입하다
□□ be supposed to-v	v하기로 되어 있다, v해야 한다	□□ irritate	통 짜증나게 하다
□□ commit	통 (범죄 등을) 저지르다; 약속하다; 전념하다	□□ litter	통 (쓰레기 등을) 버리다 몡 (길바닥에 버려진) 쓰레기
□□ complicated	혱 복잡한	□□ magnificent	혱 장엄한, 훌륭한
□□ dedicate	통 (시간 등을) 바치다, 헌신하다	□□ manual	혱 손으로 하는 몡 설명서
□□ deprive A of B	A에게서 B를 박탈하다[빼앗다]	□□ notorious	혱 악명 높은
□□ distraction	몡 주의 산만; 기분 전환	□□ prosperity	몡 번영, 번창
□□ emerge	통 모습을 드러내다; 생겨나다	□□ realm	몡 (활동·관심 등의) 영역, 범위
□□ eternal	혱 영원한	□□ sanitation	몡 위생 시설
□□ exclusive	혱 배타적인; 독점적인 몡 독점기사	□□ sculpt	통 조각하다
□□ feature	몡 특색, 특징; 이목구비; 특집 (기사)	□□ shrug off	~을 대수롭지 않게 취급하다
		□□ strive	통 노력하다, 분투하다
□□ gist	몡 요지, 요점	□□ suspicion	몡 혐의; 의심, 불신
□□ hypothesis	몡 가설; 추측	□□ sustain	통 견디다; 지속하다
□□ incense	몡 (의식에 쓰이는) 향 통 몹시 화나게 하다	□□ tease	통 놀리다, 장난하다
		□□ televise	통 텔레비전으로 방송하다
□□ inherit	통 물려받다; 상속하다	□□ withdraw	통 물러나다; (돈을) 인출하다; 철회하다

Prefixes | 부정, 반대(1) in -¹

□□ inanimate	혱 무생물의; 죽은 (것 같은)	□□ immemorial	혱 (기억·기록에 없을 만큼) 태곳적[아득한 옛적]부터의
□□ animation	몡 생기; 만화영화	□□ memorial	몡 기념비(적인 것)
□□ animism	몡 애니미즘		혱 (죽은 사람을) 기념하기 위한, 추모의
□□ inapplicable	혱 사용[적용]할 수 없는	□□ immortal	혱 죽지 않는; 불멸의
□□ incessant	혱 ((부정적)) 끊임없는, 쉴 새 없는		몡 신(神), 영생하는 존재
□□ indivisible	혱 나눌 수 없는, 분리될 수 없는	□□ immortality	몡 불사, 불멸
□□ inhumane	혱 비인간적인; 잔혹한	□□ impartial	혱 공정한, 공평한
□□ insatiable	혱 만족시킬 수 없는, 만족할 줄 모르는	□□ illiterate	혱 문맹의; 잘 모르는
□□ instability	몡 불안정		몡 문맹자
□□ instable	혱 불안정한	□□ illiteracy	몡 문맹; 무식
□□ intangible	혱 손으로 만질 수 없는, 무형(無形)의	□□ illogical	혱 비논리적인, 터무니없는
□□ invariable	혱 변함없는 몡 변치 않는 것	□□ irrelevant	혱 무관한
		□□ irrelevance	몡 무관함
		□□ irresistible	혱 저항할 수 없는; 억누를 수 없는

Essential Roots / Stems | fin(e)

□□ infinite	혱 무한한	□□ confine	동 (활동·주제 등을) 국한하다; 가두다
□□ infinity	몡 무한함	□□ confinement	몡 제한; 감금, 구금
□□ infinitive	몡 ((문법)) 부정사	□□ define	동 (범위를) 한정하다, 규정하다; (단어 뜻을) 정의하다
□□ final	몡 결승; 기말시험 혱 마지막의	□□ definition	몡 한정; 정의
□□ finalize	동 마무리 짓다	□□ definite	혱 뚜렷한, 명확한
□□ finalist	몡 결승전 진출자	□□ definitely	부 분명히; 절대로
□□ finale	몡 마지막 부분, 피날레	□□ definitive	혱 최종적인, 확정적인; 최고의

Words with Multiple Meanings | 필수 다의어의 이해

□□ fair	혱 공정한, 공평한 혱 타당한, 온당한 혱 (날씨가) 맑은 몡 박람회, 전시회
□□ fine	혱 질 높은, 좋은, 훌륭한 혱 (알갱이가) 고운; (실 등이) 가는 몡 벌금 동 벌금을 물리다
□□ arrest	동 체포하다 몡 체포 동 (무엇의 진행을) 막다, 저지하다 몡 저지, 정지 동 (시선·관심을) 끌다
□□ change	동 변하다; 변화시키다 몡 변화 동 환전하다 몡 거스름돈, 잔돈 동 (기차·비행기 등을) 갈아타다 동 (옷을) 갈아입다 동 (침대 시트·기저귀 등을) 갈다 몡 색다른 변화, 기분 전환

Phrasal Verbs | up이 포함된 구동사 1

□□ blow up   (전체적으로[완전히] 날아가다) 폭파시키다

□□ break up   (전체적으로[완전히] 부수다[깨지다]) 부수다; 끝나다; 해산하다

□□ brush up (on)   (솔질해서 나타나게 하다) 복습하다

□□ build up   (만들어 증가시키다) 기르다

□□ burn up   (완전히 타버리다[불타오르다]) 전소하다, 완전히 타버리다; 열이 나다

□□ call up   (불러서 나타나게 하다) 기억해 내다

□□ catch up with   (~을 다가가서 붙잡다) 따라잡다

Themes | 의사소통

□□ remark   동 (사실이나 의견을) 언급하다, 발언하다 명 발언

□□ remarkable   형 주목할 만한

□□ remarkably   부 현저하게, 매우

□□ blurt   동 (잘 생각해보지도 않고) 불쑥 말하다

□□ allude   동 ((to)) 암시하다, 시사하다; 넌지시 말하다

□□ allusion   명 암시

□□ avow   동 공언하다, 맹세하다

□□ avowal   명 공언, 맹세

□□ mumble   동 중얼거리다 명 중얼거림

□□ halting   형 (말이) 자꾸 끊어지는; 멈칫거리는

□□ stammer   동 말을 더듬다

□□ reserved   형 (감정·의견 등에 대해) 말을 잘 하지 않는, 내성적인

□□ maintain   동 유지하다; 지키다; (남들은 믿지 않는 것을 사실이라고) 주장하다

□□ maintenance   명 유지, 관리; 주장

□□ argue   동 논(의)하다; 말다툼하다

□□ argument   명 논의; 논거; 말다툼

□□ argumentation   명 논증

□□ discourse   동 이야기하다 명 담론, (진지한) 토론; 담화

□□ refute   동 반박하다; 부인하다

□□ convince   동 납득시키다, 확신시키다; 설득하다

□□ convincing   형 설득력 있는

□□ assure   동 장담하다; (~임을)확인하다; 보장하다

□□ assurance   명 보증; 확신

□□ eloquent   형 웅변을 잘하는; 설득력 있는

□□ eloquence   명 웅변; 유창한 화술; 설득력

□□ eloquently   부 웅변[능변]으로

□□ coax   동 구슬리다, 달래다

□□ exhort   동 권고하다, 간곡히 타이르다

□□ exhortation   명 간곡한 권고

□□ recount   동 (특히 자신이 경험한 것을) 이야기하다; (투표용지를) 재검표하다 명 (투표 등의) 재검

□□ demonstrate   동 (실례·증거를 들어가며) 보여주다; (사용법 등을) 설명하다; 시위에 참여하다

□□ demonstration   명 입증; (시범) 설명; 시위

□□ denote   동 표시하다; 의미하다

□□ denotation   명 명시적 의미

02 강

words & phrases

□□ auction	몡 경매 용 경매로 팔다
□□ biased	혱 편향된, 선입견이 있는
□□ checkpoint	몡 (특히 국경의) 검문소
□□ conservation	몡 보존; 보호
□□ contribute	용 기부하다; 기여하다; (~의) 한 원인이 되다; 기고하다
□□ corpse	몡 (사람의) 시체, 송장
□□ counterattack	몡 역습, 반격 용 역습[반격]하다
□□ currency	몡 통화, 화폐; 통용
□□ enormity	몡 엄청남; 심각함
□□ executive	몡 경영진, 중역 혱 경영의
□□ footwear	몡 신발(류)
□□ furious	혱 몹시 화가 난; 맹렬한
□□ geographical	혱 지리학의; 지리적인
□□ ghostwrite	용 대필을 해주다, 대신 써주다
□□ grip	용 움켜쥐다; 사로잡다
□□ have yet to-v	아직 v하지 않았다
□□ hypertension	몡 고혈압
□□ identification	몡 신원 확인; 신분증명서
□□ inconvenience	몡 불편(한 사람) 용 불편하게 하다
□□ modesty	몡 겸손; 보통 정도임
□□ panic	몡 (갑작스러운) 극심한 공포; 공황 (상태) 용 공황 상태에 빠지다
□□ populate	용 살다, 거주하다
□□ precaution	몡 예방 조치, 사전 대책
□□ profession	몡 전문직; 공언
□□ racism	몡 민족 우월 의식; 인종 차별(주의)
□□ radical	혱 근본적인; 과격한, 급진적인
□□ registered	혱 등록한; (우편물) 등기의; 정부 허가를 받은
□□ remote	혱 외딴; 동떨어진; 원격의
□□ soothing	혱 달래는, 진정시키는
□□ stockholder	몡 주주
□□ strain	몡 부담, 압박(감) 용 혹사하다, 무리하게 사용하다
□□ synonym	몡 동의어, 유의어
□□ xenophobia	몡 외국인 혐오(증)
□□ Yours sincerely	~ 올림

Prefixes | 부정, 반대(2) un -

□□ undue	혱 지나친, 과도한
□□ unhindered	혱 아무 방해를[제약을] 받지 않는
□□ unwilling	혱 꺼리는; 마지못해 하는
□□ unwillingly	뷔 마지못해
□□ undisturbed	혱 방해받지 않은; 누구도 손 대지 않은
□□ undaunted	혱 (곤경 등에도) 의연한, 흔들림 없는
□□ unchecked	혱 (악화되지 않도록) 억제하지 않고 놔둔; 점검받지 않은
□□ unwind	용 (감긴 것을) 풀다; 긴장을 풀다
□□ untamed	혱 길들지 않은

□□ uneven	형 평평하지 않은; (무늬 등이) 고르지 않은	□□ uninhabited	형 사람이 살지 않는
□□ unnerve	동 불안하게 만들다; 용기를 잃게 하다	□□ uninhibited	형 (행동 등에) 아무 제약을 받지 않는, 거리낌이 없는
□□ unrest	명 (사회·정치적인) 불안, 불만	□□ unintentional	형 고의가 아닌, 무심코 한
□□ unleash	동 속박을 풀다; (분노 등을) 폭발시키다	□□ unintentionally	부 무심코
□□ unidentified	형 정체불명의, 신원 미상의	□□ unattended	형 돌보는 사람이 없는; 내버려 둔

Essential Roots / Stems | equa(l) / equi

□□ unequal	형 (크기·양 등이) 다른; 불공평한	□□ equivalent	형 (가치 등이) 동등한, 맞먹는 명 (~에) 상당하는 것
□□ equalize	동 동등하게 하다; 평형을 이루다	□□ equivalence	명 동등함
□□ equalizer	명 평형[균형] 장치; (축구 등에서의) 동점 골	□□ equilibrate	동 평형을 유지하다
□□ equality	명 평등; 균등	□□ equilibrium	명 평형, 균형 (상태); (마음의) 평정
□□ equate	동 동일시하다	□□ equivocal	형 두 가지 뜻으로 해석되는; (말이) 모호한; (태도가) 애매한, 불분명한
□□ equation	명 동일시; 등식; 방정식		
□□ equator	명 (지구의) 적도	□□ equilateral	형 등변의
□□ equity	명 공평, 공정	□□ equinox	명 춘분; 추분
□□ equitable	형 공평한, 공정한		

Words with Multiple Meanings | 필수 다의어의 이해

□□ article	명 (신문·잡지의) 글, 기사 명 (합의서·계약서의) 조항 명 (특히 세트로 된 물건의 개별) 물품, 물건 명 ((문법)) 관사
□□ assume	동 (사실일 것으로) 추정하다 동 (권력·책임을) 맡다 동 (특질·양상을) 띠다, 취하다 동 ~인 척하다, 가장하다
□□ bar	명 술집, 바 명 (특정 음식·음료를 파는) 전문점, 매장 명 (일반적인) 변호사직, 변호사단 명 장애물, 차단물 동 (문을) 잠그다; 방해하다; 금하다
□□ circulate	동 (피·공기 등이) 순환하다 동 (정보·소문 등이) 퍼지다 동 (신문·책 등을) 배부하다 동 (통화를) 유통하다

Phrasal Verbs | up이 포함된 구동사 2

□□ come up with   (~을 가지고 올라오다) 생각해 내다

□□ dress up   (완전히 차려입다) 변장하다; 잘 차려입다

□□ dry up   (완전히 마르다) 바싹 마르다; 말문이 막히다

□□ end up (with)   (끝에 드러내다[드러나다]) 결국 (~하다); 얻게 되다

□□ hang up   (위에 걸다) 끊다

Themes | 언어·문학

□□ linguistic   혱 언어(학)의

□□ linguistics   몡 언어학

□□ linguist   몡 언어학자; 외국어에 능통한 사람

□□ derive   동 (~에서) 비롯되다; 유래하다

□□ lexicon   몡 어휘 (목록); 사전

□□ lexical   혱 어휘의

□□ semantic   혱 의미의; 의미론적인

□□ fluent   혱 유창한; 능란한

□□ accent   몡 (출신 지역이나 계층을 나타내주는) 말씨; 강세; 강조 동 강조하다

□□ accentuate   동 강조하다, 두드러지게 하다

□□ articulate   동 또렷이 말하다; (생각을) 분명히 표현하다 혱 (말이) 또렷한

□□ articulation   몡 (말로 하는) 표현; 발음

□□ consonant   몡 자음

□□ abbreviate   동 (어구 등을) 줄여 쓰다

□□ abbreviation   몡 (단어·구 등의) 축약(형), 약어

□□ analogy   몡 유사점; 비유; 유추

□□ analogous   혱 유사한

□□ paraphrase   동 (이해를 더 쉽게 하려고) 다른 말로 바꾸어 표현하다 몡 다른 말로 바꾸어 표현한 것

□□ formal   혱 형식상의; 격식을 차린; 공식적인

□□ formality   몡 형식상의 절차; 격식

□□ excerpt   몡 (글·음악 등의) 발췌[인용] (부분) 동 발췌하다, 인용하다

□□ proverbial   혱 속담에 나오는; 유명한, 소문이 나 있는

□□ terminology   몡 전문 용어

□□ literary   혱 문학의; (언어·문제가) 문학적인

□□ stylistic   혱 문체의; 양식의

□□ critique   몡 평론, 비평 동 평론[비평]하다

□□ verse   몡 운문, 시; (시의) 연; (노래의) 절

□□ memoir   몡 ((pl.)) (유명인의) 회고록

□□ anecdote   몡 (주로 짧고 재미있는) 일화

□□ fictional   혱 허구의; 소설적인

□□ plot   몡 (극 등의) 구성; 음모 동 구성하다; 음모하다

□□ episode   몡 (소설 등에서 중요한) 사건; (TV 등 연속 프로그램의) 1회 방송분

words & phrases

□□ ally	명 동맹국
□□ application	명 지원(서); 적용, 응용; (페인트·크림 등을) 바르기
□□ backbone	명 척추; 근간
□□ capacitor	명 축전기
□□ conviction	명 유죄 선고; 확신
□□ correspondence	명 유사함; 서신, 편지 (쓰기)
□□ crude	형 천연 그대로의, 미가공의; 조잡한 / 명 원유
□□ detergent	명 세제
□□ embrace	동 껴안다; (생각을) 받아들이다; 포괄하다
□□ ennoble	동 기품을 주다; 귀족에 봉하다
□□ issue	명 문제; 발표; 발행
□□ lightning rod	명 피뢰침
□□ mission statement	명 (기업의) 강령
□□ monk	명 수도승, 수도자
□□ outweigh	동 ~보다 더 크다[대단하다]
□□ over-the-counter	형 계산대에서의; (약을) 처방전 없이 살 수 있는
□□ parliament	명 의회, 국회; ((P-)) 영국 의회
□□ part with	(자기가 갖고 싶은 것을) 내주다
□□ patent	명 특허권 / 동 특허를 받다 / 형 특허의
□□ radiation	명 (열·에너지 등의) 복사; 방사선
□□ recession	명 불황; 물러남
□□ scheme	명 (운영) 계획, 제도; 책략 / 동 책략을 꾸미다
□□ sewage	명 하수, 오물
□□ soar	동 급등하다; (하늘 높이) 날다
□□ solute	명 용질
□□ solvent	명 용매
□□ sprinter	명 단거리 경주 선수
□□ stain	명 얼룩; 오점
□□ subsidy	명 보조금, 장려금
□□ summon	동 (법원으로) 소환하다, 호출하다; (의회를) 소집하다
□□ testimony	명 (법정에서의) 증언; 증거
□□ torture	명 고문 / 동 고문하다
□□ transaction	명 처리; 거래, 매매
□□ widow	명 미망인, 과부

Prefixes | 부정, 반대(3) dis -¹ / de -¹

□□ disapprove	동 반대하다; 못마땅해하다
□□ disapproval	명 반대; 못마땅함
□□ discontent	명 불만
□□ disregard	동 무시하다, 묵살하다 / 명 무시, 묵살
□□ disprove	동 틀렸음을 입증하다, 반박하다
□□ disproof	명 반증, 논박
□□ dissuade	동 설득해서 ~하지 않도록 하다, 단념시키다
□□ dissuasion	명 (설득하여) 단념시킴
□□ disgrace	명 망신, 수치; 불명예
□□ disintegrate	동 해체되다, 분해되다; 붕괴시키다

□□ disintegration	몡 분해; 붕괴	□□ demerit	몡 단점, 결점; 벌점
□□ disqualify	동 (규칙 등을 위반하여) 자격을 박탈하다, 실격시키다	□□ deplete	동 고갈시키다, 격감시키다
		□□ depletion	몡 (자원 등의) 고갈, 소모
□□ dispassionate	혱 감정에 좌우되지 않는; 공정한	□□ deranged	혱 (정신적으로) 정상이 아닌, 미친
□□ decode	동 (암호를) 해독하다; (외국어를) 이해하다	□□ detox	몡 해독; 약물[알코올] 중독 치료

Essential Roots / Stems 1 | clos(e) / clude

□□ disclose	동 드러내다; 폭로하다	□□ inclusive	혱 포함하는; 포괄적인
□□ disclosure	몡 폭로	□□ exclude	동 제외하다; 배제하다
□□ enclose	동 (울타리 등이) 둘러싸다; 동봉하다	□□ exclusion	몡 제외; 배제; 추방
		□□ exclusive	혱 배타적인; 독점적인
□□ conclude	동 결론을 내리다; 끝나다		몡 독점 기사
□□ conclusion	몡 결론	□□ preclude	동 못하게 하다, 불가능하게 하다
□□ include	동 포함하다		
□□ inclusion	몡 포함; 함유물	□□ seclude	동 (다른 사람들로부터) 은둔하다, 고립시키다

Essential Roots / Stems 2 | cred / creed

□□ credit	동 믿다; 입금하다 몡 신용 (거래); 입금; 칭찬, 인정	□□ incredible	혱 믿을 수 없는; 놀라운
		□□ credulous	혱 잘 믿는, 잘 속는
		□□ incredulous	혱 잘 믿지 않는; 의심 많은
□□ creditor	몡 채권자	□□ credential	몡 ((pl.)) 신임장; 신용증명서
□□ discredit	동 신임을 떨어뜨리다; 신용하지 않다 몡 불명예	□□ accredit	동 (어떤 일을) ~가 한 것으로 믿다; 승인하다, 인가하다
□□ credible	혱 믿을 수 있는	□□ creed	몡 교리; 신조, 신념
□□ credibility	몡 신뢰성		

Words with Multiple Meanings | 필수 다의어의 이해

□□ credit	몡 신용 몡 신용 거래 몡 입금 동 입금하다 몡 칭찬, 인정 몡 크레디트
□□ dissolve	동 (고체가) 녹다; (고체를) 용해하다 동 분해하다 동 분해[용해]되어 없어지다 동 (결혼생활 등을) 끝내다 동 (조직·의회 등을) 해체하다, 해산하다

□□ charge	동 (요금·값을) 청구하다 명 요금 동 신용카드로 사다; (외상으로) 달아 놓다
	동 책임을 맡기다 명 (사람·일에 대한) 책임, 담당 동 기소하다 명 (검사의) 기소
	동 충전하다 동 공격하다, 돌격하다
□□ discharge	동 (기체·액체를) 흘리다 동 (에너지를) 방출하다 명 방출 동 발사[발포]하다
	동 (전기를) 방전하다
	동 석방하다; 퇴원시키다; 제대시키다; 해고하다 명 제대; 해고 동 부채를 갚다

Phrasal Verbs | up이 포함된 구동사 3

□□ hold up	(서 있게 하다; 위로 떠받치다)	□□ look up	(봐서 드러나게 하다) 찾아보다
	지연되다; 떠받들다	□□ make up	(~을 만들어내다 / ~에 이르게
□□ keep up	(계속 위에 있게 하다) 계속하다		하다) 차지하다; 날조하다; 화해
□□ keep up with	(~에 계속해서 다가가다) 알다		하다

Themes | 인생·관계

□□ elapse	동 (시간이) 흐르다	□□ relevance	명 관련(성); 적절
□□ brevity	명 (시간이) 짧음; 간결(성)	□□ bond	명 유대; 결속; 채권
□□ temporary	형 일시적인, 임시의		동 유대감을 형성하다;
□□ sporadic	형 산발적인, 때때로 일어나는		접착시키다
□□ consecutive	형 연이은	□□ socialize	동 (사람들과) 사귀다, 어울리
□□ eternal	형 영원한		다; 사회화시키다
□□ eternity	명 영원, 영구	□□ socialization	명 사회화
□□ onset	명 (특히 불쾌한 일의) 시작;	□□ sociality	명 사교성
	(적군의) 공격	□□ intimate	형 친밀한; 개인적인
□□ retard	동 (발달·진전을) 지연시키다		동 넌지시 알리다
□□ reminiscent	형 연상시키는; 추억에 잠긴	□□ intimacy	명 친밀함
	듯한	□□ split	동 쪼개다; 분리하다;
□□ destiny	명 운명; 운명의 힘		(의견 차이로) 분열되다
□□ destined	형 (운명으로) 예정된; ~행의		명 쪼개짐; 분열
□□ doom	동 불행한 운명을 맞게 하다	□□ alienate	동 (사람을) 소원하게 하다
	명 파멸; (피할 수 없는) 비운	□□ alienated	형 소원한, 소외감을 느끼는
□□ immature	형 다 자라지 못한; 치기 어린	□□ alienation	명 소외; 멀리함
□□ longevity	명 장수; 오래 지속됨	□□ isolate	동 격리하다; 분리하다
□□ perish	동 (갑자기) 죽다; 멸망하다	□□ isolated	형 외딴; 고립된
□□ perishable	형 (특히 식품이) 잘 상하는	□□ isolation	명 고립, 격리
□□ relevant	형 관련된; 적절한	□□ peer	명 또래, 동년배
			동 유심히 보다

04 강

words & phrases

☐☐ bow	동 (고개 등을) 숙이다 명 인사 명 활; 나비 모양 (매듭)
☐☐ capitalism	명 자본주의
☐☐ competitor	명 경쟁자; (시합) 참가자
☐☐ constitution	명 구성; 체질; 헌법; 설립
☐☐ dab	동 (여러 번 가볍게) 만지다; 살짝 바르다
☐☐ dedication	명 헌신, 전념
☐☐ deduce	동 추론하다, 연역하다
☐☐ devote	동 (노력·시간 등을) (~에) 바치다, 쏟다
☐☐ diaper	명 기저귀
☐☐ donor	명 기부자, 기증자
☐☐ enthusiasm	명 열심, 의욕
☐☐ ethnic	형 민족의; 민족 전통적인
☐☐ function	명 기능; 함수 동 기능하다
☐☐ fungi	명 균류
☐☐ gigantic	형 거대한
☐☐ impractical	형 비현실적인; 비실용적인
☐☐ inopportune	형 시기가 안 좋은
☐☐ landfill	명 쓰레기 매립지
☐☐ lawmaker	명 입법자, 국회의원
☐☐ mischievous	형 짓궂은; 해를 끼치는
☐☐ misdemeanor	명 경범죄, 비행
☐☐ parallel park	(차를) 평행 주차하다
☐☐ petty	형 사소한, 하찮은
☐☐ pollen	명 꽃가루
☐☐ quarrel	동 다투다 명 다툼, 언쟁
☐☐ regime	명 제도, 체제; 정권
☐☐ respondent	명 (조사의) 응답자
☐☐ rinse	동 (물로) 씻다, 헹구다
☐☐ scar	명 흉터, 상처 동 흉터[상처]를 남기다
☐☐ set off	출발하다; 터뜨리다
☐☐ spell	동 (단어의) 철자를 말하다 [쓰다]
☐☐ spoilage	명 (음식·식품의) 부패, 손상
☐☐ vineyard	명 포도밭
☐☐ wound	명 상처, 부상 동 상처를 입히다

Prefixes | 맞섬·반대(1) ant(i) -, ob -

☐☐ antioxidant	명 항산화제, 노화 방지제; 방부제
☐☐ antidote(s)	명 해독제; 해결책
☐☐ antigen	명 항원
☐☐ antiseptic	명 소독제 형 소독[살균]이 되는
☐☐ antagonism	명 적의, 적대감
☐☐ antagonist	명 적대자
☐☐ antibacterial	형 항균성의
☐☐ obliterate	동 (흔적을) 없애다, 지우다
☐☐ obsolete	형 구식의
☐☐ obstruct	동 (진로 등을) 막다; (진행을) 방해하다
☐☐ obstruction	명 방해; (도로 등의) 차단; 장애물

Essential Roots / Stems 1 | onym

□□ antonym 명 반의어

□□ synonym 명 동의어, 유의어

□□ synonymous 형 동의어의; 아주 밀접한

□□ anonymous 형 익명의

□□ anonymity 명 익명(성)

□□ acronym 명 두문자어

□□ homonym 명 동음이의어; 동철이의어

□□ pseudonym 명 (특히 작가의) 필명

Essential Roots / Stems 2 | pos(e) / pon(e)

□□ oppose 동 (계획 등에) 반대하다; (누구와) 겨루다

□□ opposite 형 맞은편의 명 반대, 반대되는 사람[것]

□□ opposition 명 반대, 항의; 대립; 야당

□□ opponent 명 반대자; (대회 등의) 상대

□□ compose 동 구성하다; 작곡하다; 쓰다, 작문하다

□□ composition 명 구성(요소들); 작곡; 작문

□□ composite 형 합성의 명 합성물

□□ component 명 (구성)요소, 부품

□□ decompose 동 (화학작용에 의해) 분해되다; 부패하다

□□ decomposition 명 분해; 부패

□□ expose 동 (가려져 있는 것을) 드러내다; 노출시키다; 폭로하다

□□ exposure 명 노출; 폭로

□□ exposition 명 (상세한) 설명; 전시회, 박람회

□□ propose 동 제안하다; 청혼하다

□□ proposal 명 제안, 청혼

□□ proposition 명 (사업상) 제의; (처리할) 일; 명제

□□ proponent 명 제의[제안]자; 지지자

Words with Multiple Meanings | 필수 다의어의 이해

□□ offend 동 기분 상하게 하다, 불쾌하게 하다 동 범죄를 저지르다
동 (도덕·상식 등에) 위배되다, 어긋나다

□□ bear 동 (눈에 보이게) 있다, 지니다 동 (지닌 무게를) 지탱하다 동 견디다, 참다
동 (아이를) 낳다 동 (결실·열매를) 맺다 동 (~임을) 명심하다, 유념하다

□□ beat 동 (계속) 치다, 두드리다 동 (게임·시합에서) 이기다 동 더 낫다, 능가하다
동 (심장이) 뛰다, 고동치다 명 고동, 맥박
동 (북이) 둥둥 울리다 명 (북 등의) 울림 명 (음악·시 등의) 운율, 박자, 비트

□□ deal 명 거래(서) 동 거래하다 동 (문제 등을) 처리하다, 다루다 명 취급, 처리 명 많은 양, 상당량

Phrasal Verbs | up이 포함된 구동사 4

☐☐ make up for   (~을 완전하게 만들다)
보충하다; 보상하다

☐☐ pick up   (집어 올리다) 집어 들다;
(차로) 데려가다; 들어서
익히다; 좋아지다

☐☐ pile up   (쌓여서 증가하다) 쌓이다

☐☐ pull up   (완전히 끌어당기다)
(차를) 세우다

☐☐ put up with   참다

Themes | 교육

☐☐ instruct   图 지시하다; 가르치다

☐☐ instruction   명 교육; ((pl.)) 지시, 지도;
설명서

☐☐ instructive   형 교육적인; 유익한

☐☐ instructional   형 교육용의

☐☐ institute   명 (교육 관련) 기관, 협회
图 (제도 등을) 도입하다

☐☐ aptitude   명 적성, 소질

☐☐ potential   명 잠재력; 가능성
형 잠재력이 있는

☐☐ potentiality   명 잠재력

☐☐ latent   형 잠재하는; 잠복하고 있는

☐☐ faculty   명 (타고난) 능력;
(대학의) 학부; 교수단

☐☐ prodigy   명 영재

☐☐ prodigious   형 엄청난, 굉장한

☐☐ academic   형 학업의; 학구적인 명 교수

☐☐ interpret   图 (의미를) 설명하다;
해석[이해]하다; 통역하다

☐☐ interpretation   명 설명; 해석, 이해; 통역

☐☐ grasp   图 꽉 잡다; 이해하다
명 움켜잡기; 이해, 파악

☐☐ persevere   图 인내심을 갖고 계속하다

☐☐ perseverance   명 인내(심), 끈기

☐☐ exert   图 발휘하다; (영향력을) 행사
하다; 노력하다

☐☐ exertion   명 (영향력의) 행사; 노력

☐☐ quest   명 탐구, 탐색 图 탐구하다

☐☐ specialize   图 전공하다; 전문적으로 다루
다

☐☐ specialized   형 전문적인

☐☐ specialization   명 전문화; 전문 분야

☐☐ liberal arts   명 교양과목

☐☐ assess   图 평가하다; (자질 등을) 가늠
하다

☐☐ assessment   명 평가

☐☐ preliminary   형 예비의
명 예비 행위[단계]; 예선

☐☐ compliment   명 칭찬(의 말), 찬사
图 칭찬하다

☐☐ complimentary   형 칭찬하는; 무료의

☐☐ certify   图 (특히 서면으로) 증명하다;
자격증을 교부하다

☐☐ certificate   명 증명서; 자격증, 면허증

☐☐ qualify   图 자격을 주다[얻다]

☐☐ qualification   명 자격(증); 조건

☐☐ qualified   형 자격(증)이 있는

☐☐ thesis   명 학위 논문; 논지

☐☐ yearbook   명 졸업 앨범; 연감

words & phrases

□□ absentee	명 결석자, 불참자	□□ interdisciplinary	형 학제 간의
□□ aftermath	명 여파, 후유증	□□ inventory	명 물품 목록; 재고(품)
□□ allure	명 매력	□□ knob	명 손잡이
□□ ban	동 금지하다	□□ nonproliferation	명 (핵의) 확산 방지
	명 금지(법)	□□ opposition party	명 ((정치)) 야당
□□ candidate	명 입후보자, 출마자; (일자리의) 후보자		
		□□ presidency	명 대통령직[임기]; 회장직[임기]
□□ cathedral	명 대성당		
□□ compelling	형 강력한; 눈을 뗄 수 없는	□□ profoundly	부 (영향 등을) 깊이; 완전히
□□ conduct	동 수행하다; 행동하다	□□ recurrence	명 재발; 반복
□□ confirm	동 확실히 하다; 사실임을 보여주다	□□ referee	명 심판
		□□ seize	동 와락 붙잡다; 압수하다
□□ corporation	명 기업, 회사; 법인	□□ supplement	명 보충(물); 부록; 추가 요금
□□ coverage	명 적용 범위; 보도[방송] (범위); ((보험)) 보상 (범위)		동 보충하다
		□□ tariff	명 관세
□□ cover letter	명 자기소개서; 첨부서	□□ troop	명 무리; ((pl.)) 군대
□□ dawn	명 새벽, 여명		동 무리 지어 걸어가다
□□ eliminate	동 없애다	□□ twine	명 노끈 동 휘감다
□□ embark	동 (배·비행기에) 승선하다; ((on)) 시작하다	□□ unethical	형 비윤리적인
		□□ vendor	명 (거리의) 행상인, 노점상
□□ humanity	명 인류; 인간성; ((the -ies)) 인문학	□□ warrant	명 근거; 보증서; (체포) 영장

Prefixes | 맞섬 반대(2) counter -

□□ counteract 〔동〕~에 반대로 작용하다, 대응 하다; (효과 등을) 없애다

□□ counteractive 〔형〕반작용의; 중화성의 〔명〕중화제

□□ counteraction 〔명〕반작용; (약의) 중화 작용

□□ counterattack 〔명〕(전쟁·게임·논쟁 등에서의) 역습, 반격 〔동〕역습[반격]하다

□□ counterclockwise 〔형〕시계 반대 방향의 〔부〕시계 반대 방향으로

□□ counterproductive 〔형〕역효과를 낳는; 비생산 적인

□□ countermand 〔동〕(특히 다른 주문을 하여 앞의 주문을) 철회하다, 취소하다 〔명〕철회[취소] 명령

□□ countermeasure 〔명〕대응책; 보호 조치

□□ counteroffer 〔명〕대안; ((상업)) 수정 제안

□□ counterparty 〔명〕(계약 등의) 한쪽 당사자

□□ countervail 〔동〕(반대 작용으로) 무효로 만들다; 상쇄하다

Essential Roots / Stems | fac(t) / fec(t) / fic(i) / feit

□□ counterfeit 〔형〕위조의, 모조의 〔동〕위조하다, 모조하다

□□ factor 〔명〕요인, 인자; (측정) 지수

□□ artifact 〔명〕(역사적·문화적으로 의의가 있는) 인공물, 공예품

□□ affect 〔동〕영향을 주다; (질병이) 발생 하다; ~인 척하다

□□ affectation 〔명〕꾸밈; 가장

□□ defect 〔명〕결함, 결점 〔동〕(정당·국가 등을) 떠나다

□□ defective 〔형〕결함이 있는

□□ deficient 〔형〕(필수적인 것이) 부족한, 결핍된; 결함이 있는

□□ deficiency 〔명〕결핍(증); 결함

□□ effective 〔형〕효과적인

□□ efficient 〔형〕효율적인

□□ efficiency 〔명〕효율(성); 능률

□□ infect 〔동〕감염시키다; 오염시키다

□□ infection 〔명〕감염; 전염병

□□ infectious 〔형〕전염성의

□□ magnificent 〔형〕장엄한, 훌륭한

□□ magnificence 〔명〕훌륭함

□□ proficient 〔형〕능숙한, 숙달된

□□ proficiency 〔명〕능숙, 숙달

□□ sufficient 〔형〕충분한

□□ suffice 〔동〕충분하다

Words with Multiple Meanings | 필수 다의어의 이해

□□ board 〔명〕게시판, 칠판 〔명〕(숙박업소 등의) 식사(비) 〔동〕하숙하다 〔명〕위원회, 이사회 〔동〕(배·비행기 등에) 탑승하다

□□ bill 〔명〕계산서, 청구서 〔명〕지폐 〔명〕(국회에 제출된) 법안 〔명〕전단, 벽보 〔명〕(새의) 부리

□□ break 〔동〕깨다, 부수다 〔동〕고장 나다 〔동〕(법·약속 등을) 어기다 〔동〕(기록을) 깨다 〔동〕(나쁜 버릇 등을) 그만두다, 끊다 〔동〕(날이) 밝다 〔동〕휴식하다 〔명〕휴식

Phrasal Verbs | up이 포함된 구동사 5

□□ set up　(위로 세우다) 세우다; 시작하다; 만들다

□□ sign up　(서명을 해서 (이름을) 드러내다) 등록하다

□□ stay up　((몸자세가) 높은 상태로 있다) 깨어 있다

□□ take up　(완전히 취하다) 차지하다; 시작하다; 계속 (이야기)하다

□□ turn up　(돌려서 (힘·소리 등을) 증가시키다; 돌려서 나타나다) 올리다; 발견되다

Themes | 정치·외교

□□ policy　몡 정책, 방침; 보험 증권

□□ doctrine　몡 정책; 교리

□□ instill　동 (어떤 의식 등을) 서서히 주입시키다

□□ intrigue　몡 모의, 음모; 흥미진진함
　　동 음모를 꾸미다; 강한 흥미를 불러일으키다

□□ asylum　몡 망명

□□ govern　동 (국가·국민을) 통치하다; 지배하다

□□ governance　몡 통치; 관리

□□ municipal　톙 지방 자치제의; 시의

□□ federal　톙 연방제의; 연방 정부의

□□ monarchy　몡 군주제; 군주국

□□ parliament　몡 의회, 국회

□□ parliamentary　톙 의회의; 의회가 있는

□□ senate　몡 (미국·캐나다 등의) 상원

□□ senator　몡 상원 의원

□□ nominate　동 (후보자로) 지명하다, 추천하다; 임명하다

□□ nominee　몡 (직책·수상자 등에) 지명된 사람, 후보

□□ constituent　몡 유권자; 구성 성분
　　톙 구성하는

□□ ballot　몡 투표용지; 무기명 투표
　　동 무기명 투표를 하다

□□ poll　몡 투표(수); 여론조사
　　동 득표하다; 여론조사를 하다

□□ inaugural　톙 취임(식)의; 첫

□□ inauguration　몡 취임(식)

□□ tenure　몡 재임 기간; (주택) 임차 기간

□□ faction　몡 당파, 파벌

□□ propaganda　몡 (허위·과장된 정치) 선전

□□ rally　몡 (정치적) 집회
　　동 (지지를 위해) 결집하다

□□ diplomat　몡 외교관

□□ diplomatic　톙 외교의; 외교적 수완이 있는

□□ embassy　몡 대사관

□□ delegate　몡 대표(자)
　　동 대표로 보내다; (권한을) 위임하다

□□ delegation　몡 대표단; 위임

□□ treaty　몡 (국가 간의) 조약, 협정

words & phrases

□□ acute	혱 극심한; ((질병)) 급성의	□□ nausea	몡 메스꺼움
□□ account	몡 (회계) 장부; 계좌; 설명 통 설명하다	□□ navy	몡 해군
		□□ nomination	몡 지명, 추천
□□ administration	몡 관리, 행정(부); 집행	□□ outnumber	통 ~보다 수가 더 많다
□□ allegation	몡 (증거 없는) 주장; 혐의	□□ perceive	통 지각하다, 인지하다
□□ barren	혱 황폐한; 불임의	□□ plaintiff	몡 (민사 소송의) 원고, 고소인
□□ Catholicism	몡 (로마) 가톨릭교, 천주교	□□ province	몡 (수도가 아닌) 지방; (행정 단위인) 주, 도
□□ former	혱 이전의; 옛날의; (둘 중에서) 전자의 몡 ((the ~)) 전자	□□ rebel	몡 반역자 통 반란을 일으키다, 저항하다
□□ further	통 발전[성공]시키다 튄 더 멀리	□□ recession	몡 경기 후퇴, 불황
		□□ remnant	몡 나머지; 자투리(천)
□□ grin	몡 (소리 없이) 활짝 웃음 통 활짝 웃다	□□ smuggler	몡 밀수업자
		□□ storage cell	몡 축전지
□□ huddle	통 (춥거나 무서워서) 모이다; 몸을 움츠리다	□□ subtraction	몡 뺄셈
		□□ technically	튄 엄밀히 말하면; 기술적으로
□□ inflict	통 (괴로움 등을) 가하다	□□ twig	몡 잔가지
□□ lighthouse	몡 등대	□□ warehouse	몡 (판매하기 전에 보관해두는) 창고
□□ manipulate	통 조작하다, 조종하다		

Prefixes | 맞섬·반대(3) contra- / contro-

□□ contradict	통 반박하다; 모순되다	□□ contraband	몡 밀수(품) 혱 수출입 금지의
□□ contradiction	몡 반박, 모순	□□ contravene	통 (법·규칙을) 위반하다
□□ contradictory	혱 모순되는		

Essential Roots / Stems | vert / vers(e)

□□ controvert	통 반박하다, 반증하다	□□ conversation	명 대화
□□ controvertible	형 논쟁의 여지가 있는	□□ conversely	부 반대로
□□ controversy	명 논란	□□ inadvertent	형 의도하지 않은; 부주의한
□□ controversial	형 논란이 많은	□□ inadvertently	부 무심코; 부주의로
□□ versus	전 (경기 등에서) ~대	□□ inadvertence	명 부주의, 소홀
□□ version	명 (이전의 것·비슷한 종류의 다른 것들과 약간 다른) -판 [형태]; 설명, 견해	□□ introvert	명 내성[내향]적인 사람
		□□ introverted	형 내성[내향]적인
□□ versatile	형 다재다능한; 다용도의	□□ revert	통 ((to)) (~로) 되돌아가다
□□ versatility	명 다재다능; 다용도	□□ reverse	통 뒤바꾸다 형 반대의; 뒤의 명 반대; 뒷면
□□ adverse	형 거스르는; 반대하는; 불리한	□□ reversible	형 뒤집어 입을 수 있는; 되돌릴 수 있는
□□ adversity	명 역경		
□□ adversary	명 적; 상대	□□ subvert	통 (체제를) 전복시키다, 파괴하다
□□ invert	통 거꾸로 하다, 뒤집다		
□□ inverse	형 반대의; 역의	□□ pervert	통 왜곡하다; (사람을) 비뚤어지게 하다
□□ convert	통 (형태 등을)전환하다, 개조하다; 개종하다 명 전향자; 개종자	□□ perverse	형 (사고방식 등이) 비뚤어진
		□□ perversity	명 심술궂음, 괴팍함
□□ conversion	명 전환, 개조; 개종	□□ traverse	통 가로지르다, 횡단하다 명 횡단
□□ convertible	형 (다른 형태나 용도로) 전환 가능한 명 컨버터블		
		□□ vice versa	부 거꾸로[반대로]도 또한 같음
□□ converse	통 대화하다 형 정반대의 명 정반대	□□ vertigo	명 현기증

Words with Multiple Meanings | 필수 다의어의 이해

□□ chance	명 우연 명 운 명 기회 명 가능성, 가망
□□ case	명 (특정한 상황의) 경우 명 실정, 사실 명 소송 (사건) 명 (경찰이 조사 중인) 사건
□□ tip	명 끝부분 명 꼭대기, 정상 통 팁을 주다 명 정보 명 조언 통 뒤집어엎다 통 비워 없애다 통 버리다

Phrasal Verbs | away가 포함된 구동사

☐☐ **do away with** (~을 사라지게 하다) 버리다

☐☐ **get away from** (~에서 멀어지다) 벗어나다

☐☐ **pass away** (지나서 사라지다) 돌아가시다

☐☐ **pull away** (서로 멀리 끌어당기다) 밀어 내다

☐☐ **take away** (멀리 가져가다) 멎다; 빼앗다

☐☐ **throw away** (멀리 던지다) (내)버리다

☐☐ **turn away** (돌려보내다) 거절하다

Themes | 군대·전쟁

☐☐ **military** 휑 군사의, 무력의
몡 군대; 군인들

☐☐ **militant** 휑 공격적인, 전투적인
몡 투사

☐☐ **militarize** 동 군대를 파견하다;
무장시키다

☐☐ **arms** 몡 (군대의) 무기; 군비

☐☐ **armed** 휑 무장한

☐☐ **armament** 몡 ((pl.)) 군비, (대형) 무기;
군비 확충

☐☐ **enlist** 동 입대하다; 협력을 요청하다

☐☐ **enlisted** 휑 사병의

☐☐ **array** 동 (군대 등을) 정렬시키다;
배열하다
몡 배치, 배열

☐☐ **salute** 동 (거수)경례하다; 경의를 표 하다
몡 (거수)경례

☐☐ **vanguard** 몡 (군대의) 선봉, 전위;
(사회적 운동의) 선두

☐☐ **morale** 몡 사기, 의욕

☐☐ **confidential** 휑 기밀의; 은밀한; 신뢰를 받는

☐☐ **confidentiality** 휑 기밀, 비밀

☐☐ **general** 몡 (육군) 원수, 장군

☐☐ **combat** 동 싸우다 몡 전투

☐☐ **strategy** 몡 전략

☐☐ **strategic** 휑 전략상의

☐☐ **belligerent** 휑 호전적인, 공격적인; 전쟁 중인
몡 교전국

☐☐ **assault** 동 공격하다; 폭행하다
몡 공격; 폭행

☐☐ **camouflage** 동 위장하다 몡 위장

☐☐ **ally** 몡 동맹국 동 동맹시키다

☐☐ **alliance** 몡 동맹; 동맹 단체

☐☐ **vanquish** 동 (경쟁·전쟁 등에서) 완파 하다

☐☐ **triumphant** 휑 큰 승리를 거둔, 크게 성공 한; 의기양양한

☐☐ **booty** 몡 전리품

☐☐ **surrender** 동 항복하다; (권리 등을) 양도 하다
몡 항복; 양도

☐☐ **ravage** 동 황폐하게 하다, 유린하다

☐☐ **shatter** 동 산산이 부수다; 파괴하다

☐☐ **debris** 몡 (파괴된 후의) 잔해; 쓰레기

☐☐ **casualty** 몡 사상자; 피해자

☐☐ **concentration camp** 몡 포로수용소

☐☐ **armistice** 몡 휴전

words & phrases

□□ breeze	명 산들바람, 미풍
□□ collide	동 충돌하다; (의견 등이) 상충하다
□□ consequence	명 결과; (영향 등의) 중요성
□□ discrimination	명 차별
□□ domestic	형 가정의; 길든; 국내의
□□ dormitory	명 기숙사
□□ firecracker	명 폭죽
□□ forward	부 앞으로 / 동 보내다; 전달하다
□□ giggle	명 (재미, 난처함 등으로) 피식 웃음, 킥킥거림
□□ honorary	형 명예(직)의
□□ interdict	동 금지하다, 막다 / 명 (법원의) 금지 명령
□□ import	동 수입하다 / 명 수입(품)
□□ liberation	명 해방 (운동)
□□ liquor	명 (독한) 술
□□ means	명 수단, 방법
□□ meditative	형 깊은 생각에 잠긴; 명상적인
□□ merger	명 (사업체의) 합병
□□ optimism	명 낙관론, 낙천주의
□□ overdue	형 (지불 등의) 기한이 넘은; 이미 늦어진
□□ penalty	명 처벌; 벌금; 벌칙
□□ pivotal	형 중심(축)이 되는
□□ precise	형 정확한, 엄밀한
□□ racist	명 인종 차별주의자
□□ regional	형 지역의, 지방의
□□ revelation	명 폭로(된 사실)
□□ run for	~에 입후보하다[출마하다]
□□ rural	형 시골의, 전원의, 지방의
□□ spine	명 척추
□□ strive	동 노력하다; 분투하다
□□ temporarily	부 일시적으로, 임시로
□□ up-and-coming	형 전도가 유망한, 떠오르는
□□ walk away from	(사고 등을 가까스로) 피하다 [벗어나다]

Prefixes | 분리·이탈·따로(1) a(b) -, de -²

□□ avert	동 (~에서) 눈을 돌리다; 피하다
□□ abhor	동 혐오하다
□□ abhorrent	형 혐오스러운
□□ aboriginal	형 원주민의, 토착의 / 명 (호주) 원주민
□□ abortion	명 낙태, 유산
□□ abrasion	명 찰과상; 마모, 마멸
□□ absolve	동 무죄임을 선언하다; (죄를) 용서하다
□□ deregulate	동 규제를 철폐하다
□□ deregulation	명 규제 철폐
□□ deodorant	명 냄새 제거제, 데오도란트
□□ deform	동 변형시키다, 기형으로 만들다

□□ deformity	몡 기형(인 상태)	□□ deviant	혱 (정상에서) 벗어난, 일탈적인
□□ dehydrate	몽 건조시키다; (사람이) 탈수 상태가 되다	□□ deviance	몡 일탈 (행동), (사회적응 등의) 이상 (행동)
□□ dehydration	몡 건조; 탈수	□□ deviation	몡 일탈, 탈선; 편차
□□ detach	몽 떼다, 분리하다; (군인 등을) 파견하다	□□ deflect	몽 방향을 바꾸다, 빗나가게 하다; (비판 등을) 피하다
□□ deviate	몽 (일상·예상 등을) 벗어나다		

Essential Roots / Stems 1 │ duc(t) / duc(e)

□□ abduct	몽 유괴하다, 납치하다	□□ seduce	몽 (나쁜 길로) 유혹하다, 꾀다
□□ induce	몽 설득하다; 유도하다; 귀납 추론하다	□□ seduction	몡 유혹
		□□ conduce	몽 ((to)) (좋은 결과로) 이끌다; 공헌하다
□□ induction	몡 유도; ((논리학)) 귀납법		
□□ produce	몽 생산하다 몡 농산물; 제품	□□ conducive	혱 ((to)) ~에 도움이 되는

Essential Roots / Stems 2 │ fer

□□ defer	몽 연기하다; 경의를 표하다; ((to)) (의견에) 따르다	□□ transfer	몽 이동하다; 갈아타다; 전학 가다
			몡 이동; 환승
□□ deferment	몡 연기, 유예	□□ confer	몽 상의하다; (상·학위를) 수여하다
□□ deference	몡 경의, 존중		
□□ ferry	몡 페리, 연락선 몽 나르다, 수송하다	□□ conference	몡 협의; 회의
□□ infer	몽 추론하다; 암시하다	□□ conferment	몡 (학위·상 등의) 수여
□□ inference	몡 추론, 추리		

Words with Multiple Meanings │ 필수 다의어의 이해

| □□ conduct | 몽 (업무 등을) 수행하다 몡 수행, 처리 몽 행동하다, 처신하다 몡 (특정한 장소·상황에서의) 행동, 품행 몽 지휘하다 몽 (열이나 전기를) 전도하다 |
| □□ produce | 몽 생산[제조]하다 몽 (연극 등을) 제작하다 몽 (결과를) 일으키다, 초래하다 몡 생산고 몡 농산물 몡 제품 몡 작품 |

Phrasal Verbs | off가 포함된 구동사 1

□□ back off (뒤로 물러나 떨어지다) 뒤로
물러나다; 뜻을 굽히다[그만
두다]

□□ bounce off (튀어 분리되다) 튕겨 나오다

□□ break off (깨어 단절시키다) 파기하다
[파혼하다]; 중단하다

□□ brush off (빗질하여 떨어내다) 무시하다

□□ call off (중단을 말하다) 취소하다

□□ carry off (떼어서 가져가다) 수상하다

□□ come off (떨어져 나오다 / 떨어내다)
떨어지다; 중단하다; 성공하다

□□ drop off (떨어뜨려 분리시키다)
내려 주다; 잠이 들다

□□ fall off (~에서 분리되어 떨어지다)
떨어지다

□□ fight off (싸워서 제거하다) 물리쳐
없애다

□□ get off (~에서 분리되다[분리시키다])
끊다; 퇴근하다; 내리다

□□ give off (떼어 주다) (냄새가) 나다

□□ go off (폭발하며 작동하다 / 작동이
끊기다) 울리다; 터지다; 꺼지다

□□ keep off (분리된 채로 있다) 들어가지
않다

Themes | 역사·종교

□□ historic 혱 역사적으로 중요한, 역사에
남을 만한

□□ prehistoric 혱 선사시대의

□□ originate 통 시작하다, 유래하다

□□ originality 몡 원형임; 독창성

□□ milestone 몡 (돌로 된) 이정표; (역사·인
생에서) 중요한 사건

□□ era 몡 (특정한 성격의) 시대

□□ primitive 혱 원시 사회의; 원시적인

□□ tribe 몡 부족, 종족; 집단, 무리

□□ tribal 혱 부족의, 종족의

□□ barbarian 몡 미개인; 이방인

□□ barbarous 혱 야만스러운; 잔인한

□□ archaic 혱 고대의; 낡은; 구식인

□□ archive 몡 고(古)기록; ((pl.)) 기록 보
관소
통 (기록 보관소 등에) 보관하다

□□ colonize 통 식민지로 만들다; (동식물
이) 대량 서식하다

□□ colonization 몡 식민지화; (동식물의) 군체
형성

□□ colonial 혱 식민(지)의 몡 식민지 주민

□□ relic 몡 ((물건)) 유물;
((비유적)) 유물

□□ lore 몡 (전승) 지식; 구비 설화;
(민간)전통

□□ divine 혱 신[하느님]의; 신성한

□□ divinity 몡 신성; 신

□□ providence 몡 (신의) 섭리

□□ biblical 혱 성서의

□□ atheism 몡 무신론

□□ atheist 몡 무신론자

□□ pilgrim 몡 순례자

□□ pilgrimage 몡 순례, 성지 참배

□□ ritual 몡 (특히 종교상의) 의례;
(항상 하는) 의례적인 일
혱 의식상의; 의례적인

□□ sanctuary 몡 안식(처); 성역; (야생동물)
보호구역

□□ clergy 몡 ((집합적)) 성직자들

□□ salvation 몡 ((기독교)) 구원; (위험·재난
등으로부터의) 구조[구제]

□□ temporal 혱 현세의, 속세의; 시간의

□□ persecute 통 박해하다

□□ persecution 몡 박해

08 강

words & phrases

□□ accompany	통 동반하다, 동행하다; 반주하다
□□ bulk	명 대부분; (큰) 규모
□□ capacity	명 수용력; 용량; 능력; 자격
□□ celestial	형 하늘의, 천체의 명 천사
□□ civilian	명 민간인
□□ come down to	결국 ~이 되다; ~로 요약되다
□□ concave	형 오목한
□□ consideration	명 사려, 숙고; 고려사항; 보수
□□ departmental	형 부서의
□□ developing country	명 개발도상국
□□ globule	명 (액체의) 작은 방울, 작은 구체
□□ help out	(특히 곤경에 처한 ~을) 도와주다
□□ initially	부 처음에

□□ in stock	재고가 있는
□□ litter	통 (쓰레기 등을) 버리다 명 (길에 버려진) 쓰레기
□□ offshore	해안에서 멀리 떨어져서
□□ ownership	명 소유; 소유권; 회원권
□□ predictable	형 예측할 수 있는
□□ productivity	명 생산성
□□ provision	명 공급, 제공; 대비; (법률 문서의) 조항
□□ radiation	명 방사선; (열·에너지 등의) 복사
□□ radioactive	형 방사능의
□□ recurring	형 되풀이하여 발생하는; ((수학)) 순환하는
□□ soreness	명 쓰림, 아픔
□□ the chair	명 의장, 회장; 의장[회장]직

Prefixes | 분리·이탈·따로(2) di(s) –²

□□ discard	통 (불필요한 것을) 버리다
□□ discern	통 (분명하지 않은 것을) 파악하다
□□ disguise	통 변장하다; 숨기다 명 변장
□□ disinterested	형 사심이 없는, 공평한
□□ dispatch	통 (급히) 보내다; 신속히 처리하다 명 발송; 파견
□□ disperse	통 흩어지다; 해산시키다

□□ displace	통 (원래 장소에서) 옮겨놓다; 대신[교체]하다; 쫓아내다
□□ displacement	명 (제자리에서 쫓겨난) 이동
□□ dispose	통 ((of)) (~을) 없애다; 처리하다
□□ disposal	명 처리; 처분
□□ disposable	형 일회용의
□□ digest	통 소화하다 명 요약(문)

☐☐ digestive	형 소화의	☐☐ divert	동 방향을 바꾸게 하다; (생각을) 다른 데로 돌리다
☐☐ digestion	명 소화(력)	☐☐ diversion	명 (기분) 전환
☐☐ diverse	형 다른; 다양한	☐☐ diverge	동 (다른 방향으로) 갈라지다; 발산하다; (계획 등에서) 벗어나다
☐☐ diversify	동 다양화하다		
☐☐ diversity	명 다양성		
☐☐ biodiversity	명 (균형 잡힌 환경을 위한) 생물의 다양성	☐☐ divergence	명 분기; 발산; 일탈
		☐☐ dilute	동 희석하다 형 (액체가) 희석된

Essential Roots / Stems 1 | astro / aster

☐☐ disaster	명 재해, 참사; 엄청난 불행	☐☐ astronomer	명 천문학자
☐☐ disastrous	형 처참한, 피해가 막심한	☐☐ astronomical	형 천문학의; 천문학적인
☐☐ astrology	명 점성술; 점성학	☐☐ asterisk	명 별표
☐☐ astrologer	명 점성술사	☐☐ asteroid	명 소행성
☐☐ astronomy	명 천문학	☐☐ astronaut	명 우주 비행사

Essential Roots / Stems 2 | cor(d) / core

☐☐ discord	명 불화, 다툼	☐☐ accord	동 ((with)) 일치하다; 조화를 이루다 형 일치; 조화; (공식) 합의
☐☐ concord	명 ((with)) 일치; 조화, 화합		
☐☐ core	명 (과일의) 속[심]; (사물의) 중심부; 핵심 형 핵심적인	☐☐ accordance	명 일치; 조화
☐☐ cordial	형 진심 어린, 다정한	☐☐ accordingly	부 그래서; (상황에) 부응해서
☐☐ cordially	부 진심으로; 지독히		

Words with Multiple Meanings | 필수 다의어의 이해

☐☐ account	명 (회계) 장부; 외상 장부 명 단골, 고객 명 계좌 명 ((for)) 설명 동 설명하다 명 이유, 근거 명 ((컴퓨터)) 계정
☐☐ attribute (A to B)	동 A를 B의 탓[덕택]으로 돌리다 동 A(작품)가 B의 것이라고 하다 명 속성, 특성, 자질

Phrasal Verbs | off가 포함된 구동사 2

☐☐ lay off	(단절시켜 놓다) 해고하다	☐☐ take off	(~을 …에서 떼어내다 / (땅)에서 떨어지다) 떼다; 벗다; 쉬다; 깎다; 이륙하다
☐☐ pay off	(지불을 완료하다) 모두 갚다; 성공하다		
☐☐ put off	(떨어뜨려 놓다) 미루다	☐☐ turn off	(돌려서 단절시키다) 끄다; 흥미를 잃다
☐☐ see off	(~를 보고[만나고] 헤어지다) 배웅하다	☐☐ wear off	(닳게 해서 제거하다) 낫다
☐☐ set off	((있는 곳에서) 분리되게 하다) 출발하다; 터뜨리다	☐☐ work off	(~을 제거하도록 일하다) 없애다[제거하다]
☐☐ show off	(~에서 분리해 잘 보이게 하다) 자랑하다	☐☐ write off (A as B)	여기다
☐☐ shut off	(닫아서 단절시키다) 차단하다; 멈추다		

Themes | 경제

☐☐ economy	명 경제, 경기; 절약	☐☐ soar	동 (하늘 높이) 날아오르다; (물가 등이) 급등하다
☐☐ economize	동 절약하다		
☐☐ economic	형 경제의; 경제성이 있는	☐☐ invest	동 투자하다; (시간, 노력 등을) 쏟다, 들이다
☐☐ economical	형 경제적인, 절약하는		
☐☐ boom	명 쾅하는 소리; (사업·경제의) 호황; 갑작스러운 인기 동 호황을 맞다	☐☐ investment	명 투자 (자금)
		☐☐ finance	명 자금; 재정, 재무 동 자금을 대다
☐☐ boost	명 밀어 올림; 격려; 부양책 동 (경기 등을) 부양하다; 북돋우다	☐☐ financial	형 금융의, 재정의
		☐☐ treasury	명 국고; ((the T-)) 재무부; (지식 등의) 보고
☐☐ booster	명 후원자; (자신감 등을) 높이는 것	☐☐ tax	명 세금 동 세금을 부과하다
☐☐ prosper	동 (물질적으로) 번영[번창]하다	☐☐ taxation	명 과세 제도; 세수
☐☐ prosperity	명 (물질적) 번영, 번창	☐☐ loan	명 대출(금) 동 빌려주다
☐☐ prosperous	형 번영한, 번창한	☐☐ mortgage	명 담보 대출(금) 동 (재산 등을) 저당 잡히다
☐☐ stagnation	명 정체, 침체; 불경기		
☐☐ stagnant	형 (물·공기가) 고여 있는; (경기가) 침체된	☐☐ interest	명 관심; 이해관계; 이자
		☐☐ account	명 (은행) 계좌; (회계) 장부; 신용 거래; 계정
☐☐ inflation	명 팽창; 인플레이션, 물가 상승률	☐☐ currency	명 통화; (화폐의) 유통, 통용
☐☐ inflate	동 (공기 등으로) 부풀게 하다; 가격을 올리다	☐☐ monetary	형 통화의, 화폐의; 금전상의

09 강

words & phrases

□□ amphibian	몡 양서류
□□ be party to	~에 가담하다
□□ carton	몡 곽, 통
□□ companion	몡 동료; 친구
□□ detain	통 (가지 못하게) 붙들다; 구금[억류]하다
□□ draft	몡 밑그림, 초안; ((the ~)) 징병
□□ eruption	몡 폭발; 분출
□□ exile	통 추방하다, 망명을 가게 만들다
□□ exploit	통 (부당하게) 이용하다; 착취하다
	몡 위업, 공적
□□ feature	통 특징으로 삼다 몡 특색
□□ felony	몡 중죄, 흉악 범죄
□□ fine	몡 벌금 통 벌금을 부과하다
□□ flee	통 달아나다, 도망하다
□□ fume	몡 ((pl.)) (유독) 가스
□□ impulse	몡 충동; 충격, 자극
□□ mass	몡 (정확한 형체가 없는) 덩어리; ((the -es)) (일반) 대중
	혱 대중의; 대량의

□□ personable	혱 (잘생기고 성격이 좋아서) 매력적인
□□ plead	통 변호하다; 애원[간청]하다
□□ propensity	몡 (특정한 행동을 하는) 경향
□□ rebellion	몡 반란; 반대, 저항
□□ reservoir	몡 저수지; (많은 양의) 비축, 저장
□□ retina	몡 (눈의) 망막
□□ revise	통 수정하다; (책 등을) 개정하다
□□ subconscious	혱 잠재의식적인
□□ temporarily	틧 일시적으로, 임시로
□□ tin	몡 주석; 깡통
□□ traceable	혱 (기원·자취 등을) 추적할 수 있는
□□ truant	몡 무단결석생
□□ vigorous	혱 활발한; 격렬한
□□ vitality	몡 활력

Prefixes | 내부 in -²

□□ incident	몡 (특히 특이하거나 불쾌한) 일, 사건
□□ incidental	혱 부수적인, 부차적인; (자연스러운 결과로) ~에 따르기 마련인
	몡 부수적인 일
□□ influx	몡 (많은 사람·자금·물건이) 밀어닥침, 유입
□□ infuse	통 (어떤 특성을) 불어넣다; (찻잎 등을) 우려내다

□□ infusion	몡 (자금 등의) 투입; 우려낸 차[약물]
□□ inhale	통 (숨·연기 등을) 들이마시다
□□ inhalation	몡 흡입
□□ intrude	통 (가서는 안 될 곳을) 침범하다; 방해하다
□□ intrusion	몡 침범; 방해
□□ intrusive	혱 끼어드는, 거슬리는

□□ invade	图 (군사적으로) 침입[침략]하다; (권리 등을) 침해하다; (질병 등이) 침범하다	□□ impairment	图 (신체적·정신적) 장애
		□□ impose	图 ((on)) (법률 등을) 시행하다; (힘든 것을) 부과하다; (의견 등을) 강요하다
□□ invasion	图 침입, 침략		
□□ invasive	图 (질병이 체내에) 급속히 퍼지는; (치료가) 외과적인	□□ inherent	图 내재하는, 고유의
		□□ implement	图 실행[수행]하다
□□ impair	图 손상시키다, 악화시키다		图 도구, 기구

Essential Roots / Stems 1 | ject

□□ inject	图 주사하다; 주입하다; (특성을) 더하다	□□ objective	图 목적
			图 객관적인; ((문법)) 목적격의
□□ injection	图 주사; 주입	□□ subject	图 주제; 과목; 연구 대상
□□ eject	图 내쫓다; 튀어나오게 하다; (기계에서) 꺼내다		图 ((to)) (~에) 종속시키다
		□□ subjective	图 주관적인; ((문법)) 주격의
□□ ejection	图 방출; 방출물	□□ project	图 투영하다; 발사하다;
□□ object	图 물건; 목표		예상하다; 튀어나오다
	图 ((to)) (~에) 반대하다		图 계획, 기획; 과제
□□ objection	图 이의, 반대	□□ projector	图 영사기, 프로젝터

Essential Roots / Stems 2 | spir(e)

□□ inspire	图 영감을 주다; 고무하다, 격려하다	□□ conspiracy	图 공모; 음모
		□□ expire	图 (기한이) 만료되다
□□ inspiration	图 영감, 고무, 격려	□□ expiration	图 (기한) 만료, 만기
□□ spiritual	图 정신적인; 종교적인	□□ respire	图 숨 쉬다, 호흡하다
□□ aspire	图 열망하다	□□ respiration	图 호흡
□□ aspiration	图 열망, 포부	□□ respiratory	图 호흡기의
□□ conspire	图 공모하다; 음모를 꾸미다		

Words with Multiple Meanings | 필수 다의어의 이해

□□ object	图 물건, 물체 图 목적, 목표 图 (연구·관심 등의) 대상 图 반대하다
□□ subject	图 (논의 등의) 주제 图 과목, 학과 图 (그림·사진 등의) 대상, 소재 图 연구[실험] 대상 图 (특히 군주국의) 국민, 신하 图 종속시키다, 지배하다 图 (특히 나쁜 영향을 받아) ~될 수 있는

Phrasal Verbs │ in이 포함된 구동사

□□ break in (깨고 안으로 들어오다) 끼어들다; 침입하다

□□ check in (~에 들어가려고 체크하다) 탑승 수속하다

□□ count in (~을 셈에 넣다) 포함시키다

□□ drop in (on) (~ 안으로 떨어지다) 방문하다

□□ engage in (~ 안으로 관심을 끌다) 참여하다

□□ fill in (~ 안을 메우다) 채우다; 작성하다

□□ fit in,   fit in with (~ 안에 들어맞다 / ~ 안에 끼워 넣다) 잘 들어맞다; 함께 어울리다; 만나다

□□ give in (안으로 주다 / 받아들이다) 받아들이다; 항복하다; 내다

□□ hand in,   give in, turn in,   send in (안으로 건네다) 제출하다

□□ let in (on) (안으로 들어오게 하다) 끼워주다; 알려주다

□□ set in (안에 놓이다) 오다

□□ take in (안으로 취하다) 받아들이다; 포함하다; 섭취하다

Themes │ 산업

□□ cultivate 동 경작하다; 재배하다; 함양하다

□□ cultivation 명 경작; 재배; (관계) 구축; 함양

□□ fertile 형 비옥한; 생식력 있는

□□ fertility 명 비옥함; 생식력

□□ fertilize 동 ((생물)) 수정시키다; (토지에) 비료를 주다

□□ irrigate 동 관개하다, (땅에) 물을 대다

□□ irrigation 명 관개

□□ pesticide 명 살충제; 농약

□□ forage 명 (소·말의) 사료   동 (동물이) 먹이를 찾다; (사람이 손으로) 마구 뒤지며 찾다

□□ forager 명 수렵채집인; 약탈자

□□ journal 명 일기; (특정 주제를 다루는) 신문; 정기 간행물

□□ journalism 명 저널리즘

□□ coverage 명 (언론의) 보도[방송]; 보급(률); ((보험)) 보장 범위

□□ divulge 동 (비밀을) 누설하다

□□ distort 동 비틀다; (사실을) 왜곡하다

□□ distortion 명 찌그러뜨림; 왜곡

□□ censor 동 검열하다   명 검열관

□□ censorship 명 검열

□□ edit 동 (글 등을) 수정하다; (책을) 편집하다

□□ editor 명 편집자; 편집장

□□ edition 명 (출간된 책의 형태로 본) 판; (출간 횟수를 나타내는) 판

□□ streamline 동 (시스템 등을) 간소화[능률화]하다; 유선형으로 하다

□□ customize 동 주문 제작하다

□□ merchandise 명 물품, 상품   동 판매하다

□□ distribute 동 분배하다; (상품을) 유통하다

□□ distribution 명 분배 (방식); 분포; 유통

□□ barter 동 물물교환하다   명 물물교환

□□ bulk 명 대부분; (큰) 규모

□□ hub 명 (바퀴의) 중심; (특정 활동의) 중심지, 중추

□□ quota 명 (요구되거나 해야 할) 몫; (수출입 등에 공식적으로 허용되는) 한도

□□ installment 명 할부(금)

□□ commerce 명 상업, 무역

□□ commercial 형 상업의; 영리 위주의   명 광고(방송)

□□ sanction 명 허가, 승인; 제재   동 허가[승인]하다; 제재를 가하다

□□ consumerism 명 소비(문화); 소비지상주의

□□ prodigal 형 낭비하는; 방탕한

10강

words & phrases

☐☐ compel	통 강요하다; ~하게 만들다	☐☐ landlord	명 (방·집 등을 빌려주는) 주인, 임대인
☐☐ contamination	명 오염	☐☐ life imprisonment	명 종신형, 무기징역
☐☐ death sentence	명 사형 선고	☐☐ long for	~을 추구하여 바라다
☐☐ defendant	명 (재판에서) 피고	☐☐ mandatory	형 명령의; 강제의, 의무의
☐☐ donation	명 기부(금), 기증	☐☐ mutually	부 서로, 상호 간에
☐☐ endangered species	명 멸종 위기에 처한 동식물의 종	☐☐ ornate	형 화려하게 장식된
☐☐ exclaim	통 소리치다, 외치다	☐☐ overwhelming	형 압도적인, 엄청난
☐☐ expense	명 비용, 경비	☐☐ pest	명 해충; 흑사병
☐☐ extol	통 극찬[격찬]하다	☐☐ restless	형 (지루해서) 가만히 못 있는, 안절부절못하는
☐☐ facility	명 쉬움, 용이함; (편의) 시설		
☐☐ fit	명 (감정·행동의) 격발, 발작	☐☐ successor	명 계승자; 상속자; 후임자
☐☐ grant	명 (정부 등의) 보조금 통 승인하다; 인정하다	☐☐ surgeon	명 외과의사
		☐☐ sympathy	명 공감; 동정
☐☐ guilty	형 유죄의; 가책을 느끼는	☐☐ testify	통 (특히 법정에서) 증언하다, 진술하다; 증명하다
☐☐ incur	통 (좋지 못한 상황을) 가져오다; (비용을) 발생시키다		
		☐☐ unanimous	형 만장일치의
☐☐ justify	통 정당화하다, 옹호하다	☐☐ unsatisfactory	형 만족스럽지 못한
☐☐ lack	명 부족, 결핍 통 부족하다	☐☐ vacancy	명 (호텔 등의) 빈방; 결원, 공석
		☐☐ workload	명 업무량

Prefixes | 외부 (1) e(x) -

☐☐ exhibit	동 전시하다	☐☐ emigrate	동 이민을 가다
☐☐ exhibition	명 전시(회); (재능 등의) 발휘; (감정 등의) 표현	☐☐ eminent	형 저명한; 탁월한
		☐☐ eminence	명 (특히 전문 분야에서의) 명성
☐☐ expand	동 확대되다; 더 상세히 말하다	☐☐ eradicate	동 없애다, 근절하다
☐☐ expansion	명 확대, 확장	☐☐ evade	동 피하다, 모면하다; (의무·지불 등을) 회피하다
☐☐ extinct	형 멸종된; 사라진		
☐☐ extinction	명 멸종	☐☐ evasion	명 회피, 모면; 얼버무리기
☐☐ extinguish	동 (불을) 끄다; 끝내다, 없애다	☐☐ evasive	형 책임 회피의; 얼버무리는
☐☐ elaborate	형 공들인; 정교한	☐☐ evict	동 쫓아내다, 퇴거시키다
	동 정교하게 만들다; 자세히 말하다	☐☐ eviction	명 축출, 쫓아냄
☐☐ elicit	동 (정보·반응을) 끌어내다	☐☐ evoke	동 (감정·기억을) 불러일으키다, 환기시키다

Essential Roots / Stems | tend / tent(e) / tens(e)

☐☐ extend	동 확대하다, 늘이다; 포함하다	☐☐ contend	동 ((for)) (~을 얻으려고) 겨루다; ((with)) (곤란한 문제나 상황과) 싸우다; ((that)) (~을 사실이라고) 주장하다
☐☐ extension	명 (기간의) 연장, 확대; (전화의) 내선		
☐☐ extent	명 정도; (어떤 지역의) 규모		
☐☐ extensive	형 아주 넓은[많은], 대규모의	☐☐ contention	명 갈등; 논쟁
☐☐ tend	동 (~로) 향해 가다; (~하는) 경향이 있다; 돌보다	☐☐ contentious	형 논쟁을 초래하는
		☐☐ intense	형 강렬한, 극심한
☐☐ tense	형 긴장된; 팽팽한 동 긴장시키다	☐☐ intensive	형 집중적인
		☐☐ intensity	명 강렬; 강도
☐☐ tension	명 긴장, 불안	☐☐ intensify	동 강화하다
☐☐ attend	동 참석하다; ((to)) 주의를 기울이다; ((on, to)) 시중들다	☐☐ pretend	동 ~인 척하다
		☐☐ pretension	명 허세, 가식; 주장
☐☐ intend	동 의도하다	☐☐ pretense	명 허위; 구실, 핑계
☐☐ intention	명 의향; 의도	☐☐ pretentious	형 허세 부리는
☐☐ intentional	형 의도적인	☐☐ superintendent	명 감독자, 관리자; 건물 관리인

Words with Multiple Meanings | 필수 다의어의 이해

☐☐ tend	동 (길·태도 등이 ~로) 향해 가다 동 (~하는) 경향이 있다 동 돌보다, 간호하다
☐☐ attend	동 주의를 기울이다, 신경을 쓰다 동 ((on, to)) 간호하다, 시중들다 동 (~에) 다니다 동 참석하다

Phrasal Verbs | out이 포함된 구동사 1

□□ ask out — (~에게 밖으로 나가자고 청하다) 데이트를 신청하다

□□ break out — (깨고 나타나다) 발발[발생]하다; 탈출하다

□□ bring out — (가지고 나오다) 출시하다

□□ burn out — (다 타서 없어지다) 다 타버리다; 완전히 지쳐버리다

□□ burst out — (밖으로 터지다) 소리 지르다

□□ carry out — (밖으로 나르다) 실행하다

□□ check out — (나가려고 체크하다 / 확인해서 밝히다) (책을) 대출하다; 확인하다

□□ drop out (of) — ((~에서) 떨어져 없어지다) 사라지다; 중퇴하다[그만두다]

□□ drown out — (물에 잠겨서 없어지다) 들리지 않게 하다

□□ figure out — (생각해서 내놓다) 계산하다; 알아내다

□□ fill out — (완전히 채우다) 기재하다[작성하다]

□□ hand out, give out — (밖으로 건네주다) 배부하다

□□ hang out (with) — 어울려 다니다

Themes | 회사 1

□□ corporation — 몡 (비교적 큰 규모의) 기업, 회사; 법인

□□ corporate — 혱 기업의, 법인(체)의; 공동의

□□ incorporate — 동 (법인체를) 설립하다; 통합시키다

□□ incorporated — 혱 (회사가) 법인 조직의

□□ entrepreneur — 몡 기업가

□□ occupation — 몡 직업; (토지·가옥 등의) 사용, 거주

□□ recruit — 몡 신병; 신입 사원 동 (신입 사원 등을) 모집하다

□□ recruitment — 몡 신규 모집, 채용

□□ personnel — 몡 (회사 등의) 총인원; (회사의) 인사과

□□ résumé — 몡 이력서

□□ resign — 동 사직하다

□□ resignation — 몡 사직; 사직서

□□ oversee — 동 감독하다

□□ relegate — 동 격하[좌천]시키다

□□ designate — 동 가리키다; 지정[지명]하다 혱 (직책에) 지명된

□□ designation — 몡 지시; 지명; 직함

□□ rank — 몡 지위 동 지위를 차지하다

□□ ranking — 몡 순위

□□ empower — 동 권한을 주다; 자율권을 주다

□□ commute — 동 통근하다; ((법률)) 감형하다 몡 통근 (거리)

□□ commuter — 몡 통근자

□□ assign — 동 (일 등을) 할당하다; (직책에) 임명하다

□□ assignment — 몡 할당; 숙제; (임명된) 직위

□□ toil — 동 (장시간) 힘들게 일하다 몡 노고

□□ compensate — 동 ((for)) 보상하다; 보수를 주다

□□ compensation — 몡 보상; 보상금

□□ reimburse — 동 배상하다, 변상하다

□□ rewarding — 혱 돈을 많이 버는; 보람 있는

11 강

11강 MP3 🎧

words & phrases

□□ abbreviation 　명 축약(형); 약어

□□ acquaintance 　명 아는 사람; (약간의) 친분; 지식

□□ acquisition 　명 습득; (기업) 인수

□□ admission 　명 입장(료); 입학 허가

□□ bait 　명 미끼
　　　　　동 미끼를 놓다

□□ boundary 　명 경계선

□□ capital punishment 　명 사형

□□ critical 　형 비판적인; 대단히 중요한

□□ dim 　형 어둑한, 흐릿한
　　　　동 어둑해지다

□□ distract 　동 주의를 딴 데로 돌리다; 산만하게 하다

□□ dividend 　명 (주식) 배당금

□□ drastically 　부 과감하게; 철저하게

□□ eligibility 　명 적임, 적격

□□ embark 　동 (배·비행기에) 승선하다

□□ flicker 　동 (빛 등이) 깜박거리다; (생각 등이) 스치다

□□ fundamental 　형 근본적인; 필수적인

□□ glow 　명 불빛; (얼굴의) 홍조
　　　　동 빛나다; (얼굴이) 상기되다

□□ in terms of 　~에 관해서, ~의 면에서

□□ influx 　명 (많은 사람·자금·물건이) 밀려닥침, 유입

□□ inhospitable 　형 (손님에게) 불친절한; 사람이 살기 어려운

□□ initial 　형 처음의, 초기의
　　　　명 머리글자

□□ interest charge 　명 이자

□□ jurisdiction 　명 사법권; 관할권; 관할 구역

□□ prejudice 　명 편견 동 편견을 갖게 하다

□□ recommendation 　명 권고; 추천; 추천서

□□ reliability 　명 신뢰할 수 있음, 신뢰도

□□ spot 　동 발견하다, 알아채다
　　　　명 (작은) 점; 장소

□□ steep 　형 가파른; 급격한

□□ union 　명 결합; 연방; 노동조합

□□ unparalleled 　형 비할 데 없는

□□ yield 　동 (수익·농작물 등을) 생산하다; 항복하다; 양보하다
　　　　명 (농작물 등의) 산출(량); 총수익

Prefixes | 외부(2) out-¹, extra-

□□ outbreak 　명 (전쟁 등의) 발발; 발병

□□ outburst 　명 (감정의) 폭발; (특정 활동의) 급격한 증가

□□ outcast 　명 따돌림[버림]받는 사람

□□ outlaw 　동 불법화하다, 금지하다
　　　　명 (범죄를 저지른) 도망자

□□ outlay 　명 경비, 지출

□□ outskirt(s) 　명 (도시의) 변두리, 교외

□□ outspoken 　형 노골적으로[거침없이] 말하는

□□ outstanding 　형 뛰어난; 두드러진; (문제·보수 등이) 미해결[미지급]된

☐☐ utmost	형 최고의, 극도의 명 최대한도	☐☐ extraneous	형 외부로부터의; 이질적인; 관계없는
☐☐ utter	동 (입으로 소리를) 내다; (말을) 하다 형 완전한, 순전한	☐☐ extraordinary	형 기이한; 비범한; 임시의

Essential Roots / Stems 1 | cur(r)

☐☐ extracurricular	형 과외의, 정규 교육 과정 외의	☐☐ concurrent	형 동시에 일어나는
☐☐ curriculum	명 교육과정	☐☐ concurrence	명 동의; 동시 발생
☐☐ current	형 현재의; 통용하는 명 (물·공기·전기 등의) 흐름	☐☐ excursion	명 (단체로 짧게 하는) 여행, 소풍, 유람
☐☐ occur	동 발생하다; ((to)) (~에게) 떠 오르다, 생각이 나다	☐☐ incur	동 (좋지 못한 상황을) 가져오 다; (비용을) 발생시키다
☐☐ occurrence	명 발생; 사건	☐☐ recur	동 반복되다; 재발하다
☐☐ concur	동 ((with)) 동의하다; 동시에 일어나다	☐☐ recurrent	형 되풀이되는
		☐☐ recurrence	명 반복; 재발
		☐☐ precursor	명 선구자; 선임자; 전조

Essential Roots / Stems 2 | terr / terrestri

☐☐ extraterrestrial	명 외계인 형 외계의	☐☐ Mediterranean	형 지중해의
☐☐ terrestrial	형 지구의; 육지의	☐☐ subterranean	형 지하의
☐☐ territory	명 지역, 영토; 영역	☐☐ extraterritorial	형 치외법권의
☐☐ territorial	형 영토의; 세력권을 주장하는	☐☐ extraterritoriality	명 치외법권
☐☐ terrain	명 지형, 지역		

Words with Multiple Meanings | 필수 다의어의 이해

☐☐ cast	동 (시선·미소 등을) 던지다, 보내다 명 배역을 맡기다 명 (연극이나 영화의) 배역진, 출연자들 동 (빛·그림자·의혹 등을) 발하다, 드리우다 동 (~으로) …을 주조하다 명 주조물 명 깁스붕대
☐☐ current	형 현재의; 통용하는 명 해류, 기류, 전류 명 (특정 집단 사람들 사이의) 경향, 추세
☐☐ utter	동 발언하다 동 (비밀을) 누설하다 형 ((강조)) 완전한, 철저한, 전적인
☐☐ capital	명 수도 명 대문자 형 대문자의 명 자본금, 자금 형 (죄가) 사형감인, 사형의

Phrasal Verbs | out이 포함된 구동사 2

□□ keep out　(밖에 계속 두다) 차단하다

□□ lay out　(밖으로 꺼내어 놓다[펼쳐놓다])
　　　　　　설계하다; 설명하다; 쓰다

□□ leave out　(밖에 있게 하여 없애다) 빠뜨
　　　　　　리다

□□ let out　(밖으로 내보내다) 출소하다

□□ make out　(밖으로 만들어내다) 알다

□□ pass out　((의식이) 밖으로 나가다) 정신
　　　　　　을 잃다

Themes | 회사 2

□□ headquarters　몡 본사

□□ downsize　통 (비용 절감을 위해 인원을)
　　　　　　축소하다

□□ curtail　통 축소[삭감, 단축]하다

□□ merge　통 합병하다; 융합되다

□□ merger　몡 (특히 회사 등의) 합병

□□ associate　통 연합시키다 몡 동료
　　　　　　형 제휴한; ((직함)) 준[부]

□□ association　몡 협회; 연계

□□ affiliate　통 제휴하다; 가입하다
　　　　　　몡 계열사; 가입자

□□ venture　몡 (사업상의) 모험; 벤처 (사
　　　　　　업)
　　　　　　통 위험을 무릅쓰고 ~하다

□□ sabotage　통 (고의적으로) 방해하다
　　　　　　몡 사보타주

□□ offset　통 상쇄하다

□□ brainstorming　몡 브레인스토밍

□□ scheme　몡 (운영) 계획, 제도; 책략
　　　　　　통 책략을 꾸미다

□□ chamber　몡 (공공건물의) 회의실, 방;
　　　　　　(의회 상원·하원의) -원(院)

□□ ad hoc　형 특별한 목적을 위한; 임시의

□□ fund　몡 자금
　　　　　　통 자금을 제공하다

□□ asset　몡 자산, 재산

□□ stock　몡 재고품; 주식; 가축
　　　　　　통 (물품을) 비축하다

□□ audit　몡 회계 감사; (품질·수준 등에
　　　　　　대한) 검사

□□ retail　몡 소매 통 소매하다

□□ undercut　통 (경쟁자보다) 싸게 팔다;
　　　　　　약화시키다

□□ commission　몡 위원회; 수수료

□□ profitable　형 수익성이 있는; 유익한

□□ marketable　형 (상품이) 잘 팔리는, 시장성
　　　　　　이 있는

□□ margin　몡 여백; 차이; 이윤 폭

□□ marginal　형 주변부의; 미미한

□□ boycott　통 (항의의 표시로) 구매[참여]
　　　　　　를 거부하다
　　　　　　몡 불매 운동

□□ dealer　몡 상인, 중개인; (카드 게임의)
　　　　　　딜러

□□ dealership　몡 (특히 승용차) 대리점; 중개
　　　　　　인직

□□ bundle　몡 꾸러미, (함께 팔리거나 딸
　　　　　　려 나오는 물건들의) 묶음

□□ niche　몡 아주 꼭 맞는 자리[역할];
　　　　　　(수익 가능성이 큰) 틈새시장

□□ publicize　통 광고하다

□□ publicity　몡 광고

12강

words & phrases

□□ abandon	图 버리다, 유기하다; 그만두다
□□ abdominal	휑 ((신체)) 복부의
□□ advancement	圀 발전, 진보; 승진
□□ be riddled with	(특히 나쁜 것이) 가득하다
□□ bribe	圀 뇌물 图 매수하다
□□ cease-fire	圀 정전, 휴전; 사격 중지 구령
□□ competitive	휑 경쟁을 하는; 경쟁력 있는
□□ crater	圀 분화구; 큰 구멍
□□ diagonal	圀 사선; 대각선 휑 사선의; 대각선의
□□ digestion	圀 소화, 소화력
□□ distraction	圀 정신을 산만하게 만드는 것; 오락 (활동)
□□ edition	圀 (출간된 책의 형태로 본) 판; (출간 횟수를 나타내는) 판
□□ erode	图 침식시키다
□□ estimate	图 추정하다, 추산하다 圀 추정(치), 추산; 견적서
□□ excess	휑 초과한, 과도한 圀 과도
□□ formula	圀 ((수학)) 공식; 화학식; 제조법
□□ forum	圀 (고대 로마의) 광장; 토론회
□□ garment	圀 의복, 옷
□□ lava	圀 용암
□□ panel	圀 (목재, 유리, 금속) 판; 토론 위원
□□ rhombus	圀 마름모
□□ right angle	圀 직각
□□ shrink	图 줄어들다; 줄어들게 하다
□□ slanted	휑 비스듬한; 편파적인
□□ trademark	圀 (등록) 상표; (특징이 되는) 트레이드마크
□□ undertake	图 (책임을 맡아서) 착수하다; 약속하다

Prefixes | 사이·서로 inter -

□□ interchange	圀 (생각·정보의) 교환; (고속도로의) 입체 교차로 图 (생각·정보 등을) 교환하다
□□ interchangeable	휑 교환[교체]할 수 있는
□□ interfere	图 ((with)) 방해하다; ((in)) 간섭하다
□□ interference	圀 방해; 간섭
□□ internal	휑 내부의; 국내의
□□ interpersonal	휑 대인관계에 관련된
□□ interrogate	图 심문하다, 추궁하다
□□ interrogation	圀 심문, 추궁
□□ interrogative	휑 질문하는 圀 ((문법)) 의문사
□□ intersect	图 (선·도로 등이) 교차하다; 가로지르다
□□ intersection	圀 교차로; 교차 지점
□□ interval	圀 (두 사건 사이의) 간격; (연극 등의) 중간 휴식 시간

Essential Roots / Stems 1 | rupt

□□ interrupt	동 방해하다; (잠깐) 중단시키다	□□ corrupt	형 부패한, 타락한
□□ interruption	명 중단; 방해; (말을) 가로막음		동 타락시키다
□□ rupture	명 파열; 불화	□□ corruption	명 부패, 타락
	동 파열시키다; (관계를) 결렬시키다	□□ disrupt	동 방해하다; 분열시키다; 교란시키다
□□ abrupt	형 갑작스러운; 퉁명스러운	□□ disruption	명 붕괴; 분열
□□ bankrupt	형 파산한 명 파산자	□□ disruptive	형 지장을 주는
	동 파산시키다	□□ erupt	동 (화산이) 폭발하다; 분출하다
□□ bankruptcy	명 파산	□□ eruption	명 폭발; 분출

Essential Roots / Stems 2 | ven(t) / vene

□□ intervene	동 개입하다; 끼어들다; 중재하다	□□ invention	명 발명; 발명품; 지어낸 이야기
□□ intervention	명 개입, 간섭; 중재	□□ inventive	형 창의적인; 독창적인
□□ eventual	형 최종적인; 궁극적인	□□ inventory	명 물품 목록; 재고(품)
□□ eventually	부 결국, 마침내	□□ prevent	동 막다; 예방하다
□□ advent	명 출현; 도래	□□ prevention	명 예방
□□ convene	동 모이다; (회의 등을) 소집하다	□□ preventive	형 예방을 위한
□□ convention	명 (대규모) 회의; 인습, 관례		명 예방약
□□ conventional	형 관례적인; 기존의	□□ circumvent	동 (교묘히) 회피하다; 우회하다; 포위하다
□□ invent	동 발명하다; 꾸며내다	□□ revenue	명 세입; 수익; 총 매출
		□□ venue	명 (회담 등의) 장소; 개최지

Words with Multiple Meanings | 필수 다의어의 이해

□□ class	명 부류, 종류 동 분류하다 명 (사회의) 계층, 계급 명 학급 (학생들) 명 수업 명 등급
□□ column	명 세로줄; 세로 단 명 (신문 등의) 칼럼 명 원기둥, 원주

Phrasal Verbs | out이 포함된 구동사 3

□□ pull out (밖으로 끌어당기다) 뽑다; 철수하다

□□ rule out (없애기로 결정하다) 제외하다

□□ run out (of) (~ 없이 운영하다) (재고가) 떨어지다

□□ sell out (팔려서 없다) 다 팔리다

□□ set out (밖으로 놓다) 출발하다; 마음 먹다

□□ speak out (밖으로 끄집어내어 말하다) 공개적으로 말하다

□□ stand out (밖에 서 있다) 두드러지다

□□ turn out (돌려서 없애다 / 돌려서 나타나게하다) 끄다; 배출하다; 판명되다

□□ put out (밖에 놓아 없애다 / 밖에 놓다) 끄다; 내밀다

□□ wear out (닳아서 없어지다) 식상한; 지치다; 닳아 없애다

□□ wipe out (닦아서 완전히 없애다) 파괴되다; 녹초가 되다

□□ work out (일[노력]을 해서 (결과를) 내놓다) 운동하다; 내놓다; 돌아가다; 도출하다

Themes | 사회

□□ civil 〔형〕 시민의; 국내의; ((법)) 민사상의; 교양 있는

□□ citizenship 〔명〕 시민권; 국적; 시민의 자질

□□ commonality 〔명〕 일반 대중; 공통성

□□ reform 〔동〕 개혁하다 〔명〕 개혁, 개선

□□ turbulent 〔형〕 격동의; 요동을 치는

□□ turbulence 〔명〕 격동; (물·공기의) 난류, 난기류

□□ metropolis 〔명〕 대도시; 수도; 중심지

□□ metropolitan 〔형〕 대도시[수도]의; (식민지나 속령이 아닌) 본국의

□□ congestion 〔명〕 (인구의) 밀집, 과잉; (교통의) 혼잡

□□ congested 〔형〕 붐비는

□□ urban 〔형〕 도시의

□□ suburb 〔명〕 교외

□□ suburban 〔형〕 교외의; 따분한

□□ rustic 〔형〕 시골 특유의; 통나무로 만든

□□ outlying 〔형〕 중심에서 떨어진; 외딴, 외진

□□ district 〔명〕 (특정한) 지구, 지역; 구역

□□ region 〔명〕 지역, 지방

□□ regional 〔형〕 지역[지방]의

□□ province 〔명〕 (수도가 아닌) 지방; ((행정 단위)) 주, 도; (학문·활동의) 분야

□□ provincial 〔형〕 지방의; 주의; 편협한

□□ social security 〔명〕 사회보장제도; 사회보장 연금

□□ infrastructure 〔명〕 사회[공공] 기반 시설

□□ register 〔명〕 (공식) 명부, 등록부 〔동〕 (공식 명부에) 등록하다; (우편물을) 등기로 보내다

□□ registration 〔명〕 등록; (출생·혼인 등의) 신고; 우편물의 등기

□□ privatize 〔동〕 (기업·산업 분야를) 민영화 하다

□□ decentralize 〔동〕 (행정권·인구 등을) 분산시키다

□□ curfew 〔명〕 통행금지령; 통행금지 시간

□□ restrain 〔동〕 (감정 등을) 억제하다; (특히 물리력을 동원하여) 제지하다

□□ restraint 〔명〕 규제; 제지

□□ restrict 〔동〕 제한[한정]하다

□□ restriction 〔명〕 제한; 규제

□□ constrain 〔동〕 (억지로) ~하게 만들다, 강요하다

□□ constraint 〔명〕 제약; 제한

13 강

words & phrases

☐☐ appoint	동 임명하다, 지명하다; (시간·장소 등을) 정하다
☐☐ arctic	형 북극의 명 ((the A-)) 북극
☐☐ caravan	명 (사막의) 대상; 캠핑용 자동차
☐☐ charitable	형 자선(단체)의; 자선을 베푸는, 너그러운
☐☐ checkup	명 건강 검진
☐☐ culminate	동 (~로) 끝이 나다
☐☐ discrimination	명 판별(력); 차별
☐☐ flexibility	명 유연성; 적응성, 융통성
☐☐ genocide	명 집단[종족] 학살
☐☐ indicator	명 지표; 계기, 장치
☐☐ insensitivity	명 무감각, 둔감
☐☐ intrinsic	형 고유한, 본질적인
☐☐ invoke	동 (법·규칙 등을) 적용하다; 언급하다; (느낌을) 불러일으키다
☐☐ massive	형 거대한; 심각한
☐☐ occasion	명 경우, 때; (특별한) 행사
☐☐ pledge	동 약속[맹세]하다 명 약속, 맹세
☐☐ prick	동 찌르다; 따끔거리게 하다 명 찌르기; 따가움
☐☐ radically	부 완전히, 근본적으로
☐☐ revenge	동 복수[보복]하다 명 복수, 보복
☐☐ scorn	동 경멸[멸시]하다; (멸시하여) 거절하다 명 경멸(감)
☐☐ supervision	명 감독, 관리, 감시
☐☐ tickle	동 간지럼을 태우다
☐☐ tuition	명 수업; 수업료, 등록금
☐☐ veto	명 거부권; 금지 동 거부[기각]하다
☐☐ villain	명 (연극·이야기 등의) 악인, 악당
☐☐ warranty	명 (제품의) 품질 보증(서)

Prefixes | 위·넘어·과다(1) out −², over

□□ outgrow	동 ~보다 더 커지다, 많아지다
□□ outlive	동 ~보다 더 오래 살다; ~보다 더 오래 지속되다
□□ outperform	동 ~보다 더 나은 결과를 내다, 능가하다
□□ outrun	동 ~보다 더 빨리[멀리] 달리다; 넘어서다
□□ outwit	동 ~보다 한 수 앞서다
□□ outweigh	동 ~보다 더 크다[대단하다]
□□ overcharge	동 과잉 청구하다
□□ overcome	동 극복하다; (남을) 이기다
□□ overdue	형 (지불·반납 등의) 기한이 지난
□□ overhear	동 (남의 대화 등을) 우연히 듣다
□□ overlook	동 간과하다; (잘못된 것을) 눈감아주다; (건물 등이) 내려다보다
□□ override	동 (결정·명령 등을) 기각[무시]하다; ~보다 더 중요하다
□□ overshadow	동 그늘지게 하다; 빛을 잃게 하다
□□ overwhelm	동 압도하다; 제압하다
□□ overwhelming	형 압도적인; 저항하기 힘든
□□ overtake	동 추월하다, 능가하다; (불쾌한 일이) 엄습하다
□□ overthrow	동 (정부·제도 등을) 뒤엎다 명 타도, 전복

Essential Roots / Stems | val(u) / vail

□□ overvalue	동 과대평가하다
□□ valuation	명 (가치) 평가
□□ valuable	형 소중한; 값비싼; 가치가 큰
□□ invaluable	형 값을 매길 수 없는, 귀중한
□□ valid	형 타당한, 근거 있는; 유효한
□□ validity	명 타당성; 유효성
□□ validate	동 정당성을 입증하다
□□ validation	명 확인; 비준
□□ avail	동 쓸모가 있다; 이용하다 명 이익, 유용성
□□ available	형 이용할 수 있는; 시간[여유]이 있는
□□ availability	명 유용성; (입수) 가능성
□□ evaluate	동 평가하다, 감정하다
□□ evaluation	명 평가
□□ devalue	동 가치를 떨어뜨리다; 평가절하하다
□□ devaluation	명 평가절하
□□ prevail	동 만연하다; 승리하다
□□ prevailing	형 (특정 시기에) 우세한, 지배적인
□□ prevalent	형 널리 퍼진

Words with Multiple Meanings | 필수 다의어의 이해

□□ cover	동 덮다 동 다루다, 포함하다 동 취재하다, 보도하다 동 (보험으로) 보장하다 동 (무엇을 하기에 충분한 돈을) 충당하다 동 (언급된 거리를) 가다
□□ cross	동 교차하다, 엇갈리다 명 십자; 십자가 동 서로 겹치게 놓다 동 (가로질러) 건너다, 횡단하다 동 (남의 계획 등에) 반대하다 형 짜증 난, 화난
□□ due	형 ~하기로 예정된 형 (돈을) 지불해야 하는 명 ((pl.)) (회원 등으로서 정기적으로) 내야 할 돈 형 (권리나 자격이 있는 사람에게) 주어야 하는 형 마땅한, 적절한 형 ~ 때문에, ~로 인한

Phrasal Verbs | over가 포함된 구동사 1

☐☐ bring over   (가지고 건너오다) 가지고 오다

☐☐ come over   (건너오다) 오다; 느끼다

☐☐ get over   (~을 넘어서다) 극복하다; 낫다

☐☐ give over to   (~에게 넘겨주다) 이용하다

☐☐ go over   (넘어가다; 다시 가다) 검토하다; 복습하다

☐☐ look over   (~의 모든 면을 보다) 훑어보다

Themes | 사회문제

☐☐ hierarchy   몡계급, 계층; 위계질서

☐☐ status   몡(사회적) 지위; (법적) 신분, 자격

☐☐ stratify   통층을 이루게 하다; 계층화하다

☐☐ stratum   몡(암석 등의) 층; (사회) 계층

☐☐ affluent   혱부유한

☐☐ lavish   혱호화로운; 후한
통낭비하다

☐☐ deprived   혱궁핍한, 가난한

☐☐ deprivation   몡(필수적인 것의) 박탈, 부족

☐☐ ethnic   혱민족의; 민족 전통적인

☐☐ ethnicity   몡민족성

☐☐ ethnocentrism   몡자기 민족 중심주의

☐☐ racial   혱인종의, 민족의

☐☐ racism   몡민족 우월 의식; 인종 차별(주의)

☐☐ racist   몡인종 차별주의자

☐☐ segregate   통(사람을) 분리[차별]하다

☐☐ segregation   몡분리; 차별 정책

☐☐ abandon   통(특히 돌볼 책임이 있는 대상을) 버리다; 그만두다

☐☐ abandonment   몡유기; 포기

☐☐ multicultural   혱다문화의

☐☐ revolutionize   통혁명[대변혁]을 일으키다

☐☐ revolutionary   혱혁명의; 혁명적인

☐☐ rebel   통반란을 일으키다; 반항[저항]하다
몡반역자 혱반역의

☐☐ rebellion   몡반란

☐☐ mob   몡군중; 폭도; (동물의) 떼

☐☐ demo   몡시위; 설명; (음악 작품을 담은) 데모 (테이프나 음반)

☐☐ harmonize   통조화를 이루다; 비슷하게 만들다

☐☐ harmonious   혱조화로운

☐☐ integrate   통통합하다

☐☐ integration   몡통합

☐☐ assimilate   통흡수하다; 이해하다; 동화되다

☐☐ assimilation   몡흡수; 동화

☐☐ contribute   통기부하다; (~의) 한 원인이 되다; 기여하다

☐☐ contribution   몡기부금; 기여

14강

words & phrases

□□ acclaim ⑧ 환호하다; 칭찬하다
⑲ 찬사, 칭찬

□□ advocate ⑧ (공개적으로) 지지하다[옹호하다]
⑲ 옹호자, 지지자; 변호사

□□ aquatic ⑱ 물속[물가]에서 자라는; 물과 관련된

□□ barrage ⑲ 연발 사격; (질문 등의) 세례

□□ blend ⑧ 섞다; 조합되다

□□ breathtaking ⑱ (아주 아름답거나 놀라워서) 숨이 막히는

□□ camouflage ⑲ 위장 ⑧ 위장하다

□□ characterization ⑲ 인물 묘사

□□ clone ⑲ 복제(품) ⑧ 복제하다

□□ columnist ⑲ 정기 기고가, 칼럼니스트

□□ creak ⑧ 삐걱거리다

□□ cuisine ⑲ (보통 비싼 식당의) 요리; 요리법

□□ enhance ⑧ 높이다, 향상하다

□□ filtration ⑲ 여과 (과정)

□□ first mate ⑲ 일등 항해사

□□ gymnast ⑲ 체육 교사; 체조 선수

□□ imaginary ⑱ 상상의, 가상의

□□ imaginative ⑱ 상상의; 창의적인, 상상력이 풍부한

□□ incineration ⑲ 소각; 화장

□□ keen ⑱ 예리한; 열정적인; 열망하는

□□ license ⑲ 면허(증); 허가
⑧ 허가하다

□□ ornament ⑲ 장식품, 장식 ⑧ 장식하다

□□ pharmacist ⑲ 약사

□□ physical ⑱ 육체[신체]의; 물질적인

□□ predator ⑲ 약탈자; 포식 동물

□□ quarter ⑲ 4분의 1; 1분기; 구역, 지구

□□ rudimentary ⑱ 가장 기본적인; 제대로 발달하지 못한

□□ scrapyard ⑲ 폐품 처리장

□□ sophistication ⑲ 교양; 세련

□□ surrounding ⑱ 인근의, 주위의
⑲ ((pl.)) (주위) 환경

□□ sustainable ⑱ 지속 가능한

□□ trillion ⑲ 1조; 엄청난 양

□□ verdict ⑲ (배심원단의) 평결; 의견, 결정

Prefixes | 위·넘어·과다(2) super - / sover -, sur -

☐☐ superb	휑 최고의, 최상의	☐☐ sovereignty	뗑 통치권, 자주권; (국가의) 독립
☐☐ superior	휑 (~보다 더) 우수한; 상급의 뗑 상급자	☐☐ surpass	됭 능가하다
☐☐ superiority	뗑 우월성, 우세	☐☐ unsurpassed	휑 그 누구에게도 뒤지지 않는
☐☐ superficial	휑 표면[피상]적인; 얄팍한	☐☐ surplus	뗑 과잉; 흑자 휑 과잉의
☐☐ superfluous	휑 여분의; 불필요한	☐☐ surmount	됭 (산 등을) 오르다; 극복하다
☐☐ superstition	뗑 미신	☐☐ insurmountable	휑 대처[극복]할 수 없는
☐☐ sovereign	뗑 주권자; 국왕 휑 주권을 가진; (국가가) 자주적인	☐☐ surveillance	뗑 감시

Essential Roots / Stems 1 | vis(e)

☐☐ supervise	됭 감독하다, 관리하다	☐☐ envision	됭 (미래의 일을) 상상하다, 예상하다
☐☐ supervision	뗑 감독, 관리	☐☐ improvise	됭 즉석에서[즉흥적으로] 하다
☐☐ supervisor	뗑 감독관, 관리자	☐☐ improvised	휑 즉흥의, 즉흥적으로 한
☐☐ visible	휑 볼 수 있는	☐☐ improvisation	뗑 즉석에서 하기; 즉흥 연주
☐☐ visibility	뗑 시야; 눈에 잘 보임	☐☐ proviso	뗑 (합의를 보기 위한) 단서, 조건
☐☐ visual	휑 시각적인, (눈으로) 보는	☐☐ revise	됭 수정하다; (책 등을) 개정하다
☐☐ visualize	됭 시각화하다; 마음속에 그려 보다	☐☐ revision	뗑 수정; 검토; 개정(판)
☐☐ vista	뗑 (아름다운) 경치; 전망, 예상		

Essential Roots / Stems 2 | vit / viv(e)

☐☐ survive	됭 살아남다; ~보다 더 오래 살다; (위기 등을) 견뎌 내다	☐☐ revive	됭 되살리다
☐☐ survival	뗑 생존	☐☐ revival	뗑 회복; 부활; 재공연
☐☐ vital	휑 생명의; 생명 유지와 관련된; 필수적인	☐☐ vivid	휑 (기억 등이) 생생한; (색깔 등이) 선명한
☐☐ vitality	뗑 생명력, 활력	☐☐ vivacious	휑 명랑한, 쾌활한
☐☐ vitalize	됭 활력을 북돋아 주다		

Words with Multiple Meanings | 필수 다의어의 이해

☐☐ deliver	됭 (물건·편지·전언 등을) 배달하다, 전달하다 됭 (연설·강연 등을) 하다 됭 (판결 등을) 내리다 됭 (약속을) 지키다 됭 (아기를) 낳다
☐☐ dispense	됭 나누어주다, 내놓다 됭 (서비스를) 제공하다, 베풀다 됭 (약사가 약을) 조제하다 됭 ((with)) 없애다, 생략하다 됭 ~ 없이 해내다

| □□ fail | 동 실패하다 동 ~하지 않다 동 고장 나다, 작동이 안 되다 동 (은행·회사 등이) 파산하다 |
| □□ fancy | 명 상상 형 상상의 동 상상[생각]하다 명 변덕 형 변덕스러운 명 기호, 애호 명 취미 형 장식이 많은, 화려한 형 (필요 이상으로) 복잡한 형 값비싼, 고급의 형 일류의 |

Phrasal Verbs | over가 포함된 구동사 2

□□ pull over	(당겨서 저쪽으로 건너가다) 차를 길가에 대다	□□ think over	(모든 면에 걸쳐 생각하다) 숙고하다
□□ run over	(~을 뛰어넘어 달리다) 치이다	□□ turn over	(돌려서 넘기다) 물려주다, 넘기다
□□ stop over	(정거했다가 넘어가다) 잠시 머무르다	□□ win over	(~를 이기다; 이겨서 끌어들이다) 자기편으로 끌어들이다
□□ take over	(~을 넘겨받다) 인계받다		

Themes | 자연·환경

□□ tide	명 조수, 밀물과 썰물; 흐름	□□ dumping	명 (유독 물질) 투기; ((경제)) 덤핑
□□ tidal	형 조수의	□□ landfill	명 쓰레기 매립(지)
□□ ebb	명 ((the ~)) 썰물; 감퇴 동 (조수가) 빠지다; 서서히 사그라지다	□□ deforestation	명 산림 벌채
		□□ desertification	명 사막화
□□ erode	동 침식시키다; (서서히) 약화시키다	□□ global warming	명 지구 온난화
□□ erosion	명 침식; 부식	□□ resource	명 자원 동 자원을 제공하다
□□ sediment	명 침전물; ((지리)) 퇴적물	□□ exhaust	동 고갈시키다; 지치게 하다 명 배기가스
□□ devastate	동 황폐화하다; 큰 충격을 주다		
□□ devastation	명 대대적인 파괴	□□ exhaustion	명 고갈; 탈진
□□ ecology	명 생태(계); 생태학	□□ preserve	동 보호하다; 보존하다
□□ ecological	형 생태계의; 생태계를 염려하는	□□ preservation	명 보호; 보존
□□ ecologist	명 생태학자; 환경 운동가	□□ conserve	동 보호하다; 보존하다; 아껴 쓰다
□□ eco-friendly	형 친환경적인		
□□ habitat	명 (동식물의) 서식지	□□ conservation	명 보호; 보존
□□ contaminate	동 오염시키다	□□ conservationist	명 환경 보호 활동가
□□ contamination	명 오염	□□ purify	동 정화하다, 정제하다
□□ contaminant	명 오염 물질	□□ purification	명 정화, 정제
□□ radioactive	형 방사능의	□□ recycle	동 재활용하다; 재생하다
□□ radioactivity	명 방사능	□□ recyclable	형 재활용할 수 있는
□□ dump	동 내버리다; (헐값에) 팔아 치우다		

words & phrases

□□ acquisition	몡 습득; (기업) 인수
□□ appeal	동 호소하다; ((법)) 항소하다 몡 호소; 항소
□□ cabinet	몡 캐비닛, 보관장; ((the C-)) (정부의) 내각
□□ compromise	몡 타협, 절충 동 타협하다
□□ dietary	형 식사의; 식이의
□□ dizzy	형 어지러운; 아찔한
□□ expel	동 쫓아내다; 퇴학시키다; 배출하다
□□ experiment	몡 (과학) 실험; 실험 장치 동 실험하다
□□ feasible	형 실현 가능한
□□ glimpse	몡 흘끗 봄 동 흘끗 보다; 깨닫다
□□ infiltrate	동 스며들다; 잠입하다
□□ interval	몡 (두 사건 사이) 간격; (연극 등의) 중간 휴식 시간
□□ librarian	몡 (도서관의) 사서

□□ microgravity	몡 미세 중력, 극미 중력
□□ moderate	형 보통의, 중도의; 온건한; 적당한 동 누그러지다; 누그러뜨리다
□□ modification	몡 (개선을 위한) 수정
□□ on bail	보석금을 내고
□□ organism	몡 유기체, (미세한) 생물체
□□ pediatric	형 소아과(학)의
□□ posterity	몡 후세, 후대; 자손
□□ reactive	형 반응[반작용]을 보이는
□□ replicate	동 복제하다
□□ ruling party	몡 ((정치)) 여당
□□ sluggish	형 느릿느릿 움직이는; 부진한
□□ strain	동 혹사하다, 무리하게 사용하다 몡 부담, 압박(감)
□□ swelling	몡 (살갗의) 부기; (몸의) 부어오른 곳

Prefixes | 아래(1) in under -, sub -

☐☐ undercover 　 형 비밀리에 하는; 첩보 활동의

☐☐ underlie 　 동 (~의) 기초를 이루다

☐☐ underlying 　 형 밑에 있는; (겉으로는 잘 드러나지 않지만) 근본적인

☐☐ undergraduate 　 명 대학생, (대학) 학부생
　 형 대학(생)의

☐☐ underestimate 　 동 너무 적게 추정하다; 과소평가하다
　 명 과소 견적; 과소평가

☐☐ understate 　 동 (실제보다) 축소해서 말하다

☐☐ undergo 　 동 (안 좋은 일 등을) 겪다

☐☐ undermine 　 동 밑을 파다; (자신감 등을) 약화시키다

☐☐ undertake 　 동 (책임을 맡아서) 착수하다; 약속[동의]하다

☐☐ subconscious 　 명 잠재의식
　 형 잠재의식적인

☐☐ subdue 　 동 진압하다; (감정을) 억누르다

☐☐ subtitle 　 명 ((pl.)) (화면의) 자막; (책의) 부제
　 동 자막이나 부제를 달다

☐☐ subsequent 　 형 그[이]다음의, 차후의

☐☐ submerge 　 동 잠수하다, 물속에 잠기다; 몰두시키다

☐☐ subordinate 　 명 부하, 하급자
　 형 종속된; 부수적인
　 동 아래에 두다; 경시하다

☐☐ subsidiary 　 형 부수적인
　 명 자회사

☐☐ subside 　 동 가라앉다, 진정되다; 물이 빠지다; (땅 등이) 내려앉다

☐☐ supplement 　 명 추가(물), 보충(물); (신문의) 증보판; (책의) 부록
　 동 보충[추가]하다

☐☐ supplementary 　 형 추가의, 보충하는

Essential Roots / Stems | pend / pens

☐☐ suspend 　 동 매달다; 중단[유예]하다; 정학시키다

☐☐ pendant 　 명 펜던트

☐☐ pendulum 　 명 (시계의) 추; 진자

☐☐ pending 　 형 미결[미정]인; 곧 있을
　 전 ~을 기다리는 동안

☐☐ impending 　 형 (안 좋은 일이) 곧 닥칠, 임박한

☐☐ depend 　 동 ((on, upon)) 의지하다, 달려 있다

☐☐ dependence 　 명 의지, 의존

☐☐ dependent 　 형 의존하는

☐☐ appendix 　 명 부록; ((신체)) 맹장

Words with Multiple Meanings | 필수 다의어의 이해

☐☐ suspend 　 동 매달다 형 (공식적으로) 중단하다, 유예하다 동 정학시키다, 정직시키다

☐☐ support 　 동 (넘어지지 않도록) 떠받치다 명 버팀대 동 지지하다, 지원하다 명 지지, 지원
　 동 부양하다; 돈을 대다 명 부양, 후원
　 동 (사실임을) 뒷받침하다 명 (사실임을) 뒷받침하는 증거

Phrasal Verbs | down이 포함된 구동사 1

□□ blow down (불어서 아래에 놓다) 쓰러뜨리다

□□ break down (깨져서 멈추다 / 깨서 무너뜨리다) 고장 나다; 분해되다

□□ bring down (아래로 가져오다) 내리다; 실각시키다

□□ calm down 진정시키다

□□ come down with (~ 때문에 쇠약해져 오다) 걸리다

□□ cut down (on) (잘라서 감소시키다) 줄이다

□□ get down, let down (아래에 있게 하다) 낙심하다

□□ go down (아래로 가다) 가라앉다

□□ hand down (아래로 건네다) 전하다

□□ hold down (억누른 상태를 유지하다) 억제하다

□□ look down on (~을 아래로 보다) 멸시하다

□□ mark down (줄여서 표시하다) 가격이 인하되다; 점수가 깎이다

□□ narrow down (아래로 좁히다) 줄이다

□□ pass down (아래로 넘기다) 전달하다

Themes | 실험·연구·조사

□□ hypothesis 명 가설; 추측

□□ hypothetical 형 가설의

□□ plausible 형 그럴듯한, 타당한 것 같은

□□ plausibility 명 그럴듯함, 타당성

□□ formulate 동 (세심히) 만들어 내다; (의견을) 진술하다

□□ simulate 동 ~인 척하다; 모의실험하다

□□ simulation 명 모의실험, 시뮬레이션

□□ glean 동 (정보 등을 여기저기서) 모으다

□□ incidence 명 (사건 등의) 발생 정도; ((물리)) (빛의) 입사

□□ probe 명 탐침; (철저한) 조사 동 탐사하다; 조사하다

□□ statistic 명 ((pl.)) 통계(학); 통계 자료

□□ statistical 형 통계적인, 통계학상의

□□ manifest 형 (보기에) 명백한 동 (분명히) 나타내다

□□ pinpoint 동 정확히 보여주다 형 정확한

□□ ascertain 동 확인하다, 알아내다

□□ concrete 형 구체적인; 콘크리트로 만든 명 콘크리트

□□ factual 형 사실에 기반을 둔, 사실을 담은

□□ theoretical 형 이론적인

□□ generalize 동 개괄적으로 말하다; 일반화하다

□□ generalization 명 일반화

□□ specify 동 구체화하다, 구체적으로 명시하다

□□ specification 명 상술; (자세한) 설명서

□□ specific 형 구체적인; 특정한

□□ parallel 형 평행한; 아주 유사한 명 ~와 유사한 사람[것] 동 ~와 유사하다

□□ overall 형 전반적인 부 전부

□□ proportion 명 (전체에 대한) 부분; 비율; 크기; 균형

□□ diminish 동 줄어들다

□□ leap 동 (높이·멀리) 뛰다; 급증하다 명 높이[멀리]뛰기; 급증

□□ exponential 형 (증가율이) 급격한; ((수학)) 지수의

□□ exponentially 부 기하급수적으로

words & phrases

□□ barrage	명 연발 사격; (질문 등의) 세례
□□ calibrate	통 (계기 등에) 눈금을 매기다 [정하다]
□□ computation	명 계산; 컴퓨터 사용[조작]
□□ condemn	통 비난하다; 선고를 내리다; 부적격 판정을 내리다
□□ craving	명 갈망, 열망
□□ dictator	명 독재자
□□ dramatic	형 희곡의; 극적인; 인상적인
□□ fixation	명 고정, 고착; 집착
□□ friction	명 마찰
□□ fusion	명 용해; 융합
□□ hostage	명 인질
□□ hypocrite	명 위선자
□□ inference	명 추론, 추리
□□ inundate	통 감당 못할 정도로 주다[보내다]; 침수시키다
□□ loom	통 흐릿하게 보이다, 어렴풋이 나타나다
□□ make way for	~에게 자리를 내주다; ~에 길을 열어 주다
□□ malnutrition	명 영양실조
□□ nourishment	명 영양(분)
□□ obesity	명 비만
□□ perseverance	명 인내(심)
□□ purifier	명 정화 장치
□□ ruthless	형 무자비한; 인정사정없는
□□ stationary	형 움직이지 않는, 정지된; 변하지 않는
□□ stop off at	~에 잠시 들르다
□□ strike	통 치다; 공격하다; 파업하다 명 공습; 파업
□□ too much of a good thing	좋은 것이라도 지나치면 싫은
□□ trope	명 비유; 수사
□□ volume	명 (두꺼운) 책; 부피; 용량; (라디오 등의) 음량
□□ weightlessness	명 무중력

Prefixes | 아래(2) de –³

□□ decay	동 부패하다; (권력 등이) 쇠퇴하다 명 부패; 쇠퇴
□□ decadence	명 타락, 퇴폐; 쇠퇴
□□ deduce	동 추론하다, 연역하다
□□ deduction	명 추론, 연역; 공제(액)
□□ depict	동 (그림으로) 그리다; 묘사하다
□□ deflate	동 (타이어 등의) 공기를 빼다; (물가를) 끌어내리다
□□ degenerate	동 악화되다 형 타락한
□□ demolish	동 파괴하다; (건물을) 철거하다
□□ demolition	명 파괴, 폭파

□□ denounce	동 맹렬히 비난하다; 고발하다
□□ denunciation	명 맹렬한 비난
□□ delude	동 속이다
□□ delusion	명 망상; 착각
□□ deride	동 조롱하다, 조소하다
□□ derision	명 조롱, 조소
□□ deposit	동 (특정한 곳에) 두다; 예금하다; 맡기다 명 예금; 보증금; 매장층
□□ despise	동 경멸하다
□□ descend	동 내려가다
□□ descent	명 하강; 내리막; 혈통
□□ descendant	명 자손, 후손

Essential Roots / Stems 1 | press

□□ depress	동 우울하게 만들다; (경기를) 침체시키다; (물가를) 떨어뜨리다
□□ depression	명 우울증; 불경기
□□ pressing	형 긴박한
□□ compress	동 압축하다; 요약하다 명 압박 붕대
□□ express	동 (감정 등을) 나타내다, 표현하다 형 분명한; 급행의

□□ oppress	동 ((특히 정치적 상황)) 억압하다; 우울하게 만들다
□□ oppression	명 억압
□□ repress	동 (감정 등을) 억누르다; 진압하다
□□ repression	명 억압; 탄압, 진압
□□ suppress	동 (정부 등이) 진압하다; 억누르다; 멈추게 하다
□□ suppression	명 진압; 억제

Essential Roots / Stems 2 | preci / prais

□□ depreciate	동 가치가 떨어지다; 평가 절하하다
□□ depreciation	명 가치 하락; 경시
□□ appreciate	동 이해하다; 진가를 알다; 감사하다; 감상하다

□□ appraise	동 (공식적으로) 평가하다, 감정하다
□□ appraisal	명 (가치에 대한) 평가, 감정

Words with Multiple Meanings | 필수 다의어의 이해

□□ appreciate | 图 (제대로) 인식하다, 이해하다 图 진가를 알아보다 图 고마워하다 图 (문학 등을) 감상하다

□□ express | 图 (감정·의견 등을) 나타내다, 표현하다 國 분명한, 명확한 國 급행의; 신속한 圓 급행열차

□□ decline | 图 기울다 图 감소하다 图 악화되다 图 (정중히) 거절하다

□□ feature | 圓 특징, 특색 图 특징으로 삼다
圓 용모, 이목구비(의 각 부분) 圓 지세, 지형 圓 (신문·텔레비전 등의) 특집 기사[방송]

Phrasal Verbs | down이 포함된 구동사 2

□□ push down | (밀어서 누르다) 억누르다

□□ put down | (아래에 두다) 적다; 진압하다

□□ settle down | (움직이지 않게 두다)
진정시키다; 정착하다

□□ shout down | (소리 질러 정지시키다)
소리를 질러 이기다

□□ take down,
write down,
jot down | (붙들어 두다) 적다

□□ tear down | (찢어 무너뜨리다) 허물다

□□ turn down | 줄이다; 거절하다

Themes | 물리

□□ atom | 圓 원자

□□ atomic | 國 원자의; 원자력의

□□ molecule | 圓 분자

□□ molecular | 國 분자의

□□ nuclear | 國 원자력의; 원자(핵)의;
핵(무기)의

□□ nucleus | 圓 (원자)핵; 중심

□□ electron | 圓 전자

□□ electronic | 國 전자의; 전자 공학의

□□ particle | 圓 극소량; (아주 작은) 입자

□□ electric | 國 전기의 圓 전기 설비

□□ electrify | 图 (물체에) 전기를 통하게
하다

□□ electrode | 圓 전극

□□ voltage | 圓 전압

□□ polar | 國 북극[남극]의; ((자석))
양극의

□□ polarize | 图 극성을 갖게 하다; 양극화
하다

□□ magnetic | 國 자석의; 매력 있는

□□ conductor | 圓 (전기나 열의) 전도체; 지휘
자; 안내원

□□ conductivity | 圓 전도성, 전도율

□□ kinetic | 國 운동학상의; 활동적인

□□ gravitate | 图 인력에 끌리다; (물건이)
가라앉다

□□ gravity | 圓 중력; 심각성

□□ inertia | 圓 ((물리)) 관성; 타성; 무력(증)

□□ velocity | 圓 속도, 속력

□□ photon | 圓 광자

□□ infrared | 圓 적외선 國 적외선의

□□ spectrum | 圓 (빛의) 스펙트럼; 범위

□□ refraction | 圓 굴절(작용)

□□ radiate | 图 (빛·열 등을) 방출하다

□□ radiation | 圓 (열 등의) 복사; 방사선

□□ radiator | 圓 (빛·열 등의) 방사체; 난방기

□□ radiant | 國 빛[열]을 내는; 복사의

□□ luminescent | 國 발광성의

□□ thermal | 國 열의; 보온이 잘되는

□□ thermometer | 圓 온도계, 체온계

17 강

강 MP3

words & phrases

□□ abundantly	튀 풍부하게
□□ administration	몡 관리, 행정(부); 집행
□□ atomic	톙 원자(력)의
□□ aviation	몡 비행, 항공
□□ banquet	몡 (공식) 연회, 만찬
□□ collapse	동 (건물 등이) 붕괴하다; (사람이) 쓰러지다
□□ criminal	톙 범죄의, 형사상의 몡 범죄자
□□ dropout	몡 중퇴자
□□ evaporate	동 증발하다; (차츰) 사라지다
□□ fertility	몡 비옥함; 생식력
□□ flammable	톙 가연성의, 불에 잘 타는
□□ hang together	잘 들어맞다; 일치하다, 일관되다

□□ harmonious	톙 조화로운
□□ late fee	몡 연체료
□□ modernize	동 현대화하다
□□ nanotechnology	몡 나노 기술
□□ respiratory	톙 호흡기의
□□ retain	동 보유하다
□□ rigorous	톙 (규칙 적용 등이) 철저한, 엄격한; 혹독한
□□ seal	동 (봉투를) 봉하다; 밀폐하다 몡 직인; 봉인; 바다표범
□□ strand	동 좌초시키다; 오도 가도 못하게 하다
□□ trimming	몡 (테두리 등의) 장식; ((pl.)) 곁들이는 음식
□□ vigorous	톙 활발한, 활기찬; 격렬한

Prefixes | 이전·미리·먼저(1) fore-, ante-

□□ forecast	동 예측하다 몡 예측, 예보
□□ forefront	몡 맨 앞, 선두; 가장 중요한 위치[지위]
□□ foremost	톙 맨 앞에 있는; 가장 중요한; 유명한
□□ foreshadow	동 전조가 되다, 조짐을 나타내다
□□ foresight	몡 예지력, 선견지명
□□ foreword	몡 (책의 짤막한) 머리말, 서문

□□ antedate	동 (시간적으로) ~보다 먼저 일어나다
□□ antique	몡 (귀중한) 골동품 톙 골동품인
□□ antiquity	몡 고대 (유물); 아주 오래됨
□□ antiquated	톙 (더 이상 쓸 수 없게) 구식인, 오래된
□□ ancestor	몡 조상, 선조
□□ ancestry	몡 가계, 혈통
□□ ancestral	톙 조상의

□□ anticipate	동 예상하다; 기대하다
□□ anticipation	명 예상; 기대
□□ captivate	동 ~의 마음을 사로잡다
□□ capture	동 사로잡다; 점유하다; (사진이나 글로) 담아내다; ((컴퓨터)) 캡처하다 명 포획(물); (데이터의) 캡처
□□ acceptance	명 받아들임, 수락
□□ acceptable	형 받아들일 수 있는
□□ concept	명 개념
□□ conceptual	형 개념의
□□ conceive	동 (계획 등을) 마음속으로 품다, 상상하다; 임신하다
□□ conceivable	형 상상할 수 있는
□□ conception	명 구상; 이해; 신념; (난소의) 수정
□□ conceit	명 자부심; 자만
□□ deceive	동 속이다, 기만하다
□□ deceit	명 사기; 속임수
□□ deceitful	형 사기성의

□□ except	전 ~을 제외하고 동 제외하다
□□ exception	명 제외; 예외
□□ exceptional	형 예외적인; 출중한
□□ intercept	동 (중간에) 가로막다; 가로채다
□□ interception	명 차단; (통신의) 도청
□□ receive	동 받다; (격식을 차려) 환영하다
□□ receiver	명 수취인; 수신기; 수화기
□□ reception	명 수취; 접수; 환영(회)
□□ receptionist	명 접수 담당자
□□ receptive	형 잘 받아들이는; 감수성이 풍부한
□□ receipt	명 수령; 영수증
□□ recipient	명 (어떤 것을) 받는 사람, 수령인
□□ susceptible	형 (~에) 영향받기 쉬운; 민감한; 취약한
□□ susceptibility	명 민감성; 감수성; 취약성

□□ figure	명 (공식적인 자료의) 수치 명 도표 명 도형, 그림 명 (사람의) 모습, 형상 명 (중요한) 인물, 인사 동 ((out)) ~을 알아내다, 이해하다
□□ discipline	명동 규율; 훈육(하다) 명동 훈련(하다), 단련(하다) 명 자제(심), 절제력 명 (특히 대학의) 학과(목), 학문의 분야
□□ fit	동 ~에 맞다 동 (의복 등이) ~에 꼭 맞다 명 몸에 맞는 옷 형 (~하기에) 적합한, 알맞은 형 건강한
□□ exercise	명동 운동(하다) 명 (기량을 닦기 위한) 연습, 훈련 명동 (권력·권리 등을) 행사(하다)

□□ be into	(~안으로 들어가 있다) 좋아하다	□□ fall into	(~안으로 떨어지다) 시작하다; 속하다
□□ break into	(깨고 안으로 들어가다) 끼어들다; 침입하다	□□ fit into	(~안으로 꼭 맞다) 들어맞다
		□□ get into	(~안으로 들어가다) 진입하다
□□ crash into	(부수고 안으로 들어가다) 충돌하다	□□ go into	(~안으로 들어가다) 투입되다
		□□ grow into	(자라서 ~안으로 들어가다) 커지다

Themes | 화학

□□ di-	((화학)) 둘(2)의	□□ precipitate	동 (나쁜 일을) 촉발시키다; 침전하다
□□ dioxide	명 ((화학)) 이산화물		명 ((화학)) 침전물
□□ element	명 요소; ((화학)) 원소	□□ precipitation	명 강수(량); ((화학)) 침전
□□ -proof	~을 막는, 내-, 방-	□□ refine	동 정제하다; 개선하다
□□ fireproof	형 불연성의	□□ refined	형 (물질이) 정제된; 교양 있는, 세련된
□□ solvent	형 지불 능력이 있는; 용해력이 있는	□□ corrode	동 (금속이) 부식하다
	명 용매	□□ corrosion	명 부식
□□ durable	형 오래 견디는	□□ oxidize	동 산화시키다; 녹슬게 하다
□□ durability	명 내구성	□□ oxidation	명 산화
□□ volatile	형 휘발성의; 변덕스러운	□□ oxidant	명 산화제
□□ absorb	동 흡수하다; (사람의 마음을) 열중시키다	□□ residue	명 잔여, 나머지; ((화학)) 잔류물
□□ absorption	명 흡수; 전념	□□ alchemy	명 연금술; (물건을 변질시키는) 마력
□□ dense	형 빽빽한; (안개 등이) 짙은		
□□ density	명 밀도; 농도	□□ alchemist	명 연금술사
□□ solid	형 고체의; 순수한	□□ tarnish	동 (윤이 나는 것이) 흐려지다; (평판을) 손상시키다
	명 고체		명 변색
□□ solidify	동 굳어지다	□□ ignite	동 불이 붙다
□□ solidity	명 굳음; 견고함	□□ ignition	명 점화
□□ solidarity	명 연대, 결속	□□ combust	동 연료를 태우다, 연소하다
□□ saturate	동 흠뻑 적시다; 포화 상태로 만들다	□□ combustion	명 연소; 산화
□□ saturation	명 ((화학)) 포화 (상태)		

18강

words & phrases

□□ adolescent 〔명〕청소년

□□ adoption 〔명〕채택; 입양

□□ assume 〔동〕가정하다; 떠맡다; ~인 척
하다

□□ authorized 〔형〕인정받은; 공인된; 권한을
부여받은

□□ axis 〔명〕(중심) 축, 축선

□□ barrel 〔명〕(목재·금속으로 된 대형) 통;
한 통의 양

□□ cub 〔명〕(곰, 사자 등의) 새끼

□□ den 〔명〕(야생 동물이 사는) 굴, 동굴;
(부정한 행위를 하기 위한)
소굴; 은신처

□□ gender 〔명〕성, 성별

□□ go to seed 한창때가 지나다, 쇠퇴하다

□□ hazardous 〔형〕(특히 사람의 건강·안전에)
위험한

□□ individualized 〔형〕개별화된

□□ infection 〔명〕감염; 전염병

□□ instruction 〔명〕가르침, 교육;
((pl.)) 지시; 사용 설명서

□□ noted 〔형〕유명한

□□ parliament 〔명〕의회, 국회

□□ personnel 〔명〕(회사·군대 등의) 인원;
인사과

□□ primary 〔형〕초기의; 주요한

□□ qualification 〔명〕자격(증); 자질, 능력

□□ reverse 〔동〕뒤집다

□□ runaway 〔명〕도망자, (특히 청소년) 가출
자
〔형〕달아난, 고삐 풀린

□□ takeoff 〔명〕출발(점), 이륙 (지점); 제거,
분리

□□ territory 〔명〕지역, 영토; (자기 소유의)
영역

□□ vegetation 〔명〕(특정 지역의) 초목, 식물

□□ virtually 〔부〕사실상, 거의;
((컴퓨터)) 가상으로

Prefixes | 이전·미리·먼저(2) pre -

□□ predate 〔동〕~보다 선행하다

□□ predominant 〔형〕우세한; 두드러진, 눈에
띄는

□□ predominance 〔명〕우위, 우세

□□ preoccupy 〔동〕선취하다; 마음을 빼앗다

□□ preoccupation 〔명〕(생각·걱정 등에) 사로잡힘;
집착

□□ preface 〔명〕서문 〔동〕서문을 쓰다

□□ prejudice 〔명〕편견
〔동〕편견을 갖게 하다

□□ prelude 〔명〕(음악의) 서곡; (중요한 일의)
서곡, 전조

□□ premise 〔명〕(주장의) 전제

□□ prerequisite 〔명〕(필요한) 전제 조건

□□ presume 〔동〕(사실일 것으로) 추정하다

□□ presumption 〔명〕추정(되는 것)

□□ presumably 〔부〕아마, 추정컨대

□□ preview 〔명〕시사회; 예고편
〔동〕시연을 보이다; 사전 조사
하다

Essential Roots / Stems | ced(e) / ceed / cess / ceas

□□ precede	동 ~에 선행하다	□□ antecedent	형 앞서는, 선행하는
□□ precedence	명 우선(함), 우선권		명 선례; ((문법)) 선행사; ((pl.)) 조상, 선조
□□ precedent	명 선례, 전례	□□ exceed	동 초과하다
□□ unprecedented	형 전례 없는	□□ excess	명 초과; 과잉 형 초과한
□□ predecessor	명 전임자; 이전 것	□□ excessive	형 지나친, 과도한
□□ proceed	동 나아가다; (계속) 진행하다; 소송을 제기하다	□□ exceedingly	부 극도로, 대단히
□□ proceeding	명 ((pl.)) 소송 절차; 행사; 회의록	□□ concede	동 인정하다, 수긍하다; 허락하다
□□ process	명 과정; 진행 동 가공하다; 처리하다	□□ concession	명 양보; 인정
		□□ recede	동 물러가다; 퇴각하다; (가치 등이) 감소하다
□□ processed	형 가공한	□□ recess	명 휴회 (기간), (학교 등의) 쉬는 시간 동 휴회를 하다
□□ procession	명 행렬; 행진		
□□ procedure	명 절차, 방법; 수술		
□□ procedural	형 절차상의	□□ recession	명 후퇴; 불경기, 불황
□□ access	명 ((to)) (~로의) 접근(권) 동 (컴퓨터에) 접속하다	□□ succeed	동 계승하다; 상속하다; 성공하다
□□ accessible	형 접근하기 쉬운	□□ decease	명 사망 동 사망하다
□□ accessibility	명 접근성		

Words with Multiple Meanings | 필수 다의어의 이해

□□ occupy	동 (공간·지역·시간을) 차지하다, 사용하다 동 점령[점거]하다 동 (지위·일자리를) 차지하다
□□ succeed	동 (자리·지위 등을) 계승하다; 상속하다 동 (하려던 일에) 성공하다 동 (부·명예 등을 얻어) 성공하다, 출세하다
□□ withdraw	동 철수시키다 동 (제공 등을) 중단하다, 취소하다 동 (활동·조직에서) 탈퇴[기권]하다 동 (계좌에서 돈을) 인출하다
□□ present	형 (사람·사물이) 있는, 존재하는; 참석한 명 현재 형 현재의 동 증정[수여]하다 명 선물 동 제시하다, 제출하다 동 (문제 등을) 일으키다, 겪게 하다

Phrasal Verbs | into가 포함된 구동사 2

□□ put into	(~안으로 집어넣다) 더하다	□□ turn into	(돌아서 ~으로 되다) 변하다
□□ run into	(~안으로 뛰어들다) 부딪히다	□□ come into effect	(효력 안으로 들어오다) 시행 되다
□□ talk into	(말해서 ~을 하게 하다) 말해서 하게 하다	□□ take into consideration	(생각 속으로 데리고 가다) 고려하다
□□ throw into	(~안으로 던지다) 전념하다		

Themes | 지구과학·생물

□□ cosmos	몡 (질서 있는 시스템으로서의) 우주	□□ adapt	동 적응하다; 개작[각색]하다
□□ cosmic	형 우주의; 무한한	□□ adaptation	명 적응; 각색
□□ eclipse	명 (일식·월식의) 식; (중요성 등이) 빛을 잃음	□□ adaptability	명 적응성
		□□ breed	동 새끼를 낳다; 사육[재배]하다
□□ celestial	형 하늘의		명 (가축의) 품종
□□ orbit	명 궤도 동 궤도를 돌다	□□ microbe	명 미생물; 세균
□□ hemisphere	명 (지구·뇌의) 반구	□□ ferment	동 발효되다
□□ latitude	명 위도		명 발효균, 효소; (사회적) 동요
□□ rotate	동 회전하다; (일을) 교대로 하다	□□ fauna	명 (특정 지역·시대의) 동물군
		□□ nocturnal	형 야행성의
□□ organism	명 유기체	□□ hibernate	동 동면하다
□□ organic	형 유기체의; 유기농의	□□ hibernation	명 동면
□□ species	명 종	□□ sprout	동 싹이 나다
□□ evolve	동 진화하다; (점진적으로) 발달하다	□□ luxuriant	형 (식물이) 무성한; 풍부한
□□ evolution	명 ((생물)) 진화; (점진적) 발달	□□ luxuriance	명 (식물의) 무성함; 풍부함; (문체의) 화려함
□□ mutant	형 돌연변이의 명 변종	□□ wither	동 시들다; 말라 죽다

19강 MP3

words & phrases

□□ cast	동 던지다; (빛 등을) 발하다, 드리우다
□□ convention	명 (대규모) 회의, 집회; 조약, 협약; 관습
□□ copyright	명 저작권, 판권 동 저작권[판권]을 얻다 형 저작권 보호를 받는
□□ deem	동 (~으로) 여기다, 생각하다
□□ eviction	명 쫓겨남, 퇴거
□□ get off the ground	이륙하다; 순조롭게 출발하다
□□ inevitable	형 불가피한, 필연적인
□□ integrity	명 고결, 성실; 완전한 상태, 온전함
□□ irrigation	명 관개, 물을 끌어들임
□□ judiciary	명 사법부
□□ laureate	명 (뛰어난 업적으로 상을 받은) 수상자
□□ lease	명 임대차 계약 동 (부동산·장비를) 임대[임차·대여]하다
□□ lessee	명 ((법률)) 임차인
□□ mediator	명 중재인; 중재[조정] 기관
□□ mugger	명 노상강도
□□ omen	명 징조, 조짐
□□ paradigm	명 패러다임, 이론적 틀; 전형적인 예[양식]
□□ prominence	명 중요성; 명성
□□ prompt	형 즉각적인, 신속한; 시간을 엄수하는 동 촉발하다
□□ radius	명 반지름; 반경, 범위
□□ referendum	명 국민투표, 총선거
□□ regulation	명 규칙; 조절
□□ reluctant	형 꺼리는, 마지못한
□□ scrap	명 (종이 등의) 조각; 남은 음식; 폐품 동 폐기하다
□□ stipulate	동 규정하다, 명기하다
□□ unsporting	형 (특히 경기에서) 정정당당하지 않은

Prefixes | 이동·관통(1) dia -, 이후·뒤·다음 post -

□□ diagonal	형 (직선이) 사선의; 대각선의
□□ diagram	명 도표, 도해
□□ diameter	명 직경, 지름
□□ diametric(al)	형 지름의; 정반대의
□□ dialect	명 방언, 사투리
□□ dialectal	형 방언의; 방언 특유의
□□ posterity	명 후세, 후대; 자손
□□ posterior	형 ((명사 앞)) 뒤의, 뒤쪽에 있는
□□ postdate	동 실제보다 날짜를 늦추어 적다; (시간상으로) 뒤에 일어나다
□□ postindustrial	형 탈공업화의, 탈공업 시대의
□□ postpone	동 연기하다, 미루다
□□ posthumous	형 사후의

Essential Roots / Stems | scrib(e) / script

□□ postscript	몡(편지 등의) 추신; (책 등의) 후기	□□ transcription	몡필사(본); 복사(본)
□□ script	몡대본; 글씨 동대본을 쓰다	□□ transcript	몡사본; ((미)) 성적증명서
□□ scripture	몡((pl.)) (특정 종교의) 경전; ((S- 혹은 the Scriptures)) 성서	□□ prescribe	동(의사가) 처방하다; 규정 하다
		□□ prescription	몡처방(전); 처방된 약; 규정
□□ scribble	동휘갈겨 쓰다; 낙서하다 몡휘갈겨 쓴 글씨; 낙서	□□ prescriptive	혱규정하는, 지시하는; 규범 적인
□□ describe	동묘사하다, 서술하다	□□ inscribe	동(이름 등을 돌이나 금속에) 새기다
□□ description	몡묘사, 서술		
□□ descriptive	혱묘사적인	□□ inscription	몡새겨진 글
□□ ascribe	동((A to B)) A의 원인을 B에 두다, A를 B의 탓으로 돌리 다	□□ circumscribe	동주위에 선을 긋다; (권리·자유 등을) 제한하다
		□□ subscribe	동((to, for)) 서명하여 동의 하다; (서비스를) 신청하다; 정기구독하다; 기부하다
□□ ascription	몡원인이 있다고 여김; 치부		
□□ transcribe	동기록하다; 옮겨 적다; 복사 하다	□□ subscription	몡정기구독(료); 기부금
		□□ subscriber	몡정기구독자; 기부자

Words with Multiple Meanings | 필수 다의어의 이해

□□ flat	혱평평한 몡평원, 평지 몡개펄 혱납작한 혱바람이 빠진 혱몡펑크 난 (타이어) 혱김이 빠진; 생기가 없는 혱(요금이) 균일한, 고정된 몡아파트식 주거지
□□ foster	동(수양 자식으로 아이를) 기르다 동육성[촉진]시키다 동(감정 등을) 마음에 품다
□□ game	몡경기, 게임 몡(대규모 스포츠) 대회 몡사냥감 몡재미로 하는 일, 장난
□□ ground	몡땅 몡(특정 용도를 위한) 장소, -장 몡운동장 몡(건물 주위의) 뜰, 구내 몡바닥 몡근거, 기초 동근거[기초]를 두다 몡입장, 의견 동(벌로) 외출을 금지하다

Phrasal Verbs | along이 포함된 구동사

□□ bring along (~을 가지고 같이 오다) 가지고 오다

□□ come along (~을 따라오다[가다]) 따라가다

□□ get along (따르게[같이 하게 되다]) 잘 어울려 지내다

□□ go along (with) ((~을 함께) 따라가다) 진행되다; 따르다

□□ play along (with) (~을 따라 연주하다) 함께 연주하다; 동조하다

□□ take along (~을 가지고[데리고] 같이 가다) 데려가다

Themes | 법

□□ constitution 명 구성; 체질; 헌법

□□ justice 명 공정성; 사법; 재판

□□ norm 명 ((the ~)) 표준; ((pl.)) 규범; 기준

□□ moral 형 도덕상의; 도덕적인 명 교훈

□□ morality 명 도덕(성)

□□ conscience 명 양심

□□ conscientious 형 양심적인; 성실한

□□ legislate 동 법률을 제정하다

□□ legislation 명 법률 제정, 입법

□□ legislative 형 입법의, 입법부의

□□ legislature 명 입법부, 입법 기관

□□ regularize 동 규칙화하다; 합법화하다

□□ legitimate 형 합법적인; 정당한

□□ amend 동 (법 등을) 개정하다 ; (행실 등을) 고치다

□□ amendment 명 개정; 변경

□□ abolish 동 (법률·제도·조직을) 폐지하다

□□ abolition 명 (법률·제도·조직의) 폐지

□□ comply 동 (법·명령 등에) 따르다

□□ compliance 명 (법 등의) 준수; (명령 등에) 따름

□□ uphold 동 (법 등을) 유지시키다; (이전의 판결을) 확인하다

□□ abide by 동 (규칙 등을) 지키다

□□ abiding 형 지속적인, 변치 않는

□□ breach 명 위반; 파괴 동 (합의나 약속을) 위반하다

□□ infringe 동 (법률 등을) 위반하다; (법적 권리를) 침해하다

□□ infringement 명 (법규) 위반; (특허권 등의) 침해

□□ enforce 동 (법을) 집행[시행]하다; 강요하다

□□ enforcement 명 (법) 집행[시행]

□□ grant 동 (특히 공식적·법적으로) 승인하다; (내키지 않지만) 인정하다 명 (정부나 단체에서 주는) 보조금

□□ prohibit 동 (법으로) 금지하다

□□ prohibitive 형 (법으로) 금지하는; 엄두를 못 낼 만큼 비싼

□□ banish 동 (국외로) 추방하다; 사라지게 만들다

□□ exile 명 망명(자); 추방 동 추방하다

□□ forfeit 명 벌금; 몰수품 형 몰수된 동 몰수당하다

□□ rigid 형 뻣뻣한; (규칙 등이) 엄격한

□□ rigidity 명 단단함; 엄격

20 강

words & phrases

□□ actionable	형 소송을 제기할 수 있는
□□ alibi	명 알리바이; 변명
□□ allergy	명 알레르기
□□ as per A	(미리 결정된) A에 따라
□□ autopsy	명 (시체) 부검, 검시
□□ bribe	명 뇌물 동 뇌물을 주다, 매수하다
□□ capital	명 수도; 대문자; 자본
□□ contrast	명 차이; 대조; 화면의 명암 대비 동 대조하다, 대비하다
□□ cue	명 신호, 단서 동 신호를 주다
□□ custody	명 양육권, 보호권; (재판 전의) 유치, 구류
□□ death with dignity	명 존엄사
□□ embezzlement	명 (위탁금 등의) 횡령
□□ handcuff	명 ((pl.)) 수갑 동 수갑을 채우다

□□ intricate	형 (여러 부분[내용]으로 되어 있어) 복잡한, 정교한
□□ investigator	명 수사관, 조사관
□□ jury	명 배심원단; 심사위원단
□□ lawsuit	명 소송, 고소
□□ odor	명 냄새, (특히) 악취; 낌새; 평판, 인기
□□ patrol	명 순찰(대) 동 순찰하다
□□ snorer	명 코 고는 사람
□□ statement	명 성명(서), 진술(서)
□□ strained	형 긴장한; (상황이) 불편한
□□ terminally ill	말기의, 위독한
□□ typographic	형 인쇄상의, 인쇄술의
□□ vegetarian	명 채식주의자 형 채식주의(자)의; 채식의
□□ veterinarian	명 수의사
□□ witness	명 목격자, 증인 동 목격하다; 증명하다

Prefixes | 방향·접근 ad -

☐☐ adjust — 동 조절하다; 적응하다

☐☐ adjustment — 명 조정, 조절; 적응

☐☐ administer — 동 (회사·조직 등을) 관리하다; 집행하다; (약을) 투여하다

☐☐ adhere — 동 ((to)) 들러붙다; (규칙 등을) 지키다, 고수하다

☐☐ adherence — 명 고수, 집착

☐☐ adhesive — 명 접착제 형 들러붙는

☐☐ adjacent — 형 인접한, 가까운

☐☐ advocate — 명 옹호자, 지지자; 변호사 동 지지하다

☐☐ advocacy — 명 (공개적인) 지지, 옹호

☐☐ accelerate — 동 가속하다

☐☐ accelerator — 명 (자동차의) 액셀, 가속 장치

☐☐ accumulate — 동 (서서히) 모으다; 늘어나다

☐☐ accumulation — 명 축적

☐☐ accumulative — 형 누적되는, 늘어나는

☐☐ appease — 동 달래다; (상대의) 요구를 들어주다

☐☐ approximate — 형 거의 정확한, 근사치인 동 근사치를 내다; (성격·자질 등이) 근접하다

☐☐ approximation — 명 근사치

☐☐ assemble — 동 모이다, 집합시키다; 조립하다

☐☐ assembly — 명 집회; 의회; 조립

☐☐ attest — 동 증명하다; (법정에서) 증언하다

☐☐ attain — 동 이루다, 획득하다; (특정한 수준에) 이르다

☐☐ attainment — 명 달성

☐☐ attainable — 형 이룰 수 있는

Essential Roots / Stems | tract

☐☐ attract — 동 끌어당기다; 매혹하다

☐☐ attraction — 명 인력; 매력; (사람을 끄는) 명소

☐☐ attractive — 형 매력적인

☐☐ traction — 명 끌기, 견인(력)

☐☐ abstract — 형 추상적인, 관념적인 명 개요, 발췌; 추상화 동 추출하다; 요약하다

☐☐ abstraction — 명 추상적 개념; 추출

☐☐ detract — 동 ((from)) (가치·명예를) 손상시키다

☐☐ distract — 동 (주의를) 딴 데로 돌리다; 산만하게 하다

☐☐ distraction — 명 집중을 방해하는 것; 오락(활동)

☐☐ extract — 동 뽑다, 추출하다 명 발췌; 추출물

☐☐ extraction — 명 추출

☐☐ retract — 동 (전에 한 말, 약속, 합의 등을) 취소하다, 철회하다

☐☐ subtract — 동 (수·양을) 빼다

☐☐ subtraction — 명 뺄셈

Words with Multiple Meanings | 필수 다의어의 이해

☐☐ administer — 동 (회사·조직·국가 등을) 관리[운영]하다 동 (공정하게) 집행하다 동 (약을) 투여하다 동 (타격을) 가하다, 치다

☐☐ address — 동 우편물을 보내다 명 주소 동 말을 걸다 명 연설 동 연설하다 동 (문제·상황 등에 대해) 고심하다, 다루다

☐☐ direct — 동 (~로) 향하다, 겨냥하다 형 직접적인 형 (열기·빛이) 직접 닿는 형 직행의, 직통의 형 정확한 동 지시하다, 명령하다 동 지휘하다 동 감독하다

Phrasal Verbs | to가 포함된 구동사

☐☐ lead to	(~을 향해 인도하다) 이어지다	☐☐ stick to,	(~에 들러붙다) 지키다	
☐☐ refer to	(~에 대해 말하다 / ~을 조회하다) 나타내다; 언급하다; 참조하다	cling to, adhere to, hold to		
☐☐ resort to	(~에 의존하다) 의존하다	☐☐ turn to	(~으로 방향을 돌리다) 바뀌다; 의지하다; 구하다	

Themes | 범죄·재판

☐☐ vice	명 악; 악덕 행위	☐☐ allegation	명 (증거 없는) 주장, 혐의
☐☐ vicious	형 나쁜, 잔인한	☐☐ alleged	형 (증거 없이) 주장된
☐☐ felony	명 중죄, 흉악 범죄	☐☐ allegedly	부 주장한[전해진] 바에 의하면
☐☐ misdemeanor	명 경범죄; 비행	☐☐ confess	동 자백하다
☐☐ delinquency	명 (특히 청소년의) 비행, 범죄	☐☐ confession	명 (죄의) 자백; 고백, 인정
☐☐ criminal	명 범인, 범죄자 형 범죄의; 형사상의	☐☐ plead	동 변호하다; (법정에서 피고가) 답변하다; 간청[탄원]하다
☐☐ forensic	형 범죄 과학 수사의; 법정의		
☐☐ apprehend	동 체포하다	☐☐ plea	명 (피고인의) 답변; (법원에 제출하는) 사유서; 간청, 탄원
☐☐ apprehension	명 우려, 불안; 체포		
☐☐ indict	동 기소하다	☐☐ verdict	명 (배심원단의) 평결; 의견, 결정
☐☐ indictment	명 기소; 기소장; 비난		
☐☐ prosecute	동 기소[고발, 소추]하다; 검사가 사건을 담당하다	☐☐ convict	동 유죄를 선고하다 명 재소자
☐☐ prosecution	명 기소[고발, 소추]; 검사 측	☐☐ conviction	명 유죄 선고; 확신
☐☐ prosecutor	명 기소 검사	☐☐ innocent	형 순진한, 순결한; 무죄인, 결백한
☐☐ petition	동 진정하다, 청원하다 명 진정(서), 청원(서)	☐☐ innocence	명 무죄, 결백
☐☐ testify	동 증명하다; (법정에서) 증언하다	☐☐ overrule	동 기각하다
☐☐ allege	동 (증거 없이) 혐의를 제기하다[주장하다]	☐☐ amnesty	명 사면; (범행·무기의) 자진 신고 기간

21 강

words & phrases

□□ algae	몡 조류
□□ applause	몡 박수(갈채)
□□ aroma	몡 (기분 좋은) 향기
□□ artificial respiration	몡 인공호흡
□□ brisk	혱 활발한; (바람·날씨가) 상쾌한; (말투 등이) 무뚝뚝한
□□ bump into	~와 우연히 마주치다
□□ bygone	혱 지나간, 옛날의 몡 ((pl.)) 지난 일
□□ complaint	몡 불평, 항의; 고소
□□ CPR	몡 심폐소생술
□□ customary	혱 관례적인; 습관적인
□□ decline	몡 감소, 하락 동 감소하다; 거절하다
□□ electrical current	몡 전류
□□ eloquently	뷔 (유창한) 웅변으로

□□ errand	몡 심부름; 용건, 볼일
□□ excessive	혱 지나친, 과도한
□□ nectar	몡 (꽃의) 꿀; (진한) 과일즙
□□ personnel	몡 (조직의) 인원, 직원들; (회사의) 인사과
□□ pollen	몡 꽃가루, 화분
□□ pollinate	동 수분하다
□□ retro	혱 복고풍의
□□ saliva	몡 침, 타액
□□ scheme	몡 계획, 책략 동 책략을 꾸미다
□□ squeeze in	(스케줄에) ~을 간신히 끼워 넣다, ~을 위한 짬을 내다
□□ stalk	몡 (식물의) 줄기, 대
□□ thrilled	혱 (너무 좋아서) 아주 흥분한, 신이 난
□□ turnout	몡 참가자의 수; 투표자의 수, 투표율

Prefixes | 전방·전진 pro -

□□ provision	몡 제공; 대비; (법률 관련 문서의) 조항, 단서; ((pl.)) (여행) 식량
□□ prominent	혱 돌출된; 눈에 잘 띄는; 중요한; 유명한
□□ prominence	몡 두드러짐; 중요성; 명성
□□ prologue	몡 프롤로그
□□ prophecy	몡 (특히 종교적·마법적인) 예언; 예언력

□□ prophesy	동 예언하다
□□ prophet	몡 예언자
□□ prompt	혱 신속한, 시간을 엄수하는 동 유도하다
□□ promptness	몡 재빠름, 신속; 시간 엄수
□□ protest	동 항의하다 몡 항의; 시위

Essential Roots / Stems 1 | mov(e) / mo(b) / mot(e)

☐☐ promote   동 증진하다, 촉진하다;
                  홍보하다; 승진시키다

☐☐ mobile   형 이동하는
                  명 휴대전화; 모빌

☐☐ mobility   명 이동성, 기동성

☐☐ mobilize   동 (사람·물자·군대 등을) 동원
                  하다

☐☐ motivate   동 동기를 부여하다

☐☐ motivation   명 동기 부여; 자극

☐☐ motive   명 동기, 이유
                  형 ((명사 앞)) 원동력이 되는

☐☐ commotion   명 동요; 소동, 소란

☐☐ locomotive   형 운동의, 이동의
                  명 기관차

☐☐ locomotion   명 운동[이동](능력)

Essential Roots / Stems 2 | spec(t) / spic / specul

☐☐ prospect   명 기대; 가망, 가능성; 예상

☐☐ prospective   형 장래의; 유망한

☐☐ spectator   명 (특히 스포츠 행사의) 관중;
                  구경꾼

☐☐ spectacle   명 장관, 구경거리; ((pl.)) 안경

☐☐ spectacular   형 장관을 이루는; 극적인

☐☐ inspect   동 검사하다; 사찰하다

☐☐ inspection   명 검사; 사찰

☐☐ inspector   명 조사관, 감독관; (경찰) 경위

☐☐ aspect   명 측면, 모양

☐☐ introspective 형 자기 성찰적인; 내성적인

☐☐ introspection 명 자기 성찰; 내성적 성질

☐☐ suspect   동 (좋지 않은 일이 있을 것으
                  로) 의심하다; 혐의를 두다
                  명 용의자

☐☐ suspicious   형 의심스러운, 수상한

☐☐ suspicion   명 혐의; 의심

☐☐ specify   동 (구체적으로) 명시하다

☐☐ specification 명 (자세한) 설명서

☐☐ specific   형 구체적인, 명확한; 특정한;
                  특유의

☐☐ specimen   명 견본, 샘플; 표본

☐☐ conspicuous   형 눈에 잘 띄는

☐☐ speculate   동 추측하다; 투기하다

☐☐ speculation   명 추측, 짐작; 투기

Words with Multiple Meanings | 필수 다의어의 이해

☐☐ move   동 옮기다, 이사하다 명 이사 동 (~의 길·방향으로) 나아가다, 진행되다
                  동 조치를 취하다 명 조치, 행동 동 감동시키다 동 (안건 등을) 제안하다, 제출하다

☐☐ promote   동 증진하다, 촉진하다 동 홍보하다 동 장려하다, 고무하다 동 (결과를) 조장하다
                  동 승진시키다, 진급시키다

☐☐ respect   명 존경; 존중 동 존경[존중]하다 명 (측)면, 점, 사항

☐☐ commit   동 맡기다 동 (범죄를) 저지르다 동 (엄숙히) 약속하다 동 전념하다, 헌신하다

Phrasal Verbs │ on이 포함된 구동사 1

□□ act on	(~을 근거로 행동하다) 의거하여 행동하다	□□ count on, depend on, rely on	(~에 의지하여 셈하다) 의지하다
□□ catch on	(붙잡아서 접하다) 유행하다; 이해하다	□□ dwell on	(~에 계속 살다) 연연하다
□□ call on	(들러서 접하다 / ~을 향해 말하다) 방문하다; 요구하다	□□ feed on	(~에 의지하여 먹고 살다) 먹다
□□ carry on	(계속 나르다[전달하다]) 계속하다		

Themes │ 감정 1

□□ kindle	통 불붙이다; (감정을) 자극하다	□□ outrageous	형 난폭한; 매우 모욕적인; 터무니없는
□□ rouse	통 (잠든 사람을) 깨우다; (감정을) 불러일으키다; 성나게 하다	□□ infuriated	형 극도로 화가 난, 노발대발하는
□□ invoke	통 기원하다; (법 등을) 적용하다; (느낌을) 불러일으키다	□□ indignant	형 분개한, 성난
		□□ indignation	명 분개, 분노
□□ rejoice	통 크게 기뻐하다	□□ irritable	형 짜증을 (잘) 내는
□□ exhilarated	형 아주 신나는	□□ glare	통 노려보다; (불쾌하게) 눈부시다
□□ hilarious	형 아주 우스운[재미있는]		명 노려봄; 눈부심
□□ festive	형 축제의; 축하하는		
□□ festivity	명 축제 행사; 축제 기분	□□ retort	통 쏘아붙이다, 대꾸하다
□□ quizzical	형 (표정이) 약간 놀란[재미있어하는] 듯한	□□ soothe	통 (특히 화난 마음을) 달래다; (통증을) 누그러뜨리다
□□ grin	통 (소리 없이) 활짝 웃다	□□ grief	명 큰 슬픔, 비통
□□ temper	명 (걸핏하면 화내는) 성질; 기분	□□ grieve	통 크게 슬퍼하다, 비통해하다
	통 완화시키다; (쇠를) 단련하다	□□ lament	통 슬퍼하다; 후회하다
			명 애도
□□ tempered	형 ((보통 복합어)) (~한) 기질의; 완화된; 단련된	□□ bemoan	통 한탄하다
		□□ weep	통 울다, 눈물을 흘리다
□□ temperament	명 기질; 신경질적임	□□ console	통 위로하다
□□ rage	명 격노	□□ consolation	명 위안(을 주는 사람[것])
	통 몹시 화를 내다		

22 강

words & phrases

□□ accentuate	통 강조하다, 두드러지게 하다
□□ apply oneself	전념하다, 정진하다
□□ assess	통 평가하다; (자질 등을) 가늠하다
□□ boisterous	형 활기가 넘치는, 명랑하고 떠들썩한
□□ brutality	명 잔인성
□□ cactus	명 선인장
□□ conserve	통 보호[보존]하다; 아껴 쓰다
□□ contemporary	형 동시대의; 현대의 명 동년배, 동시대 사람
□□ corrosive	형 부식을 일으키는; 좀먹는
□□ elicit	통 (정보·반응을) 끌어내다
□□ exceedingly	부 극도로, 대단히
□□ generosity	명 너그러움
□□ graciously	부 우아하게; 상냥하게; 고맙게도
□□ grasp	명 꽉 쥐기; (확실한) 통제; 이해 통 꽉 잡다; 완전히 이해하다

□□ greed	명 탐욕; 식탐
□□ inequality	명 불평등
□□ limb	명 팔, 다리; (새의) 날개; (큰) 나뭇가지
□□ make every effort to-v	v하려고 온갖 노력을 다하다
□□ outnumber	통 ~보다 수가 더 많다, 수적으로 우세하다
□□ partially	부 부분적으로; 불공평하게
□□ pawnshop	명 전당포
□□ scent	명 향기, 냄새; (냄새를 통해 남아 있는) 자취 통 몸을 굽히다[구부리다]
□□ stoop	
□□ supplement	명 보충(물), 추가(물) 통 보충[추가]하다
□□ tune out	~을 듣지 않다, 무시하다
□□ wreck	명 난파선; 망가진 차량[사람] 통 난파시키다; 망가뜨리다

Prefixes | 다시·반복·뒤로 re -

□□ recite	통 (시 등을) 암송하다, 낭독하다	□□ recline	통 비스듬히 기대다[눕다]; (의자 등받이를) 뒤로 넘기다
□□ recitation	명 낭독; 설명	□□ redeem	통 (저당물을 돈을 주고) 되찾다; (주식·상품권 등을) 현금[상품]으로 바꾸다; (결함 등을) 보완하다
□□ reconcile	통 화해시키다; 조화시키다		
□□ reinforce	통 강화하다; 보강하다; 증원하다		
□□ reinforcement	명 강화; ((pl.)) (군대 등의) 증강 병력	□□ reflex	명 반사 작용[운동]
		□□ refund	통 환불하다 명 환불(금)
□□ reproduce	통 복사[복제]하다; 재생하다; 번식하다	□□ rehabilitate	통 회복시키다; 재활 치료를 하다
□□ reproduction	명 복사, 복제; 재생; 번식	□□ retreat	통 후퇴하다; 물러가다 명 후퇴; 물러섬
□□ resume	통 다시 시작하다, 재개되다		
□□ resumption	명 재개	□□ retrograde	형 역행하는, 퇴보하는
□□ retrieve	통 되찾아오다, 회수하다; ((컴퓨터)) (정보를) 검색하다	□□ retrospect	명 회상, 회고
		□□ retrospective	형 회고하는; ((법률)) 소급 적용되는
□□ retrieval	명 회수		

Essential Roots / Stems 1 | nov

□□ renovate	통 (낡은 건물 등을) 수리[보수]하다; 혁신하다	□□ novel	형 새로운 명 (장편) 소설
		□□ nova	명 ((천문)) 신성
□□ renovation	명 수리, 보수; 혁신	□□ innovate	통 혁신하다; 획기적으로 하다
□□ novice	명 초보자	□□ innovation	명 혁신; 획기적인 것

Essential Roots / Stems 2 | tain / ten

□□ retain	통 (계속) 보유하다, 유지하다	□□ detention	명 억류; 구금
□□ retention	명 보유, 유지	□□ sustain	통 지탱하다; 뒷받침하다; 지속하다
□□ abstain	통 ((from)) 삼가다; (투표에서) 기권하다		
		□□ sustainable	형 (환경 파괴 없이) 지속 가능한; 오랫동안 유지 가능한
□□ contain	통 포함하다; (감정을) 억누르다; (안 좋은 일을) 방지하다	□□ obtain	통 (노력 끝에) 얻다
□□ detain	통 (가지 못하게) 붙들다; 억류하다		

Words with Multiple Meanings | 필수 다의어의 이해

□□ content 　휑 만족하는 　동 만족시키다 　명 만족
　　　　　　명 ((pl.)) (어떤 것의) 내용물 　명 함유량 　명 ((pl.)) (책의) 목차

□□ reduce 　동 (크기·양 등을) 줄이다, 축소하다 　동 (간단하게) 정리하다 　동 ((to)) 바꾸다
　　　　　　동 ((to)) (가격을) 낮추다, 할인하다

□□ novel 　휑 새로운 　휑 참신한, 신기한 　명 (장편) 소설

□□ reflect 　동 (빛 등을) 반사하다 　동 (거울 등에 이미지를) 비추다 　동 (속성·태도·감정을) 나타내다, 반영
　　　　　　하다 　동 반성하다 　동 깊이 생각하다

Phrasal Verbs | on이 포함된 구동사 2

□□ get on with 　(~와 함께 계속하다) 계속하다

□□ go on 　(계속 가다) 계속하다

□□ hang on (to) 　(~에 단단히 매달리다)
　　　　　　고수하다; 기다리다;
　　　　　　끊지 않고 기다리다

□□ hit on 　(~에 부딪치다[맞닥뜨리다])
　　　　　　떠오르다; 발견하다

□□ hold on (to) 　(계속[단단히] 붙들고 있다 /
　　　　　　(시간을) 붙들고 있다)
　　　　　　단단히 붙들고 있다; 기다리다

□□ let on 　말하다

□□ live on 　(~에 의존하여 살다) 주식으로
　　　　　　하다

Themes | 감정 2

□□ adore 　동 흠모하다; 아주 좋아하다

□□ adorable 　휑 사랑스러운

□□ cherish 　동 소중히 여기다

□□ esteem 　명 (대단한) 존경
　　　　　　동 (대단히) 존경하다

□□ emulate 　동 (흠모하여) 모방하다

□□ enchant 　동 매혹하다; 마법을 걸다

□□ endear 　동 사랑받게 하다

□□ endearment 　명 애정을 담은 말[표현]

□□ idol 　명 우상

□□ idolize 　동 우상화하다, 숭배하다

□□ nostalgic 　휑 향수의, 향수를 불러일으
　　　　　　키는

□□ nostalgia 　명 향수

□□ lure 　명 매력; 미끼
　　　　　　동 꾀다, 유혹하다

□□ averse 　휑 ((to)) (~을) 싫어하는,
　　　　　　반대하는

□□ disgusted 　휑 역겨워하는

□□ disgusting 　휑 역겨운

□□ hideous 　휑 흉측한, 끔찍한

□□ hateful 　휑 혐오스러운

□□ hatred 　명 증오(감), 혐오(감)

□□ irritated 　휑 짜증이 난; (몸에) 염증이 난

□□ reluctant 　휑 꺼리는, 마지못한

□□ reluctantly 　부 마지못해서

□□ compassionate 　휑 연민 어린, 동정하는

□□ miserable 　휑 비참한

□□ misery 　명 비참(함); (심신의) 고통

□□ deplorable 　휑 한탄스러운; 비참한

□□ ambivalent 　휑 반대 감정이 병존하는

□□ burdensome 　휑 부담스러운; 힘든

□□ gratitude 　명 고마움; 감사

□□ gloomy 　휑 음울한, 어두운; (표정이)
　　　　　　우울한

□□ gloom 　명 어두침침함; 우울

□□ solitary 　휑 혼자의; 외로운; 외딴

□□ solitude 　명 (편안한) 고독

23 강

words & phrases

□□ accusation 몡 혐의 (제기); 고발, 고소; 비난

□□ angelic 휑 천사 같은

□□ bottom line 몡 (결산서의) 맨 밑줄; 최종 결과, 총결산; 핵심

□□ breakthrough 몡 돌파구; (과학 등의) 큰 발전

□□ chronicle 몡 연대기 동 연대순으로 기록하다

□□ cling to ~을 고수하다, ~에 집착하다

□□ conform 동 (규칙·관습 등을) 따르다

□□ confront 동 직면하다; 맞서다

□□ contaminant 몡 오염 물질

□□ counterintuitive 휑 직관에 반하는, 반직관적인

□□ coverage 몡 적용 범위; ((보험)) 보상 (범위); 보도[방송] (범위)

□□ dependency 몡 의존 (상태), 종속

□□ dictatorship 몡 독재 국가[정권]

□□ fingerprinting 몡 지문 채취

□□ human resources department 몡 인력개발부, 인사부

□□ in session 개회 중의

□□ inn 몡 (보통 시골 지역의) 여관

□□ intruder 몡 불법 침입자, 불청객

□□ joint 휑 공동의 몡 관절; 연결 부위

□□ lab 몡 실험실

□□ leopard 몡 표범

□□ merit 몡 가치; 장점 동 (칭찬·관심 등을) 받을 만하다[가치가 있다]

□□ modest 휑 겸손한; 얌전한; (크기·가격 등이) 보통의, 적당한

□□ perpetrator 몡 (범행·과실 등을 저지른) 가해자, 범인

□□ plagiarism 몡 표절

□□ pony 몡 조랑말

□□ principally 부 주로, 대개

□□ safeguard 동 보호하다 몡 안전장치

□□ silver lining 몡 구름의 흰 가장자리; 밝은 희망[전망]

□□ stroll 몡 산책 동 산책하다, 한가로이 거닐다

□□ toll 몡 요금, 통행료; (재난 등의) 사상자 수

□□ wrongdoing 몡 범법[부정] 행위, 비행

Prefixes | 이동·관통 (2) trans-

□□ transient 휑 일시적인; 잠깐 머무르는 몡 단기 체류자

□□ transit 몡 수송; (다른 곳으로 가기 위한) 환승

□□ transition 몡 (다른 상태로의) 변화, 이행

□□ transitional 휑 변천하는; 과도기의

□□ transaction 몡 처리; 거래, 매매

□□ transcend 동 초월하다; 능가하다

□□ transcendence 몡 초월(성); 탁월

□□ transcendental 휑 초월적인; 탁월한

□□ transform 동 변형시키다; (더 좋게) 완전히 바꿔 놓다

□□ transformation 몡 (완전한) 변화, 변신; (곤충의) 변태

□□ transfuse	동 수혈하다; (액체를) 주입하다; (사상 등을) 불어넣다	□□ transcontinental	형 대륙 횡단의
		□□ transgenics	명 유전자 이식(학)
□□ transfusion	명 수혈; (추가 자금의) 투입	□□ transgenic	형 (동식물이) 이식 유전자를 가진
□□ transparent	형 투명한; 알기 쉬운, 명료한		명 유전자 이식 식물[동물]
□□ transplant	동 (식물을) 옮겨 심다; 이식하다		
	명 이식		

Essential Roots / Stems | grad / gress / gred

□□ transgress	동 (도덕적·법적 한계를) 넘어서다, 벗어나다	□□ aggress	동 공격하다; 시비를 걸다
		□□ aggressive	형 공격적인; 진취적인, 적극적인
□□ transgression	명 위반, 범죄; (종교·도덕적) 죄	□□ aggression	명 공격
□□ grade	명 등급; 성적; 학년	□□ aggressor	명 (먼저) 공격[침략]을 한 사람[국가]
	동 등급을 나누다		
□□ gradation	명 단계적 차이, 점진적 변화	□□ progress	동 (앞으로) 나아가다; 진보하다
□□ gradual	형 점진적인		명 전진; 진행
□□ gradually	부 서서히	□□ progression	명 전진, 진보; ((수학)) 수열
□□ degrade	동 비하하다; 강등시키다; (질적으로) 저하하다; (화학적으로) 분해하다	□□ progressive	형 진보적인; 점진적인
		□□ regress	동 퇴행하다, 퇴보하다
□□ degradation	명 비하; 강등; 저하; (화학적) 분해	□□ regression	명 퇴행; 회귀
□□ biodegradable	형 생분해될 수 있는	□□ congress	명 의회, 국회; 회의
□□ nonbiodegradable	형 생분해성이 아닌	□□ ingredient	명 (요리) 재료, 성분; 구성 요소

Words with Multiple Meanings | 필수 다의어의 이해

□□ degree	명 정도 명 (각도·온도 단위인) 도 명 학위
□□ hold	동 (손에) 들다, 잡다 동 (어떤 상태·위치에) 유지하다 동 (지위에) 재직하다 동 (기록·타이틀 등을) 보유하다 동 (사람·사물을) 수용하다, 담다 동 (신념·의견 등을) 가지다 동 (회의 등을) 개최하다, 열다
□□ intelligence	명 지능 명 지성 명 (기밀) 정보 명 정보기관[요원]
□□ issue	명 (걱정거리가 되는) 문제 명 쟁점, 주제, 사안 명 발표 동 발표하다 명 (우표·동전·주식의) 발행(물) 동 발행하다 명 (정기 간행물의) 호

☐☐ put on   (~을 (몸에) 접촉하여 두다) 착용하다

☐☐ take on   (취해서 접하다) 떠맡다

☐☐ tell on   영향을 끼치다; 고자질하다

☐☐ turn on   (돌려서 연결하다) 틀다

☐☐ try on   (시험 삼아 (몸에) 접촉시키다) 입어 보다

☐☐ wait on   (~에 대해 기다리다 / ~을 (돕기 위해) 기다리다) 기다리다; 돌보다

☐☐ work on   (~에 대하여 일하다) 작성하다; 노력하다

Themes | 태도·성격 1

☐☐ demeanor   몡 처신, 품행; 태도

☐☐ hospitable   혱 환대하는; 쾌적한

☐☐ hospitality   몡 환대; 접대

☐☐ committed   혱 헌신적인

☐☐ candid   혱 솔직한; (사진이) 자연스러운 모습 그대로 찍은

☐☐ candor   몡 솔직함

☐☐ sincere   혱 진실한

☐☐ sincerity   몡 진실, 성실

☐☐ exemplary   혱 모범적인; ((법)) (처벌이) 가혹한

☐☐ loyal   혱 충성스러운; (약속 등에) 충실한; 성실한

☐☐ loyalty   몡 충실; 충성심

☐☐ meticulous   혱 세심한, 꼼꼼한

☐☐ altruistic   혱 이타적인

☐☐ altruism   몡 이타주의

☐☐ tolerant   혱 관대한; 내성이 있는

☐☐ tolerance   몡 관용; 내성

☐☐ merciful   혱 자비로운

☐☐ mercy   몡 자비

☐☐ leisurely   혱 여유로운, 느긋한 / 뷔 느긋하게

☐☐ docile   혱 유순한, 온순한

☐☐ spontaneous   혱 자발적인; 저절로 일어나는; 즉흥적인

☐☐ spontaneity   몡 자발적임; 자연스러움, 자연 발생

☐☐ bold   혱 대담한, 용감한

☐☐ humble   혱 겸손한; 미천한

☐☐ decent   혱 적절한; 품위 있는

☐☐ noble   혱 귀족의; 고귀한

☐☐ nobility   몡 ((the ~)) 귀족; 고귀함

☐☐ nobleman   몡 귀족(인 사람)

☐☐ sophisticated   혱 세련된; (기계 등이) 정교한

☐☐ sophisticate   몡 세련된 사람

☐☐ sophistication   몡 교양; 세련

☐☐ zealous   혱 열성적인, 열렬한

☐☐ zeal   몡 열성, 열의

☐☐ strenuous   혱 격렬한, 열렬한; 몹시 힘든

☐☐ agile   혱 (동작이) 민첩한; (생각이) 기민한

☐☐ agility   몡 민첩함; 기민함

☐☐ vibrant   혱 진동하는; 활기찬

☐☐ steady   혱 (발달·전개 등이) 꾸준한; 변함없는, 한결같은

☐☐ steadiness   몡 착실함; 끈기

24 강

words & phrases

□□ abortion	명 낙태, 임신중절
□□ armchair	명 안락의자 형 (책이나 텔레비전 등을 통해) 간접적으로 아는, 탁상공론식의
□□ artifice	명 책략, 계략
□□ assumption	명 가정, 추측; (권력·책임의) 인수, 취임
□□ auditory	형 청각의
□□ babysitter	명 (보통 돈을 받고) 아기를 봐 주는 사람
□□ challenging	형 도전적인; 힘든; 저항하는
□□ confirm	동 (증거를 들어) 사실임을 보여주다; 확정하다, 공식화하다
□□ criticism	명 비판, 비난; 비평, 평론
□□ deforestation	명 삼림 벌채[파괴]
□□ desertification	명 사막화
□□ documentation	명 증거 서류 (제출); 기록, 문서화
□□ eating disorder	명 식이 장애
□□ extent	명 정도; (어떤 지역의) 규모

□□ grind	동 (곡식 등을) 갈다, 빻다; (날을) 갈다 명 고된 일, 따분한 일
□□ illusion	명 착각; 환상
□□ inspiration	명 영감; 영감[자극]을 주는 것
□□ mess	명 엉망인 상태[상황] 동 엉망으로 만들다
□□ misspelling	명 틀린 철자
□□ oncoming	형 다가오는
□□ orphan	명 고아 동 (아이를) 고아로 만들다
□□ perseverance	명 인내(심)
□□ persistent	형 끈질긴; 끊임없는
□□ remind A of B	(유사한 점 때문에) A에게 B를 연상시키다
□□ remorse	명 회한, 자책
□□ sensitivity	명 민감함
□□ temptation	명 유혹; 유혹하는 것
□□ tune	명 곡(조), 선율 동 (악기의) 음을 맞추다; 조정하다
□□ tyrant	명 폭군, 독재자

Prefixes | 이동·관통 (3) per -, 멀리 tele -

□□ perpetual	형 (오랫동안) 끊임없이 계속되는
□□ perspective	명 전망; 관점; 원근법
□□ perspire	동 땀을 흘리다
□□ perspiration	명 땀(흘리기); 노력
□□ pervade	동 (구석구석) 스며들다, 만연하다

□□ pervasive	형 (구석구석) 스며드는, 만연하는
□□ telecommuting	명 (컴퓨터 등의 통신 시설을 이용하는) 재택근무
□□ telegraph	동 전보를 보내다 명 전보, 전신
□□ telescope	명 망원경
□□ televise	동 텔레비전으로 방송하다

Essential Roots / Stems 1 │ mit / miss

□□ permit   동 허락하다 명 허가증

□□ permission   명 허락

□□ admit   동 (입학·입장을) 허가하다; (마지못해) 인정하다

□□ admission   명 입장(료); 입학 (허가)

□□ admittedly   부 인정하건대

□□ dismiss   동 해산시키다; 해고하다; 묵살하다

□□ dismissal   명 해고; 묵살; (소송) 기각

□□ emit   동 (빛·열 등을) 방출[배출]하다

□□ emission   명 (빛·열 등의) 발산; (대기 속의) 배출물

□□ intermit   동 일시적으로 중단하다

□□ intermission   명 (연극·수업 등의) 중간 휴식 시간; 중지

□□ intermittent   형 간헐적인, 간간이 일어나는

□□ omit   동 생략하다

□□ omission   명 생략

□□ remit   동 송금하다, 보내다; (빚 등을) 면제하다; 완화하다

□□ remittance   명 송금(액)

□□ submit   동 ((to)) 굴복하다; (보고서 등을) 제출하다

□□ submission   명 항복; 제출

□□ submissive   형 순종적인

□□ transmit   동 전송하다; 전염시키다; (열·전기 등을) 전도하다

□□ transmission   명 전송; 전염; 전도

Essential Roots / Stems 2 │ path

□□ telepathy   명 텔레파시

□□ sympathy   명 공감; 동정

□□ sympathize   동 ((with)) 공감하다; 동정하다

□□ sympathetic   형 공감하는; 동정적인

□□ empathy   명 감정 이입, 공감

□□ empathize   동 ((with)) 감정 이입하다, 공감하다

□□ empathic   형 감정 이입의

□□ antipathy   명 반감

□□ apathy   명 무관심; 냉담함

□□ apathetic   형 무관심한; 냉담한

□□ pathetic   형 불쌍한; 비참한; 한심한

□□ pathos   명 비애; 페이소스

Words with Multiple Meanings │ 필수 다의어의 이해

□□ perspective   명 전망 명 관점, 시각 명 원근법; 원근감

□□ yield   동 (수익·결과·농작물 등을) 생산하다, 산출하다 명 산출량 동 굴복하다 동 (도로에서 다른 차에게) 양보하다

□□ last   형 마지막의 형 가장 최근의, 지난 형 결코 ~할 것 같지 않은 동 계속하다, 지속되다

□□ leave   동 (사람·장소에서) 떠나다 동 (살던 집·직장·학교 등을) 그만두다 명 휴가 (기간) 동 ~한 상태로 계속 놓아두다 동 (어떤 결과를) 남기다 동 (일을 즉각 하지 않고) 미루다

Phrasal Verbs | through가 포함된 구동사

□□ be through	(끝까지 한 상태이다) 끝내다	□□ get through	(~을 통과하여 나가다) 통과하다; 빠져나가다
□□ browse through	(처음부터 끝까지 둘러보다) 훑어보다	□□ go through	(처음부터 끝까지 가다) 길을 건너다; 경험하다; 자세히 살펴보다
□□ come through	(~을 통과하여 오다) 뚫고 나오다	□□ look through	(처음부터 끝까지 보다) 죽 살펴보다

Themes | 태도·성격 2

□□ cynical	혱 냉소적인	□□ fitful	혱 발작적인; 변덕스러운
□□ pessimistic	혱 비관적인	□□ stingy	혱 인색한
□□ pessimist	몡 비관주의자	□□ solemn	혱 (표정이) 근엄한; (행동 등이) 엄숙한
□□ complacent	혱 현실에 안주하는, 자기만족적인	□□ sluggish	혱 느릿느릿한; 부진한
□□ contemptuous	혱 경멸하는	□□ stern	혱 엄격한, 단호한
□□ contempt	몡 경멸, 멸시	□□ coward	몡 겁쟁이
□□ sinister	혱 사악한, 해로운; 불길한	□□ cowardice	몡 겁, 비겁
□□ wicked	혱 못된, 사악한; 짓궂은	□□ cowardly	혱 겁 많은
□□ brutal	혱 잔인한, 잔혹한	□□ daunt	통 겁먹게[기죽게] 하다
□□ brutality	몡 잔인성	□□ timid	혱 소심한, 자신감 없는
□□ ruthless	혱 무자비한; 인정사정없는	□□ hesitant	혱 주저하는
□□ relentless	혱 냉혹한, 잔인한; 수그러들지 않는	□□ hesitate	통 주저하다, 망설이다
□□ fierce	혱 사나운, 맹렬한; (기상 조건이) 극심한	□□ hesitation	몡 주저, 망설임
		□□ indecisive	혱 우유부단한; (결과가) 뚜렷하지 않은
□□ egocentric	혱 자기중심적인		
□□ stubborn	혱 완고한, 고집스러운	□□ indecision	몡 (결정을 못 내리고) 망설임, 우유부단
□□ picky	혱 까다로운	□□ naive	혱 ((주로 부정적)) 순진해 빠진
□□ demanding	혱 요구가 많은; (일이) 부담이 큰	□□ masculine	혱 남자의; 사내다운

25 강

words & phrases

☐☐ acrobatic	형 곡예의, 곡예적인
☐☐ audacity	명 대담함, 뻔뻔함
☐☐ colony	명 식민지; 집단, 거주지; (동식물의) 군집
☐☐ dart	명 다트, 던지는 화살 동 (시선·화살 등을) 던지다; (화살처럼) 날아가다
☐☐ draft	명 밑그림, 초안 동 초안을 작성하다; 선발하다; 징병하다
☐☐ formality	명 형식상의 절차; 형식적인 일
☐☐ humiliating	형 굴욕적인
☐☐ indigenous	형 토착의; 고유한
☐☐ irresistible	형 저항할 수 없는; 억누를 수 없는
☐☐ literally	부 문자 그대로; 사실상
☐☐ manipulation	명 (교묘한) 조작
☐☐ mosquito	명 모기
☐☐ overwhelmed	형 압도된

☐☐ particulate	명 ((pl.)) 미립자, 입자성 물질 형 미립자의; 미립자로 된
☐☐ phenomena	명 ((phenomenon의 복수형)) 현상
☐☐ plaque	명 (기념) 명판; (치아에 끼는) 플라크
☐☐ pneumonia	명 폐렴
☐☐ primarily	부 주로
☐☐ proceeding	명 행사; 소송 절차; 회의록
☐☐ radical	형 근본적인; 급진적인 명 급진주의자
☐☐ render	동 ~이 되게 하다; 제공하다; 표현하다
☐☐ representative	명 대표(자); 대리인 형 대표하는
☐☐ residence	명 주택, 거주지; 거주
☐☐ sulfur dioxide	명 아황산가스
☐☐ swallow	명 한 입[모금]; 제비 동 (음식 등을) 삼키다
☐☐ theft	명 절도

Prefixes | 함께·같이 (1) com -

☐☐ commemorate	동 기념하다
☐☐ commemoration	명 기념 (행사)
☐☐ commence	동 ((격식)) 시작하다
☐☐ commencement	명 시작, 개시; ((미)) 학위 수여식, 졸업식
☐☐ communal	형 공동의, 공용의; (공동체 내의) 집단이 관련된
☐☐ compatible	형 양립[화합]할 수 있는; 호환이 되는
☐☐ commensurate	형 (크기나 액수가) 어울리는, 상응하는, 적당한
☐☐ compile	동 (여러 출처에서 자료를 따위) 엮다, 편집하다, 편찬하다

☐☐ compilation	명 (책이나 음반의) 모음집, 편집본
☐☐ complement	명 보완물; ((문법)) 보어 동 ~을 완전하게 하다; 보완하다
☐☐ complementary	형 상호 보완적인
☐☐ complex	형 복잡한 명 복합 건물; 콤플렉스, 강박 관념
☐☐ complexity	명 복잡함
☐☐ compound	명 (화학적) 화합물; 복합체 형 합성의 동 혼합하다; 구성하다; (문제 등을) 악화시키다

Essential Roots / Stems 1 | ply / plic

□□ complicate	통 (더) 복잡하게 만들다	□□ implicate	통 (범죄 등에) 연루시키다; 암시하다
□□ complication	명 복잡함; 합병증	□□ implication	명 (범죄에의) 연루; 함축, 암시; 영향
□□ apply	통 신청하다; 적용하다; (페인트·크림 등을) 바르다		
		□□ replicate	통 모사하다, 복제하다
□□ explicate	통 (사상·작품 등을) 설명하다, 해석하다	□□ replication	명 복제
□□ explicable	형 설명[해명]되는	□□ replica	명 모사품, 복제품
□□ explicit	형 명시적인, 분명한		

Essential Roots / Stems 2 | pel / puls(e)

□□ compel	통 강요하다; ~하게 만들다	□□ impel	통 (생각·기분이) ~해야만 하게 하다
□□ compulsion	명 강요, 강제		
□□ compulsory	형 강제적인, 의무적인, 필수의	□□ impulse	명 충동; 충격, 자극
		□□ impulsive	형 충동적인
□□ compulsive	형 강박적인, 조절이 힘든	□□ propel	통 나아가게 하다; (특정한 상황으로) 몰고 가다
□□ pulse	명 맥박; 고동; (음향 등의) 진동		
		□□ propeller	명 프로펠러, 추진기
□□ dispel	통 (느낌 등을) 떨쳐 버리다, 없애다	□□ repel	통 물리치다; 쫓아버리다; 혐오감을 주다
□□ expel	통 쫓아내다; 퇴학시키다; 배출하다	□□ repellent	형 혐오감을 주는 명 방충제; 방수제

Words with Multiple Meanings | 필수 다의어의 이해

□□ apply	통 신청하다, 지원하다 통 적용하다 통 쓰다, 사용하다 통 (페인트·크림 등을) 바르다
□□ company	명 함께 있음, 동반 명 함께 있는 사람들 명 회사
□□ mean	통 의미하다 통 의도하다, 작정하다 통 (결국) ~하게 되다 형 보통의, 평균의 형 비열한, 못된 명 ((pl.)) 수단, 방법
□□ command	통 명령하다 통 명령 통 (군대에서) 지휘하다 명 지휘, 통솔 통 (관심·존경 등을) 받다 명 전문적 기술[지식]; (언어) 구사 능력 명 ((컴퓨터)) 명령어

Phrasal Verbs | with가 포함된 구동사

☐☐ cope with   (~과 함께 맞서다) 대처하다

☐☐ contend with   (~과 함께 겨루다) 싸우다

☐☐ deal with   (~과 상대하다) 처리하다
[다루다]

☐☐ go with   (~과 함께 가다) 어울리다;
공존하다[동반되다]; 동조하다

☐☐ dispense with, 없애다
do without,
go without

☐☐ identify with   (~과 동일시하다)
동일시하다[일체감을 갖다]

Themes | 기분

☐☐ astonished   (형) (깜짝) 놀란

☐☐ astonish   (동) 깜짝 놀라게 하다

☐☐ astounded   (형) 경악한, 몹시 놀란

☐☐ astound   (동) 경악시키다, 큰 충격을
주다

☐☐ stunned   (형) (놀라서) 할 말을 잃은

☐☐ stun   (동) (소식 등이) 망연자실하게
만들다; 기절시키다

☐☐ startled   (형) (약간 공포의 감정을 동반
하여) 놀란

☐☐ startle   (동) 깜짝 놀라게 하다

☐☐ intimidated   (형) 겁이 난

☐☐ intimidate   (동) 겁을 주다, 위협하다

☐☐ agonize   (동) 고민하다, 고뇌하다

☐☐ agony   (명) (심신의) 극심한 고통,
괴로움

☐☐ inflict   (동) (괴로움 등을) 가하다

☐☐ fret   (동) 초조해하다, 안달하다

☐☐ fretful   (형) 초조해하는, 안달하는

☐☐ disheartened   (형) 실망한, 낙담한

☐☐ bewilder   (동) 어리둥절하게 만들다, 당황
하게 하다

☐☐ flounder   (동) (어쩔 줄 몰라) 허둥대다;
허우적대다

☐☐ confound   (동) 어리둥절하게 하다; 틀렸음
을 입증하다

☐☐ sulk   (동) 부루퉁하다, 샐쭉하다
(명) 부루퉁함

☐☐ sulky   (형) 부루퉁한

☐☐ envy   (명) 부러움, 선망
(동) 부러워하다

☐☐ envious   (형) 부러워하는, 선망하는

☐☐ longing   (형) 갈망하는 (명) 갈망, 동경

☐☐ implore   (동) 애원[간청]하다

☐☐ indulge   (동) 마음껏 하다; (욕구·관심
등을) 채우다

☐☐ indulgent   (형) 멋대로 하게 하는; 관대한

☐☐ deter   (동) 단념시키다, 그만두게 하다

☐☐ deterrent   (형) 제지하는 (명) 제지하는 것

☐☐ forgo   (동) (하거나 갖고 싶은 것을)
포기하다

26 강

words & phrases

☐☐ aftermath	몡 (전쟁·사고 등의) 여파, 후유증
☐☐ Antarctica	몡 남극 대륙
☐☐ assumption	몡 추정; (권력·책임의) 인수
☐☐ confirm	동 (증거를 들어) 사실임을 보여주다
☐☐ crooked	형 비뚤어진, 구부러진; 부정직한
☐☐ defective	형 결함이 있는
☐☐ dine	동 식사를 하다
☐☐ enact	동 (법을) 제정하다; (연극을) 상연하다
☐☐ inequality	몡 불평등, 불균등
☐☐ investigator	몡 수사관, 조사원
☐☐ inquiry	몡 연구, 탐구; 조사; 문의
☐☐ in (a) ~ fashion	~한 방식으로
☐☐ leading	형 가장 중요한; 선두의
☐☐ leisurely	형 한가한, 여유로운
☐☐ lodge	몡 오두막 동 숙박하다
☐☐ monument	몡 (동상 등의) 기념물; 기념비적인 건축물
☐☐ out and about	(병을 앓고 난 후에) 다시 나다니는; (어디를) 돌아다니는
☐☐ reconcile	동 화해시키다; (두 가지 이상의 생각 등을) 조화시키다
☐☐ recurring	형 되풀이하여 발생하는; ((수학)) 순환하는
☐☐ rug	몡 깔개, 양탄자
☐☐ run low on	~이 고갈되다, 모자라게 되다
☐☐ site	몡 (건물 등의) 위치, 장소; (건설) 현장, 부지; (사건 등의) 현장
☐☐ standby	몡 의지할 만한 것; 예비품, 대기자 형 대기의
☐☐ stationery	몡 문구류; 편지지
☐☐ tackle	동 (힘든 상황과) 씨름하다; 태클하다 몡 태클
☐☐ transmit	동 전송하다; 전염시키다
☐☐ yawn	몡 하품 동 하품하다

□□ concentrate	동(정신을) 집중하다; (한 곳에) 모으다 명농축물	□□ consistent	형일관된, 변함없는
		□□ consistency	명일관성
□□ concentration	명집중; 농도	□□ constitute	동구성하다, 이루다; 제정하다; 설립하다
□□ concerted	형(둘 이상의 사람·국가가) 합심한, 결연한		
□□ conform	동(규칙·관습 등에) 따르다; (~에) 일치하다	□□ constituent	형구성하는 명구성 성분; (특정 선거구) 유권자
□□ conformity	명(규칙·관습 등에) 따름, 순응; 일치	□□ consume	동소비하다; 섭취하다
		□□ consumption	명소비
□□ confront	동직면하다, 맞서다; (문제가) 닥치다	□□ consolidate	동통합하다; (권력·지위 등을) 강화하다, 굳건하게 하다
□□ confrontation	명대치, 대립	□□ contagious	형전염성의
□□ condemn	동비난[규탄]하다; 선고를 내리다	□□ configure	동(틀에 맞추어) 배열하다; (컴퓨터의) 환경을 설정하다
□□ congregate	동모이다		
□□ consequent	형~의 결과로 일어나는	□□ configuration	명배열; (컴퓨터) 환경 설정
□□ consequently	부그 결과, 따라서	□□ context	명맥락, 전후 사정; (글의) 문맥
□□ consequence	명결과	□□ converge	동모여들다, 집중되다
		□□ convergence	명(한 점으로의) 집중

Essential Roots / Stems | gen

□□ congenial	형같은 성질의, 마음이 맞는; 적합한; 친절한	□□ genesis	명기원, 발생; ((G-)) 창세기
		□□ generic	형일반적인, 포괄적인; 통칭의
□□ generate	동만들어내다; (전기·열 등을) 발생시키다	□□ homogeneous	형동종의; 동질적인
		□□ homogeneity	명동종; 동질성
□□ generator	명발전기	□□ indigenous	형토착의; 고유한
□□ generation	명세대; (전기·열 등의) 발생	□□ ingenious	형기발한; 독창적인
□□ gene	명유전자	□□ ingenuity	명기발한 재주; 독창성
□□ genetic	형유전의; 유전학의	□□ ingenuous	형솔직한; 순진한
□□ gender	명성, 성별		

Words with Multiple Meanings | 필수 다의어의 이해

□□ measure	동측정하다 동치수를 재다 동~의 길이[폭, 높이]이다 동평가[판단]하다 명척도, 기준 명수단, 대책, 조치; 법안, 정책
□□ meet	동만나다 동(힘들거나 불쾌한 일을) 만나다, 겪다 동~에 닿다 동(필요·요구 등을) 충족시키다 동(비용을) 지불하다, 부담하다
□□ odd	형(두 개가 한 벌이 되는 것 중) 한 짝의 형홀수의 형이상한, 기묘한 형이따금의; 임시의
□□ order	명순서 명정돈 동정돈하다 명질서 명명령 동명령하다 동주문하다 명주문; 주문품

□□ bring about	(~을 가져오다)	□□ move about	(주변을 옮겨 다니다) 이동하다
□□ come about	(~ 주위에 오다) 발생하다	□□ see about	(~의 주위를 보다) 고려하다;
□□ go about	(~ 주위에 가다) 시작하다;		돌보다
	계속 해나가다	□□ set about	(~의 주위에 놓다) 시작하다

Themes │ 사고

□□ mentality	영 사고방식	□□ logic	영 논리(학)
□□ contemplate	동 생각하다; 심사숙고하다; (오래) 응시하다	□□ causal	형 인과 관계의
		□□ causation	영 인과 관계; (다른 사건의) 야기
□□ contemplation	영 사색, 명상; 응시		
□□ obsess	동 (어떤 생각이 사람의 마음을) 사로잡다, 집착하게 하다	□□ ensue	동 (결과가) 뒤따르다
		□□ classify	동 분류하다; (정보·문서 등을) 기밀 취급하다
□□ obsession	영 집착, 강박 상태		
□□ standpoint	영 견지, 관점	□□ classified	형 분류된; 기밀의
□□ stereotype	영 고정관념; 정형화된 표현 동 고정관념을 형성하다; 정형화하다	□□ distinct	형 구별되는; 뚜렷한, 분명한
		□□ distinction	영 구별; 차이; 특징; 우수성
		□□ distinctive	형 독특한
□□ flip side	영 뒷면; (생각 등의) 다른 면	□□ priority	영 우선 (사항)
□□ fallacy	영 (많은 사람이 믿는) 그릇된 생각; 오류	□□ prioritize	동 우선순위를 매기다
		□□ disparate	형 (본질적으로) 다른; 이종의
□□ criteria	영 ((criterion의 복수형)) (판단) 기준, 표준	□□ disparity	영 (특히 한쪽에 불공평한) 차이, 불일치
□□ conscious	형 의식하는; 지각 있는		
□□ consciousness	영 의식; 자각	□□ option	영 선택(권)
□□ oblivious	형 의식하지 못하는	□□ optional	형 선택적인
□□ oblivion	영 의식하지 못하는 상태; 망각	□□ acknowledge	동 인정하다; (공식적으로) 감사를 표하다
□□ unwittingly	부 자신도 모르게		

27강

words & phrases

☐☐ arthritis	몡 관절염
☐☐ auction house	몡 경매장; 경매 전문 회사
☐☐ bilateral	혱 쌍방의; 좌우 양측의
☐☐ coma	몡 혼수상태
☐☐ confidential	혱 기밀의; 은밀한; 신뢰를 받는
☐☐ curator	몡 큐레이터
☐☐ deficiency	몡 결핍(증); 결함
☐☐ dimension	몡 (공간의) 크기, (높이 등의) 치수; 규모, 범위; 차원
☐☐ expense	몡 비용, 경비
☐☐ fat-soluble	혱 지용성의
☐☐ hype up	과대광고하다, 과장하여 선전하다
☐☐ immune	혱 면역성이 있는; ~의 영향을 받지 않는; ~이 면제되는
☐☐ inhale	동 (숨·연기 등을) 들이마시다
☐☐ integration	몡 통합
☐☐ irritation	몡 짜증 나게 함; 자극하는 것, 염증
☐☐ measles	몡 홍역
☐☐ mistress	몡 (하인을 부리는) 여주인; ((비유)) (~의) 여왕
☐☐ profitability	몡 수익성, 이윤율
☐☐ rearing	몡 양육; (가축) 사육
☐☐ remark	몡 발언, 논평; 주목 동 언급하다, 논평하다
☐☐ revive	동 되살리다, 부활시키다; (예전 연극·영화를) 재상연하다
☐☐ secondhand smoke	몡 간접흡연
☐☐ shade	몡 그늘; 색조; 음영
☐☐ spatial	혱 공간의, 공간적인
☐☐ stimuli	몡 ((stimulus의 복수형)) 자극; 자극이 되는 것
☐☐ untried	혱 경험이 없는; 검증되지 않은
☐☐ vivid	혱 (기억 등이) 생생한; (색깔 등이) 선명한

Prefixes | 함께·같이 (3) co -, syn -

□□ coalition 　명 연립 정부; (정치적) 연합체

□□ coherent 　형 일관성 있는

□□ coherence 　명 일관성

□□ cohesive 　형 화합하는, 결합하는

□□ cohesion 　명 화합, 결합; 응집력

□□ coincide 　동 동시에 일어나다; (의견 등이) 일치하다

□□ coincidence 　명 우연의 일치; 동시 발생; (의견 등의) 일치

□□ coexist 　동 공존하다

□□ coexistence 　명 공존

□□ correspond 　동 서신을 주고받다; ((with, to)) 일치하다; 상응하다

□□ correspondent 　명 편지를 쓰는 사람; (특정 지역이나 주제 담당) 기자, 특파원

□□ correspondence 　명 서신, 편지; 일치; 관련성

□□ collaborate 　동 협력하다

□□ collaboration 　명 협력; 공동 작업

□□ collaborative 　형 협력적인; 공동의

□□ collateral 　형 서로 나란한, 평행한; 부수적인, 이차적인
　　　　　　　　명 담보물

□□ colloquial 　형 구어의, 일상적인 대화체의

□□ collide 　동 충돌하다; (의견 등이) 상충하다

□□ collision 　명 충돌

□□ collusion 　명 공모, 결탁; 유착

□□ collusive 　형 공모의, (미리) 결탁한

□□ syndrome 　명 증후군; 일련의 증상[태도]

□□ synergy 　명 시너지 효과, 동반 상승효과

□□ synthetic 　형 (인위적으로) 합성한, 인조의; 종합적인

□□ synthesize 　동 합성하다; 종합하다

□□ synthesis 　명 합성

□□ symmetry 　명 대칭; 균형

□□ symposium 　명 심포지엄, 학술 토론회

□□ symptom 　명 증상; (특히 불길한) 징후

□□ symptomatic 　형 증상을 보이는

Essential Roots / Stems | chron(o), tempor

□□ synchronize 　동 동시에 발생하다

□□ chronicle 　명 연대기, 연대표
　　　　　　　동 연대순으로 기록하다

□□ chronology 　명 연대순, 연대표

□□ chronological 　형 (여러 사건이) 연대순의, 시간 순서대로 된

□□ chronic 　형 (병 등이) 장기간에 걸친, 만성적인; 상습적인

□□ temporal 　형 시간의; 세속적인

□□ temporary 　형 일시적인

□□ contemporary 　형 동시대의; 현대의
　　　　　　　　명 동시대인

Words with Multiple Meanings | 필수 다의어의 이해

□□ party 　명 일행, 단체, 무리 　명 (사교 상의) 모임, 파티 　명 정당 　명 (계약·소송 등의) 당사자

□□ pay 　동 (비용·임금 등을) 지불하다 　명 보수, 임금 　동 (~에게) 이득이 되다 　동 수익을 내다
　　　　동 (자신의 신념·행동에 대한) 대가를 치르다

□□ plain 　명 평원, 평지 　형 무늬가 없는 　형 예쁘지 않은, 못생긴 　형 솔직한 　형 (음식이) 담백한
　　　　형 (보거나 이해하기에) 분명한, 명백한

□□ practice 　명 실행, 실천 　명 습관 　명 관행, 관례 　명 연습 　동 연습하다 　명 (의사·변호사 등의) 개업; 영업

Phrasal Verbs | around가 포함된 구동사

☐☐ come around, come to one's senses   (방향을 바꿔서 오다) 의식이 돌아오다

☐☐ get around   (주위를 다니다) 돌아다니다

☐☐ hang around   (주위에 매달려 있다) 주위를 어슬렁거리다

☐☐ show around   (주위를 보여 주다) 두루 안내하다

☐☐ shop around   (주위를 둘러 쇼핑하다) 가게들을 둘러보다

☐☐ turn around   (방향을 바꿔 돌리다) 돌아서다; 바뀌다; 회복시키다

Themes | 건강

☐☐ complexion   명 안색

☐☐ metabolism   명 신진[물질]대사

☐☐ metabolic   형 신진대사의

☐☐ metabolize   동 대사 작용을 하다

☐☐ robust   형 원기 왕성한; 튼튼한

☐☐ vigorous   형 활발한, 격렬한; 활기찬

☐☐ vigor   명 힘, 활력

☐☐ inert   형 기력이 없는; 움직이지 않는

☐☐ vulnerable   형 (~에) 취약한, 연약한

☐☐ vulnerability   명 상처받기 쉬움; 취약성

☐☐ weary   형 (몹시) 지친; ((of)) (~에) 싫증 난

☐☐ debilitate   동 (심신을) 약화시키다

☐☐ disabled   형 장애를 가진

☐☐ disability   명 (신체적) 장애

☐☐ frail   형 노쇠한; 부서지기 쉬운

☐☐ detrimental   형 해로운

☐☐ obese   형 비만인

☐☐ obesity   명 비만

☐☐ sanitary   형 위생의; 위생적인

☐☐ sanitation   명 위생; 위생시설[관리]

☐☐ sanitize   동 위생 처리하다, 살균하다

☐☐ hazardous   형 (특히 건강·안전에) 위험한

☐☐ hazard   명 위험 (요소)

☐☐ inoculate   동 예방 접종하다; (사상 등을) 주입하다

☐☐ vaccinate   동 (특히 백신으로) 예방 접종하다

☐☐ vaccination   명 백신[예방] 접종

☐☐ intuition   명 직관(력), 직감, 육감

☐☐ intuitive   형 직관에 의한; 직관력이 있는

☐☐ tactile   형 촉각의; 촉감의

☐☐ acoustic   형 청각의; 음향의; 전자 장치를 쓰지 않는

☐☐ acoustics   명 ((단수 취급)) 음향학; ((복수 취급)) 음향시설

☐☐ resonate   동 소리가 울려 퍼지다, 공명이 잘되다

☐☐ resonant   형 소리가 깊이 울리는

☐☐ resonance   명 소리의 울림

28강

words & phrases

☐☐ asthma	명 천식
☐☐ bet	명 내기 (돈); 짐작 동 (내기에) 돈을 걸다; (~이) 틀림없다
☐☐ celebrity	명 유명 인사; 명성
☐☐ communion	명 친교, 교감; 성찬식; 종교 단체
☐☐ consult	동 상담하다; (참고서 등을) 찾아보다
☐☐ diagnose	동 (질병·문제의 원인을) 진단하다
☐☐ district	명 구역, 지구
☐☐ dweller	명 거주자, 주민
☐☐ exemplify	동 전형적인 예가 되다; 예를 들다
☐☐ extension	명 연장, 확대; (전화의) 내선
☐☐ humanitarian	형 인도주의적인, 인도주의자의
☐☐ obligate	형 필수[의무]적인; 불가피한 동 의무를 지우다; 강요하다

☐☐ ointment	명 연고
☐☐ operate	동 (기계 등이) 작동하다; 작용하다; 수술하다
☐☐ on grounds of	~을 이유[근거]로
☐☐ persist	동 고집하다; 지속하다
☐☐ pharmaceutical	형 약학의; 제약의
☐☐ pill	명 알약
☐☐ pneumonia	명 폐렴
☐☐ prevalent	형 일반적인, 널리 퍼져 있는
☐☐ repressive	형 억압적인, 탄압하는
☐☐ sign up for	~을 등록[가입]하다
☐☐ steering wheel	(자동차의) 핸들
☐☐ temperament	명 기질, 성질
☐☐ tolerate	동 참다; 견디다; 용인하다
☐☐ validity	명 유효함; 타당성
☐☐ virulent	형 악성의, 치명적인; 매서운, 맹렬한
☐☐ wound	명 상처, 부상 동 상처를 입히다

Prefixes | 하게 함 en -, 스스로, 자동 auto -

□□ enact   동 (법을) 제정하다; 상연하다

□□ encompass   동 둘러싸다; (많은 것을) 포함하다

□□ entail   동 (필연적 결과로) 수반하다

□□ entrench   동 (변경이 어렵게) 단단히 자리 잡게 하다

□□ enroll   동 등록하다, 입학시키다

□□ entrust   동 (일을) 맡기다

□□ embattled   형 공세에 시달리는; 교전 중인

□□ embed   동 (단단히) 박다, 끼워 넣다; (마음에) 깊이 새겨두다

□□ embody   동 구현하다, 구체화하다; 포함하다

□□ embodiment   명 구체화; 전형, 본보기

□□ embark   동 (배·비행기에) 승선하다; ((on)) (~에) 착수하다

□□ impoverish   동 가난하게 하다; 저하시키다

□□ automatic   형 (기계가) 자동의; 반사적인

□□ automation   명 자동화

□□ autonomy   명 자치권; 자주성, 자율성

□□ autonomous   형 자주적인, 자율적인

□□ autocracy   명 독재 정치; 독재 국가

□□ autocrat   명 전제 군주, 독재자

Essential Roots / Stems 1 | graph / gram

□□ autograph   명 (유명인의) 사인, 자필 서명 동 사인을 해주다

□□ phonograph   명 축음기, 레코드플레이어

□□ calligraphy   명 서예; 달필

□□ demographic   형 인구학의; 인구통계학의

□□ demographics   명 인구통계학

□□ polygraph   명 거짓말 탐지기

□□ pictogram   명 그림 문자; 상형 문자

Essential Roots / Stems 2 | bio

□□ autobiography   명 자서전

□□ biology   명 생물학

□□ biological   형 생물학의; 생물체의

□□ antibiotic(s)   명 항생제, 항생물질

□□ antibiosis   명 항생작용

□□ biosphere   명 생물권

□□ biomass   명 (특정 지역의) 생물량; 바이오매스

□□ symbiosis   명 공생 (관계)

□□ symbiotic   형 공생하는

□□ symbiont   명 공생자, 공생 동물

Words with Multiple Meanings | 필수 다의어의 이해

□□ race	몡 달리기 동 달리다 몡 (급히) 서두름 동 서두르다 몡 경주 동 경주하다
	몡 경쟁 동 경쟁하다 몡 선거전; ((pl.)) 경마
	몡 인종; 민족, 국민
□□ reason	몡 사고력, 이성 동 추론하다; 논리적으로 생각하다 몡 이유, 원인, 근거
□□ regard	동 생각[간주]하다 동 고려하다 몡 고려 몡 점, 사항
	동 존중[중요시]하다 몡 존경, 존중 몡 관심
□□ relief	몡 (고통·불안 등의) 경감[완화] 몡 안심, 안도 몡 구호(품) 몡 (업무 등의) 교대자[팀]

Phrasal Verbs | for가 포함된 구동사 1

□□ account for	(~에 대해 설명하다) 설명하다; 차지하다	□□ ask for	(~에 대해 묻다[요청하다]) 청하다
□□ allow for	(~을 받아들이다) 고려하다	□□ call for	(~을 위해 부르다) 요구하다; 예상하다
□□ answer for	(~에 대해 답변하다) 책임을 지다	□□ care for	(~을 위해 돌보다 / ~을 좋아하다) 돌보다; 좋아하다

Themes | 의료

□□ insomnia	몡 불면증	□□ alleviation	몡 완화
□□ diabetes	몡 당뇨병	□□ sterilize	동 살균[소독]하다; 불임이 되게 하다
□□ sharp[acute] pain	몡 심한 통증		
		□□ sterile	혱 소독한; 척박한; 불임의
□□ fatal	혱 치명적인, 죽음을 초래하는	□□ hospitalize	동 입원시키다
□□ fatality	몡 사망자; 치사율	□□ hospitalization	몡 입원; 입원 기간
□□ throb	동 (규칙적으로) 고동치다; 욱신거리다	□□ irreparable	혱 (손실·부상 등이) 회복할 수 없는
	몡 진동; 욱신거림	□□ dose	몡 (약의) 복용량
□□ ail	동 괴롭히다; 병들게 하다		동 (약을) 투여하다
□□ ailment	몡 (가볍거나 만성적인) 질병	□□ dosage	몡 (약의) 복용량
□□ trauma	몡 외상; 정신적 충격[외상], 트라우마	□□ abuse	몡 남용, 오용; 학대
			동 남용[오용]하다; 학대하다
□□ traumatic	혱 정신적 외상의; 대단히 충격적인	□□ abusive	혱 남용[오용]하는; 모욕적인
□□ remedy	몡 치료(약); 해결책	□□ ingest	동 (음식·약 등을) 삼키다[먹다]
	동 바로잡다; 개선하다	□□ side effect	몡 부작용
□□ heal	동 고치다, 치유하다	□□ medicinal	혱 약효가 있는
□□ alleviate	동 완화하다	□□ placebo	몡 플라세보, 위약

29강 MP3

words & phrases

□□ additive	명 첨가물, 첨가제
□□ appetizer	명 전채 요리, 애피타이저, 식욕을 돋우기 위한 것
□□ broth	명 (걸쭉한) 수프
□□ canning	명 통조림 제조(업)
□□ component	명 구성 요소; 성분
□□ dent	명 움푹 들어간 곳 동 움푹 들어가게 하다; 훼손하다
□□ faultless	형 흠잡을 데 없는
□□ fetal	형 태아의, 태아 상태의
□□ firmly	부 단호히, 확고히
□□ food group	명 식품군
□□ inheritance	명 유산; 유전
□□ inhibit	동 억제하다; 못하게 하다
□□ margarine	명 마가린
□□ negotiation	명 협상
□□ on occasion	이따금, 가끔
□□ plump	형 통통한; (물건·과일 등이) 불룩한, 속이 가득 찬
□□ queue	명 (차례를 기다리는 사람의) 줄 동 줄을 서다
□□ relentlessly	부 가차 없이
□□ resign oneself	체념하다
□□ retailer	명 소매상, 소매업
□□ spice	명 양념, 향신료
□□ spread	동 펼치다; 확산되다; (얇게 펴서) 바르다 명 확산, 전파; 스프레드
□□ stand trial	((for)) (~의 혐의로) 재판을 받다
□□ stew	명 스튜 동 뭉근히 끓이다; 마음 졸이다, 애태우다
□□ stranglehold	명 목 조르기; 옥죄기
□□ vegetarian	명 채식주의자 형 채식주의자의
□□ victorious	형 승리를 거둔
□□ villain	명 (연극·이야기 등의) 악인, 악당
□□ wrinkle	명 주름; (천 등의) 구김살 동 주름이 생기다

Prefixes | 좋은 bene -, 나쁜 mal(e) -, 잘못 mis -

□□ benevolent	형 자애로운, 인정 많은	□□ malignant	형 악의에 찬; (종양·병이) 악성의
□□ benefactor	명 선행자; 기부자, 후원자	□□ malpractice	명 (전문 직종에서의) 위법 행위; 의료 과실
□□ benefaction	명 기부금, 후원금	□□ malformation	명 (몸의) 기형 (상태)
□□ beneficent	형 선행하는; 자비로운		
□□ beneficence	명 선행; 자선	□□ misbehave	동 못된 짓을 하다, 비행을 저지르다
□□ beneficial	형 유익한, 이로운	□□ misbehavior	명 버릇없음; 비행, 부정행위
□□ beneficiary	명 수혜자; (유산) 수령인	□□ misconception	명 (옳지 않은 정보에 근거한) 오해; 잘못된 통념
□□ malady	명 (만성적인) 병; 심각한 문제, 병폐	□□ mishap	명 작은 사고; 불행
□□ maladaptive	형 순응성이 없는, 부적응의	□□ mislead	동 잘못 인도하다; 오해하게 하다, 속이다
□□ malefactor	명 악인, 악한		
□□ malnutrition	명 영양실조(증)	□□ misplace	동 제자리에 두지 않다 (그래서 찾지 못하다)
□□ maltreat	동 학대하다, 혹사하다	□□ misplaced	형 부적절한, 잘못된
□□ malevolent	형 악의적인	□□ misdirect	동 엉뚱한 곳으로 보내다; 적절하지 못하게 이용하다
□□ malice	명 악의, 적의		
□□ malicious	형 악의적인		

Essential Roots / Stems | dic(t)

□□ benediction	명 축복; 축복 기도	□□ dictator	명 독재자
□□ malediction	명 저주, 비방	□□ dictatorship	명 독재 (정권)
□□ dictate	동 받아쓰게 하다; 지시[명령]하다; 영향을 주다	□□ diction	명 발음; 말투; 어휘 선택
		□□ predict	동 예측[예언]하다
□□ dictation	명 받아쓰기	□□ prediction	명 예측, 예언

Words with Multiple Meanings | 필수 다의어의 이해

□□ refer to	동 ~을 참고하다 동 ~에게 문의하다 동 ~에 관하여 언급하다, 설명하다 동 가리키다, 나타내다
□□ reference	명 언급 명 (정보를 얻기 위해) 찾아봄, 참고, 참조 명 참고 문헌 명 추천서
□□ represent	동 나타내다; 상징하다 동 대리[대표]하다 동 표현하다, 묘사하다 동 (분명히) 말하다, (의견을) 제기하다
□□ resolve	동 분해하다 동 해결하다 명동 결심(하다), 결의(하다)

□□ feel for	(~을 느끼다 / ~을 (찾으려고) 만져보다) 공감하다; 더듬어 찾다	□□ make for	(~을 위해 만들다 / ~을 향해 가다) 도움이 되다; 쪽으로 가다
□□ go for	(~에게 가다) 좋아하다; 해당되다; 선택하다	□□ speak for	(~을 대신하여 말하다) 대변하다
□□ long for, yearn for, be anxious for, be eager for	(~을 추구하여 원하다) 갈망하다	□□ stand for	(~을 대신하여 서 있다) 의미하다; 지지하다

□□ chore	몡 (정기적으로 하는) 일; 하기 싫은 일	□□ grind	동 (곡식을) 분쇄하다; (날을) 갈다
□□ junk	몡 쓸모없는 물건, 폐물 동 폐물로 처분하다	□□ dietary	혱 음식물의; 식이 요법의
□□ clothing	몡 ((집합적)) 의류	□□ portion	몡 부분; (음식의) 1인분 동 (부분·몫으로) 나누다
□□ ragged	혱 누더기가 된; (표면이) 고르지 못한	□□ gourmet	몡 미식가, 식도락가 혱 미식가를 위한
□□ drape	동 (옷·천 등을 느슨하게) 걸치다, 씌우다 몡 휘장	□□ sip	동 (음료를) 홀짝거리다
		□□ fast	동 단식[금식]하다 몡 단식, 금식
□□ fad	몡 (일시적인) 유행	□□ fasting	몡 단식, 금식
□□ fabric	몡 직물, 천; 구조	□□ edible	혱 먹을 수 있는
□□ recipe	몡 조리법	□□ succulent	혱 즙이 많은
□□ season	몡 계절 동 양념[간]하다	□□ nourish	동 영양분을 공급하다
		□□ nourishment	몡 영양(분)
□□ grain	몡 곡물; 낟알; 티끌 (천 등의) 결	□□ nourishing	혱 자양분이 많은
□□ granular	혱 낟알의; 오돌토돌한	□□ feast	몡 연회, 잔치 동 (아주 즐겁게) 맘껏 먹다

words & phrases

□□ abolish	图(법률·제도·조직 등을) 폐지하다	□□ just in case	(혹시라도) (~할) 경우에 대비해서
□□ accidentally	图우연히, 뜻하지 않게	□□ make it	성공하다; 참석하다; (간신히) 시간 맞춰 가다
□□ candidate	閔(선거의) 입후보자, 출마자; (일자리의) 후보자	□□ overinterpret	图확대해석하다
□□ declaration	閔선언(문); 신고(서)	□□ pole	閔막대기; (지구·자석의) 극
□□ dispute	閔분쟁, 논쟁	□□ pose	图(문제 등을) 제기하다; 자세를 취하다
	图반박하다, 이의를 제기하다; 논란을 벌이다	□□ reassure	图안심시키다
□□ distort	图(형체 등을) 비틀다; (사실을) 왜곡하다	□□ rescuer	閔구조자, 구출자
□□ equator	閔((the ~)) 적도	□□ scarcity	閔부족, 결핍
□□ evict	图(주택이나 땅에서) 쫓아내다	□□ shelter	閔주거지; 대피(처), 보호소
□□ faction	閔당파, 파벌		图막아 주다, 보호하다; 피하다
□□ grease	閔기름; (기계의) 윤활유	□□ simultaneously	图동시에, 일제히
	图기름을 바르다	□□ stream	閔개울; (계속 이어진) 줄, 흐름
□□ hedge	閔(정원 등의) 울타리; ((against)) (금전 손실에 대한) 대비책		图줄줄 흘러나오다
		□□ subsidy	閔(국가·기관이 제공하는) 보조금[장려금]
	图울타리를 치다; 얼버무리다; (손실에) 대비하다	□□ tariff	閔관세(율)
□□ have a way of v-ing	흔히 v하게 되어 가다	□□ virtual	웹사실상의, 거의 ~과 다름없는; ((컴퓨터)) 가상의

Prefixes | 수·양(1) mon(o)-, un(i)-, du-, bi(n)-

□□ monotone	閔단조로운 소리	□□ monolingual	웹단일 언어의
	웹(소리·색깔이) 단조로운		閔단일 언어 사용자
□□ monotony	閔단조로움	□□ monogamous	웹일부일처의
□□ monotonous	웹단조로운; 지루한	□□ monogamy	閔일부일처제
□□ monopoly	閔(시장의) 독점; 전매권	□□ monoxide	閔((화학)) 일산화물
□□ monopolize	图독점하다	□□ unanimous	웹만장일치의
□□ monopolist	閔독점기업, 전매자	□□ unify	图통합하다, 통일하다

□□ unification	명 통일	□□ duplicate	동 복사[복제]하다
□□ unity	명 통합, 통일(성)		형 똑같은; 사본의 명 사본
□□ unilateral	형 일방적인, 단독의	□□ duplicity	명 이중성, 표리부동
□□ dual	형 두 부분으로 된; 이중의	□□ binary	형 2진법의; 2진수의; 두 부분
□□ duality	명 이중성		으로 이루어진
		□□ binoculars	명 쌍안경

Essential Roots / Stems 1 | ann(u) / enn

□□ biannual	형 연 2회의	□□ centennial	명 100주년
□□ annual	형 매년의; 연간의		형 100년마다의
□□ annually	부 매년; 일 년에 한 번	□□ millennium	명 천 년; 새로운 천 년이 시작
□□ annals	명 연대기; 연보		되는 시기
□□ anniversary	명 (매년의) 기념일	□□ perennial	형 영원한; 계속 반복되는;
			(식물이) 다년생인
			명 다년생 식물

Essential Roots / Stems 2 | ped(e) / pedi

□□ biped	명 두발짐승	□□ pedestal	명 받침대; 기초, 근거
□□ peddle	동 (물건을) 팔러 다니다, 행상 하다	□□ expedition	명 탐험(대), 원정(대)
		□□ impede	동 (진행을) 방해하다
□□ peddler	명 행상; 잡상인	□□ impediment	명 장애(물)
□□ pedestrian	명 보행자 형 보행자의		

Words with Multiple Meanings | 필수 다의어의 이해

□□ scale	명 비늘; 치석 동 비늘[치석]을 벗기다
	명 (특히 다른 것과 비교해서 본) 규모, 범위 명 (측정용) 등급 명 저울 동 저울로 달다
	동 (아주 높고 가파른 곳을) 오르다
□□ settle	동 정착하다 동 직업에 종사하게 하다 동 (마음 등을) 진정시키다
	동 해결하다 동 결정하다, 결심하다 동 (주어야 할 돈을) 지불[정산]하다
□□ serve	동 (식당 등에서 음식을) 제공하다, 상에 차려주다 동 (상품·서비스를) 제공하다
	동 도움이 되다, 기여하다 동 (특정 용도로) 이용할 수 있다, 적합하다
	동 (사람·국가 등을 위해) 일하다, 복무하다 동 (교도소에서) 복역하다
	동 (테니스 등에서) 서브를 넣다
□□ sound	명 소리 동 ~처럼 들리다; ~인 것 같다
	형 믿을 만한; 견실한 형 정통한; 철저한 형 (신체·정신이) 건강한, 온전한 형 (수면이) 깊은

Phrasal Verbs | across, against가 포함된 구동사

□□ come across (오다가 서로 교차하다) 우연히 보게 되다; 이해되다; 인상을 주다

□□ get across (~을 건너서 옮기다) 이해시키다

□□ run across (가다가 서로 교차하다) 우연히 발견하다

□□ go against (~에 맞서서 가다) 거스르다; 불리하다; 어긋나다

□□ set against (~에 맞서 배치하다) 대립하다

Themes | 일상생활2

□□ reside 图 (특정한 곳에) 살다, 거주하다

□□ residence 图 거주(지)

□□ resident 图 거주자 图 거주하는

□□ residential 图 거주하기 좋은

□□ inhabit 图 살다, 서식하다

□□ inhabitant 图 주민; 서식 동물

□□ inhabitable 图 살기에 적합한

□□ ventilate 图 환기하다

□□ ventilation 图 통풍; 환기

□□ vent 图 통풍구 图 (감정을) 발산하다

□□ illumination 图 조명; 계몽

□□ insulate 图 절연[단열/방음] 처리를 하다; 격리하다

□□ insulation 图 절연; 절연체

□□ cozy 图 편안한; 친밀한

□□ spacious 图 (방·건물이) 널찍한

□□ tenant 图 세입자, 임차인

□□ estate 图 사유지; 재산

□□ lease 图 임대차 계약 图 임대[임차/대여]하다

□□ rent 图 집세, 임대료 图 임대[임차/대여]하다

□□ rental 图 임대(료); 임대물

□□ utility 图 유용; (수도·전기 등의) 공익 사업

□□ furnish 图 (가구를) 비치하다

□□ furnished 图 가구가 비치된

□□ furnishing 图 (집·방의) 가구

□□ clog 图 막다; 막히다 图 나막신

□□ leak 图 새는 곳[틈]; 누설 图 새다

□□ leakage 图 누출

□□ leaky 图 새는, 구멍이 난

□□ mow 图 (잔디를) 깎다; (풀 등을) 베다

□□ mower 图 (잔디) 깎는 기계

□□ trim 图 다듬다; 장식하다 图 다듬기; 테두리

□□ trimming 图 (테두리 등의) 장식; ((pl.)) 곁들이는 음식

□□ decorate 图 장식하다

□□ decoration 图 장식(품)

□□ decorative 图 장식용의

□□ decor 图 (실내) 장식

□□ install 图 설치하다

□□ installation 图 설비, 설치

□□ drain 图 물을 빼다; 따라 내다 图 배수관

□□ drainage 图 배수 (시설)

□□ drained 图 진이 빠진

words & phrases

□□ diminish	동 줄이다; (중요성을) 깎아내리다
□□ excavation	명 발굴(지); 땅파기
□□ extant	형 (아주 오래된 것이) 현존하는, 남아 있는
□□ fiscal year	명 회계 연도
□□ flurry	명 (잠시 한바탕 벌어지는) 소동; 한차례 흩뿌리는 눈[비]
□□ formula	명 공식; 방식
□□ fugitive	명 도망자, 탈주자 형 도망 다니는
□□ grudge	명 원한, 유감 동 (무엇을 하거나 주는 것을) 아까워하다; 샘내다
□□ hay	명 건초
□□ impair	동 손상시키다, 악화시키다
□□ impose	동 ((on)) (법률 등을) 도입하다; (힘든 것을) 부과하다; (의견을) 강요하다
□□ insignificant	형 대수롭지 않은, 하찮은
□□ marshal	동 (사람 등을) 집결시키다, 모으다
□□ mitigate	동 완화시키다, 경감시키다
□□ monumental	형 기념비적인; 엄청난, 대단한
□□ outskirts	명 (도시의) 변두리, 교외
□□ perpetual	형 (오랫동안) 끊임없이 계속되는; 빈번한
□□ porch	명 현관; 베란다
□□ ram	동 (차량 등이) 들이받다; (억지로) 밀어 넣다 명 숫양
□□ retrieve	동 되찾아오다, 회수하다
□□ secluded	형 (장소가) 한적한, 외딴
□□ sequel	명 (영화 등의) 속편; 뒤이어 일어난 일
□□ solidarity	명 연대, 결속
□□ take the chance of	~을 운에 맡기고 해보다; ~의 기회를 이용하다
□□ territorial	형 영토의; 세력권을 주장하는
□□ turning point	명 전환점, 전기
□□ unspoiled	형 (장소가) 자연 그대로의, 훼손되지 않은
□□ vessel	명 (대형) 선박; 그릇; 혈관

Prefixes | 수·양(2) tri-, multi-

□□ triple
- 혱 3배의; 3개로 이뤄진
- 동 3배로 만들다

□□ trillion
- 명 1조; 엄청난 양

□□ trilogy
- 명 (책·영화 등의) 3부작

□□ tridimensional
- 혱 3차원의, 입체의

□□ multilateral
- 혱 다자간의; 다국가 간의; 다각적인

□□ multiply
- 동 곱하다; (수·양이) 많이 증가하다

□□ multiplier
- 명 증가시키는 것; 승수, 곱하는 수

□□ multiple
- 혱 많은, 다수의
- 명 ((수학)) 배수

□□ multitasking
- 명 (컴퓨터) 다중 작업; 동시에 여러 가지 일을 하는 능력

□□ multitude
- 명 다수; 군중

Essential Roots / Stems | medi

□□ multimedia
- 명 멀티미디어, 다중매체
- 혱 멀티미디어의

□□ medium
- 명 수단; (대중 전달용) 매체
- 혱 중간의

□□ median
- 명 중앙값
- 혱 중앙의; 중간값의

□□ medieval
- 혱 중세의

□□ mediate
- 동 (해결책을 위해) 중재하다; 타결을 보다

□□ mediation
- 명 조정, 중재

□□ mediator
- 명 중재자

□□ intermediate
- 혱 중간의, 중급의 명 중급자

□□ mediocre
- 혱 평범한, 보통밖에 안 되는

□□ mediocrity
- 명 ((부정적)) (썩 뛰어나지 않은) 보통, 평범; 보통 사람

Words with Multiple Meanings | 필수 다의어의 이해

□□ quarter
- 명 4분의 1 명 15분 명 25센트 명 1분기 (3개월) 명 방위 명 지역, 지구

□□ spell
- 동 (단어의) 철자를 말하다[쓰다]
- 명 주문, 마법 명 마력, (강한) 매력 동 (보통 나쁜 결과를) 가져오다
- 명 한동안; 한동안의 일[활동]

□□ stake
- 명 말뚝 명 지분 명 (사업·계획 등에 대한 개인적인) 이해관계
- 명 (내기에) 건 돈 동 (돈을) 걸다

□□ stand
- 동 (~에 대해 특정한) 입장에 있다 명 입장, 태도 동 참다 명 저항, 반항 명 판매대, 매점

Phrasal Verbs | aside, by가 포함된 구동사

□□ push aside (밀어서 옆에 두다) 제쳐놓다

□□ put aside, (옆에 두다) 따로 떼어 두다;
set aside 무시하다

□□ step aside (옆으로 비켜서다) 옆으로 비
켜주다; 물러나다

□□ live by (~에 따라 살다)

□□ pass by (옆을 지나가다) 놓치다

□□ stop by, (옆에 멈추다) 잠깐 들르다
drop by[in]

Themes | 교통·수송

□□ detour 몡 우회도로
동 돌아서 가다

□□ tow 동 (줄로) 잡아당기다; (차를)
견인하다

□□ honk 동 (자동차 경적을) 울리다

□□ skid 동 (보통 차량이) 미끄러지다
몡 미끄러짐

□□ junction 몡 접합(점); 교차로

□□ airway 몡 항공로; ((pl.)) 항공사;
(코에서 폐까지의) 기도

□□ altitude 몡 (해발) 고도; 고지

□□ aviation 몡 비행, 항공

□□ landing 몡 상륙; 착륙

□□ runway 몡 활주로; (패션쇼장의) 무대

□□ anchor 몡 닻; (뉴스) 앵커
동 닻을 내리다; 고정시키다

□□ anchorage 몡 닻을 내림; 고정시키는 곳

□□ canal 몡 운하, 수로; (체내의) 관

□□ dock 몡 부두 동 (배를) 부두에 대다;
(급여에서) 공제하다

□□ harbor 몡 항구; 피난처
동 숨겨 주다; (생각을) 품다

□□ shipping 몡 ((집합적)) 선박; 선적; 해운

□□ adrift 혱 표류하는; 떨어져 나간

□□ wreck 몡 난파(선); 망가진 차량
동 난파시키다

□□ cargo 몡 (선박·비행기의) 화물

□□ freight 몡 화물; 화물 운송
동 화물로 보내다

□□ load 몡 짐; 작업량 동 (짐을) 싣다

□□ loaded 혱 (짐을) 실은; 가득한

□□ compartment 몡 (열차 안의 칸막이) 객실

□□ postal 혱 우편의; 우편에 의한

32 강

words & phrases

□□ abolition	명 폐지	□□ intensify	동 강화하다
□□ aristocrat	명 귀족(인 사람)	□□ layout	명 (책·건물 등의) 배치
□□ artwork	명 삽화; (박물관의) 미술품	□□ masterpiece	명 걸작, 대표작
□□ bump	동 부딪치다	□□ muse	명 (예술적 영감을 주는) 뮤즈
	명 충돌; 혹, 타박상		동 사색하다, 생각에 잠기다
□□ cattle	명 ((집합적)) 소	□□ occasion	명 (특정한) 때[경우]; (특별한)
□□ dexterity	명 (손이나 머리를 쓰는) 재주		행사[의식] 동 일으키다
□□ draft	명 밑그림, 초안; ((the ~))	□□ perform	동 실행하다; 성과를 내다;
	징병		공연[연주]하다
	동 선발하다	□□ pledge	명 (굳은) 약속, 서약, 공약
□□ exploitation	명 착취; 부당한 이용; (토지 등	□□ populous	형 인구가 많은
	의) 개발	□□ ranch	명 (대규모) 목장
□□ GNP	명 국민 총생산	□□ rapturous	형 황홀해하는, 열광적인
(Gross		□□ robe	명 예복, 가운
National			동 예복[가운]을 입히다
Product)		□□ sealing	바다표범[물개] 사냥
□□ illuminate	동 불을 비추다; 계몽하다	□□ subantarctic	형 아남극의, 남극에 가까운
□□ immortal	형 죽지 않는 명 신	□□ vocalist	명 가수

Suffixes | 동사화 접미사

□□ harden	동 굳히다, 굳어지다; (태도가)	□□ magnify	동 확대하다; 과장하다
	단호해지다	□□ notify	동 알리다, 통지하다
□□ madden	동 정말 화나게 하다	□□ notification	명 알림, 통지
□□ amplify	동 확대하다; 증폭시키다	□□ authorize	동 권한을 부여하다; 인가하다
□□ clarify	동 명확하게 하다; 분명히 말	□□ fertilize	동 (토지에) 비료를 주다;
	하다		((생물)) 수정시키다
□□ clarification	명 설명, 해명	□□ fertilizer	명 (인공적인) 비료
□□ dignify	동 위엄 있어 보이게 하다	□□ immunize	동 (특히 백신 주사로) 면역력
□□ dignity	명 위엄, 품위		을 갖게 하다
□□ exemplify	동 예를 들다; 전형적인 예가	□□ penalize	동 처벌하다; 벌칙을 부과하다
	되다		

☐☐ domesticate	동 (동물을) 길들이다, 가축화하다; (작물을) 재배하다	☐☐ excavate	동 (구멍 등을) 파다; 발굴하다
☐☐ evacuate	동 (위험한 장소를) 떠나다, 대피하다	☐☐ excavation	명 땅파기; 발굴(지)
		☐☐ exterminate	동 몰살시키다, 전멸시키다
☐☐ evacuation	명 피난, 대피		

Essential Roots / Stems | man(u) / mani

☐☐ emancipate	동 (법적·사회적 제약에서) 해방하다	☐☐ manageable	형 관리할 수 있는
		☐☐ mandate	명 명령; (선거에 의해 주어진) 권한
☐☐ manual	형 손으로 하는; 육체노동의 명 설명서		동 명령하다; 권한을 주다
☐☐ manuscript	명 (자필) 원고; 필사본, 사본	☐☐ mandatory	형 법에 정해진; 의무[명령]의
☐☐ manufacture	명 제조, 생산; ((pl.)) 제품 동 생산하다	☐☐ manipulate	동 (능숙하게) 조작하다; (교묘하게) 조종하다
☐☐ manufacturer	명 제조 회사, 제조자	☐☐ manipulation	명 조작; 조종
☐☐ manage	동 (어떻게든) 해내다; 운영[관리]하다	☐☐ maneuver	명 (기술적) 동작, 움직임; 책략; ((군사)) 작전행동
☐☐ managerial	형 경영[관리]의		동 (능숙하게) 움직이다; 책략을 쓰다

Words with Multiple Meanings | 필수 다의어의 이해

☐☐ declare	동 선언하다, 공표하다 동 분명히 말하다, 단언하다 동 (세관에 소득이나 과세 물품을) 신고하다
☐☐ identify	동 ((with)) (~와) 동일시하다 동 이해하고 공감하다 동 (신원 등을) 확인하다 동 ~임을 알려주다 동 찾다, 발견하다
☐☐ note	명 메모, 쪽지 명 필기, 노트 명 지폐 명 음, 음표 명 어조; (특정한) 기색, 분위기 동 ~에 주목[주의]하다 동 언급하다
☐☐ state	명 상태 명 (미국·호주 등의) 주 형 주립의 명 정부, 국가 형 국가의 동 진술하다, (정식으로) 말하다[쓰다]

□□ repertoire	명 레퍼토리, 공연[연주] 목록	□□ lyric	형 서정(시)의; 노래의
□□ rehearsal	명 리허설, 예행연습		명 서정시; ((pl.)) (노래의) 가사
□□ rehearse	동 리허설을 하다; 연습하다	□□ lyrical	형 서정적인, (표현이) 아름다운
□□ debut	명 데뷔, 첫 출연 동 데뷔하다	□□ anthem	명 (국가 등의) 노래; 성가, 찬송가
□□ applause	명 박수(갈채); 칭찬		
□□ applaud	동 박수를 치다; 칭찬하다	□□ chant	명 노래; (연이어 외치는) 구호
□□ ovation	명 (열렬한) 박수		동 (노래를) 부르다; (구호를) 외치다
□□ acclaim	동 칭송하다, 환호를 보내다	□□ tune	명 곡(조); 선율
	명 (특히 예술적 업적에 대한) 찬사		동 (악기를) 조율하다; 맞추다
□□ acclamation	명 환호, 박수갈채	□□ attuned	형 익숙한, 적절히 대응하는
□□ encore	명 앙코르, 재청; 앙코르 곡 [연주]	□□ chord	명 ((음악)) 코드, 화음
	동 앙코르를 요청하다	□□ chorus	명 합창; 후렴; 이구동성
□□ drama	명 드라마, 극; 연극; 극적인 사건		동 합창하다; 이구동성으로 말하다
□□ dramatic	형 희곡의; 극적인	□□ choral	형 합창의
□□ dramatize	동 각색하다; (실제보다 더) 극적으로 보이게 하다, 과장하다	□□ virtuoso	명 (음악 연주의) 거장
			형 기교가 뛰어난
□□ theatrical	형 연극의; 연극조의, 과장된	□□ podium	명 지휘대; 연단
□□ protagonist	명 (연극·영화 등의) 주인공; (정책·운동의) 지지자, 주동 인물	□□ fine art	명 ((pl.)) (순수) 미술
		□□ portray	동 그리다; 나타내다
□□ puppet	명 꼭두각시, 인형	□□ portrayal	명 묘사
□□ tearjerker	명 (눈물을 흘리게 하는) 최루성 영화[연극]	□□ portrait	명 초상화; (생생한) 묘사
		□□ aesthetic	형 (예술적) 미의; 미학의
□□ sequel	명 (책·영화 등의) 속편; 뒤이어 일어난 일		명 ((pl.)) 미학
		□□ exquisite	형 매우 아름다운, 정교한
□□ dub	동 (다른 언어로) 재녹음하다, 더빙하다; 별명을 붙이다	□□ patron	명 (예술가 등에 대한) 후원자; (상점·식당 등의) 고객
□□ dubbing	명 재녹음, 더빙	□□ patronage	명 후원; 단골
□□ notate	동 (특히 악보에) 기록하다	□□ auction	명 경매 동 경매로 팔다
□□ notation	명 (특히 음악 등에서) 표기법, 기호	□□ bid	동 (경매에서) 값을 부르다; 입찰하다; 애쓰다
			명 입찰; 가격 제시; 노력
		□□ bidding	명 (경매의) 가격 제시; 입찰; 명령

33 강

words & phrases

□□ abnormality	몡 이상, 기형
□□ acoustics	몡 ((단수 취급)) 음향학; ((복수 취급)) 음향시설
□□ adept	혱 능숙한
□□ capability	몡 능력; 역량; 가능성
□□ carve	동 조각하다; (글씨를) 새기다; (노력해서) 이루다
□□ cast	동 던지다; (빛·의혹 등을) 드리우다; 주조하다 몡 거푸집; 주조물; 깁스붕대
□□ clay	몡 점토, 찰흙
□□ clumsy	혱 어설픈; 서투른
□□ crack	몡 (갈라진) 금; 틈 동 금이 가다; 날카로운 소리가 나다
□□ devise	동 고안하다, 만들다
□□ dynamics	몡 ((물리)) 역학 (관계); ((음악)) 강약법; 원동력, 활력
□□ file	몡 파일, 서류철 동 (문서를 정리하여) 보관하다; (소송을) 제기하다
□□ infrared	혱 적외선의

□□ inspiration	몡 영감; 영감[자극]을 주는 것
□□ installation	몡 설치; 장치; 시설
□□ interference	몡 간섭, 방해
□□ limestone	몡 석회암, 석회석
□□ mill	몡 (제조) 공장; 방앗간; 제분소; 제분기 동 분쇄하다
□□ neurologist	몡 신경학자, 신경과 전문의
□□ offend	동 기분 상하게 하다; (도덕·상식 등에) 위배되다
□□ publicity	몡 홍보, 광고; 언론의 관심[주목]
□□ room	몡 방; 공간; 여지, 여유
□□ scaffolding	몡 (건축장의) 발판, 비계
□□ shortcut	몡 지름길; 손쉬운 방법
□□ skyscraper	몡 마천루, 초고층 빌딩
□□ stretch	동 늘리다; 내뻗다 몡 뻗침; 신축성; (길게 뻗은) 지역; 기간
□□ upload	동 업로드하다
□□ verify	동 확인하다; 입증하다

Suffixes | 형용사화 접미사

☐☐ accessible 　형 접근[이용]하기 쉬운
☐☐ legible 　형 (필적·인쇄가) 읽기 쉬운
☐☐ fruitful 　형 생산적인
☐☐ mindful 　형 의식하는, 염두에 두는
☐☐ flawless 　형 흠 없는; 완벽한
☐☐ optimal 　형 최선의, 최적의
☐☐ optimize 　동 최적화하다

☐☐ desolate 　형 (장소가) 황량한, 적막한
☐☐ advisory 　형 권고의; 자문의
　　　　　　　 명 주의보, 경보
☐☐ affirmative 　형 긍정하는, 동의하는
　　　　　　　　 명 긍정, 동의
☐☐ affirm 　동 단언하다
☐☐ costly 　형 많은 돈이 드는; 대가가 큰

Essential Roots / Stems 1 | aud

☐☐ audible 　형 들을 수 있는, 들리는
☐☐ audition 　명 (가수·배우 등의) 오디션
☐☐ auditorium 　명 강당; 객석

☐☐ auditory 　형 청각의
☐☐ audiovisual 　형 시청각의; 시청각 교재의

Essential Roots / Stems 2 | sens(e) / sent

☐☐ senseless 　형 의식이 없는; 무분별한; 무의미한
☐☐ sensitive 　형 민감한; 예민한; 감수성이 풍부한
☐☐ sensuous 　형 (심미적으로) 감각적인; 감각을 만족시키는
☐☐ sensual 　형 (육체적) 감각의; 쾌락적인
☐☐ sensible 　형 분별력 있는, 현명한; 의식하고 있는
☐☐ sensibility 　명 (문학·예술적) 감상; ((pl.)) (영향·상처를 쉽게 받는) 감정
☐☐ sensor 　명 센서, 감지기
☐☐ sensory 　형 감각의, 지각의
☐☐ sensation 　명 느낌, 감각; 선풍적 반응, 센세이션

☐☐ sensational 　형 선풍적 인기의; 인기 끌기 위주의
☐☐ sentiment 　명 감정, 정서; (지나친) 감상
☐☐ sentimental 　형 감정적인; 감상적인
☐☐ assent 　명 찬성, 승인 　동 찬성하다
☐☐ dissent 　명 반대 (의견) 　동 반대하다
☐☐ consent 　명 동의, 허락
　　　　　　　 동 동의하다, 허락하다
☐☐ consensus 　명 합의, 의견 일치
☐☐ resent 　동 분개하다
☐☐ resentment 　명 분개
☐☐ resentful 　형 분개하는

Words with Multiple Meanings | 필수 다의어의 이해

☐☐ still	형 조용한; 정지한 부 아직(도) (계속해서) 명 스틸 부 ((비교급 수식)) 훨씬, 더욱; 그럼에도 불구하고
☐☐ suit	명 (특정한 활동 때 입는) 옷, 정장 명 소송 동 (~에게) 맞다, 편리하다 동 (옷·색상 등이) 어울리다
☐☐ term	명 (정해진) 기간 명 학기; 임기 명 용어 명 조건, 조항 명 ((pl.)) 관계, 사이

Themes | 문화·예술 2

☐☐ sculpt	동 조각하다; 형태를 만들다	☐☐ blueprint	명 청사진; (상세한) 계획
☐☐ sculpture	명 조각(품)	☐☐ construct	동 건설하다; 구성하다
☐☐ mold	명 틀, 거푸집; 곰팡이 동 (틀에 넣어) 만들다	☐☐ construction	명 건설; 건물; 구조
		☐☐ constructive	형 건설적인
☐☐ craft	명 기술, 기교; (수)공예; 항공기, 우주선 동 공들여 만들다	☐☐ collapse	동 (건물 등이) 붕괴하다; (사람이) 쓰러지다; 접다 명 붕괴; 쓰러짐
☐☐ craftsman	명 (수)공예가, 장인	☐☐ collapsible	형 접을 수 있는
☐☐ craftsmanship	명 손재주; 솜씨	☐☐ quarry	명 채석장 동 (돌을) 캐내다
☐☐ apprentice	명 수습생, 도제	☐☐ timber	명 목재
☐☐ apprenticeship	명 수습 기간; 수습직	☐☐ vault	명 아치형 천장; 금고 동 아치형 천장으로 만들다; 뛰어넘다
☐☐ foundation	명 창설, 설립; 기초, 토대		
☐☐ architect	명 건축가; 설계자	☐☐ framework	명 (건물 등의) 뼈대, 골조; 틀, 구조; 체계
☐☐ architecture	명 건축(학); 건축 양식; 구조		
☐☐ architectural	형 건축(학)의		

34강

words & phrases

□□ agile	혱 민첩한	□□ on a budget	한정된 예산으로, 불필요한 지출을 피해
□□ applicant	몡 지원자	□□ outermost	혱 가장 바깥쪽의
□□ awe	몡 경외감	□□ permanent	혱 영구적인
	동 경외심을 갖게 하다	□□ remote	혱 먼, 외딴
□□ circuit	몡 순환(로), 순회; (전기) 회로	□□ rock	혱 바위; 록 음악
□□ civilization	몡 문명 (사회)		동 흔들리다; 동요하다; 록을 연주하다
□□ chore	몡 (정기적으로 하는) 일; 하기 싫은[따분한] 일	□□ scenic	혱 경치가 좋은; (연극) 무대 장치의
□□ clinical	혱 임상[치료, 진찰]의	□□ sheer	혱 (직물 등이) 얇은; 순수한, 순전한; 가파른
□□ drastic	혱 과감한, 극단적인; 급격한	□□ sparkle	동 반짝이다; 생기 넘치다
□□ deluxe	혱 호화로운, 고급의		몡 반짝거림; 생기
□□ excavate	동 (구멍 등을) 파다; 발굴하다	□□ sway	동 (전후좌우로) 흔들다
□□ externally	부 외부적으로, 외부에서	□□ tow	몡 견인, 예인
□□ filter	동 여과하다; 스며들다; 서서히 이동하다		동 (줄로) 잡아당기다; (차를) 견인하다
	몡 필터, 여과 장치	□□ verdant	혱 파릇파릇한, (풀 등이) 녹색의
□□ individuality	몡 개성, 특성		
□□ meteorite	몡 운석		

Suffixes | 명사화 접미사

□□ interviewer	몡 면접관, 인터뷰 진행자	□□ delicacy	몡 연약함; 섬세함; 미묘함; (특정 지역의) 진미, 별미
□□ interviewee	몡 면접 받는 사람	□□ delicate	혱 연약한; 섬세한; 미묘한
□□ immersion	몡 (액체 속에) 담금; 몰입, 몰두	□□ alignment	몡 가지런함; 일직선; (정치적) 지지
□□ immerse	동 (액체에) 담그다; (~에) 몰두하다	□□ replenishment	몡 (원래처럼) 다시 채움, 보충
□□ procrastination	몡 (해야 할 일을 하기 싫어서) 꾸물거림; 지연	□□ replenish	동 다시 채우다, 보충하다
□□ procrastinate	동 미루다, 질질 끌다	□□ authorship	몡 저술 작업; (원)저자
□□ immensity	몡 광대함; 막대함	□□ ownership	몡 소유(권)
□□ sensitivity	몡 감수성; 민감함	□□ factionalism	몡 파벌주의
□□ mastery	몡 숙달, 통달; 지배(력)	□□ livelihood	몡 생계 (수단)
□□ burial	몡 매장; 장례식		

Essential Roots / Stems | geo

☐☐ geologist	몡 지질학자	☐☐ geographic(al)	혱 지리적인; 지리학의
☐☐ geology	몡 지질학	☐☐ geometry	몡 기하학; 기하학적 구조
☐☐ geologic(al)	혱 지질의, 지질학의	☐☐ geometric	혱 기하학의, 기하학적인
☐☐ geographer	몡 지리학자	☐☐ geostationary	혱 (인공위성이) 지구 정지 궤도 상에 있는
☐☐ geography	몡 지리학; (한 지역의) 지형	☐☐ geothermal	혱 지열의

Words with Multiple Meanings | 필수 다의어의 이해

☐☐ toll　　몡 통행료 몡 (사고·재해 등의) 사상자 수
　　　　　 동 (죽은 사람을 애도하는 종 등을) 울리다

☐☐ touch　 동 (손 등으로) 만지다, 건드리다 몡 만지기, 손길 몡 촉각 몡 (마무리) 손질
　　　　　 동 (둘 이상의 사물·표면 등이) 접촉하다, 닿다 동 감동시키다

☐☐ treat　 동 (특정한 태도로) 다루다, 대우하다 동 (문제 등을) 처리하다; 논의하다 동 치료하다
　　　　　 동 대접하다 몡 대접, 한턱; (대접하여 주는) 특별한 선물

☐☐ trial　 몡 시도 몡 (품질·성능 등의) 시험, 실험 몡 시련, 고난; 골칫거리 몡 재판, 공판

Themes | 여가·여행

☐☐ pastime	몡 취미	☐☐ hitchhike	몡 히치하이크
			동 히치하이크하다
☐☐ avocation	몡 취미, 여가 활동; 부업	☐☐ accommodate	동 수용하다; 숙박시키다
☐☐ stroll	몡 산책	☐☐ accommodation	몡 숙소, 숙박 시설
	동 산책하다, 한가로이 거닐다	☐☐ accommodating	혱 (기꺼이 남을) 도와주는, 친절한
☐☐ outing	몡 소풍; (짧은) 여행		
☐☐ serene	혱 고요한, 평화로운	☐☐ suite	몡 (물건의) 한 벌; (호텔의) 스위트룸
☐☐ serenity	몡 고요함, 평온함		
☐☐ itinerary	몡 여행 일정표	☐☐ exotic	혱 이국적인; 외래의
☐☐ reconfirm	동 (예약을) 재확인하다	☐☐ ripple	동 잔물결을 이루다; (소식 등이) 파문처럼 퍼지다
☐☐ jet lag	몡 시차증		
☐☐ high[peak] season	몡 (관광지 등의) 성수기		몡 잔물결; 파문
		☐☐ horizon	몡 시평선, 수평선; (사고 등의) 시야
☐☐ trek	동 트레킹을 하다, (힘들게 오래) 걷다	☐☐ horizontal	혱 수평의; 가로의
	몡 트레킹, 오지 여행	☐☐ memento	몡 기념품
☐☐ hitchhiker	몡 히치하이커	☐☐ caravan	몡 캠핑용 자동차; (사막의) 대상

35강

words & phrases

□□ anthropology	명 인류학
□□ disagreeable	형 불쾌한; 마음에 들지 않는; 무뚝뚝한
□□ dwindling	형 줄어드는, 감소하는
□□ execute	동 실행하다; 사형[처형]하다
□□ falsify	동 (문서를) 위조하다
□□ flesh	명 (사람·동물의) 살, 고기
□□ formidable	형 가공할, 무시무시한
□□ gleam	동 어슴푸레[희미하게] 빛나다
□□ hit A up for B	A에게 B를 달라고 부탁하다
□□ identical	형 동일한
□□ increment	명 (수·양의) 증가; 정기적인 임금 인상
□□ insert	동 끼우다, 삽입하다 명 삽입물; 삽입 광고
□□ installment	명 할부금; (전집의) 1권
□□ intricacy	명 복잡한 사항[내용]; 복잡함
□□ lay-off	명 정리 해고; 중단 기간
□□ legitimize	동 정당화하다; 합법화하다
□□ loom	동 어렴풋이[흐릿하게] 보이다; (거대한 것이) 불쑥 나타나다
□□ migratory	형 이주[이동]하는
□□ minute	형 극미한, 극히 작은; 대단히 상세한
□□ perceptible	형 감지[지각]할 수 있는
□□ prey on	~을 먹이로 하다
□□ quote	동 인용하다; 견적을 내다; 시세를 매기다
□□ resilient	형 회복력 있는; 탄력 있는
□□ scrutiny	명 정밀 조사, 철저한 검토
□□ set up shop	사업을 시작하다
□□ shaggy	형 털북숭이의; 텁수룩한
□□ signature	명 서명; 특징
□□ stained	형 얼룩투성이의, 얼룩이 묻은
□□ stink	동 (고약한) 냄새가 나다; 수상쩍다
□□ testability	명 시험[검사] 가능성
□□ trapper	명 (특히 모피를 얻기 위해) 덫을 놓는 사냥꾼
□□ unaided eye	명 육안, 맨눈
□□ well off	형 잘사는, 부유한; 형편이 좋은

□□ cost-effective   [형]비용 대비 효율적인

□□ qualifier   [명]자격을 주는 사람[것]; 한정하는 것; 예선 통과자; 예선 경기; ((문법)) 수식어구

□□ off limits   [명]출입 금지 (지역)
[형]출입 금지의

□□ hit one's stride   본래 컨디션을 되찾다

□□ sedentary   [형]주로 앉아서 하는; 한곳에 머물러 사는

□□ demoralized   [형]사기가 저하된

□□ wind down   긴장을 풀고 쉬다; (기계가) 서서히 멈추다

□□ hallmark   [명](전형적인) 특징, 특질; (귀금속의) 품질 보증 마크

□□ align   [동](~에 맞춰) 조정하다; 나란히 만들다, (일직선으로) 맞추다

□□ come to naught   무효화하다, 실패로 끝나다

□□ monocropping   [명]단일 재배, 단종 재배

□□ convoluted   [형]대단히 난해한[복잡한]; 구불구불한

□□ disengage   [동]풀다, 분리하다; (의무·속박에서) 해방하다

□□ crafty   [형]약삭빠른, 교활한

□□ impart   [동](정보·지식 등을) 나눠주다

□□ interdisciplinary   [형]학제 간의

□□ diffusion   [명]발산, 유포; ((물리)) 확산 (작용); (문화 등의) 전파, 보급

□□ weed out   (불필요하거나 부족한 대상 등을) 제거하다[뽑아 버리다]

□□ quantitative   [형]양적인, 정량적인

□□ downplay   [동]경시하다, 대단치 않게 생각하다

□□ acupuncture   [명]침술 (요법)

□□ devour   [동]게걸스레 먹다; 삼켜버리다

□□ err   [동]실수를 범하다

□□ amortization   [명]((법)) 법인에의 부동산 양도; ((경제)) (부채의) 할부 상환(액)

□□ trifling   [형]하찮은, 사소한

□□ obtrusive   [형](보기 싫게) 눈에 띄는, 두드러지는

□□ premonition   [명](특히) 불길한 예감; 전조, 징후

□□ defy   [동]무시하다; 반항하다; 맞서다

□□ underprivileged   [형](사회·경제적으로) 혜택을 못 받는

□□ non-shedding   [형]흘리지[떨어지지] 않는; 발산하지 않는

□□ exact   [동]무리하게 요구하다; (나쁜 일을) 일으키다 [형]정확한

□□ plasticity   [명]가소성; 유연성, 적응성

FINAL 실전

한눈에 보는
현대문학사
+
사자성어 150

SD에듀
(주)시대고시기획

현대문학사

⊕

사자성어 150

한눈에 보는 현대문학사

01 갑오개혁 이후 가장 크게 나타난 문학 현상: 구어체(=일상용어체, 대화체) 문장

① 언문일치 시작(1900년대): 유길준의 「서유견문」
② 언문일치 발전(1910년대): 이광수의 「무정」
③ 언문일치 완성(1920년대): 김동인의 「약한 자의 슬픔」

02 1900년대(1894~1908)

① 창가가사
　㉠ 개화가사와 찬송가의 영향
　㉡ 형식: 초기에 '3 · 4, 4 · 4조'에서 후기에 '6 · 5, 7 · 5, 8 · 5조'로 발전함
　㉢ 내용: 계몽(독립신문), 항일(대한매일신보)
　㉣ 최초의 7 · 5조 작품: 최남선의 「경부철도가」
② 신소설(원래 뜻은 '고소설'의 반대 개념)
　㉠ 내용: 개화, 계몽, 신교육
　㉡ 개념: 고대 소설에서 근대 소설로의 과도기
　㉢ 창작 신소설: 일반적인 의미의 신소설
　　• 이인직: 「은세계」, 「치악산」, 「귀의 성」, 「혈의 누」
　　• 이해조: 「빈상설」, 「구마검」, 「자유종」
　　• 안국선: 「금수회의록」
　　• 최찬식: 「안의성」, 「추월색」
　㉣ 번안 신소설: 조중환의 「장한몽」(이수일과 심순애 등장)
　㉤ 개작 신소설: 이해조의 「역할」
　　• 「춘향전」 → 「옥중화(獄中花)」
　　• 「흥부전」 → 「연(燕)의 각(却)」
　　• 「토끼전」 → 「토(兎)의 간(肝)」
　　• 「심청전」 → 「강상련(江上蓮)」

③ 역사 전기 소설
    ㉠ 내용: 민족주의적 역사의식, 자보ㆍ자강, 항일구국의 이념
    ㉡ 대표작품: 신채호의 「을지문덕」
④ 신문
    ㉠ 한성순보: 최초 신문, 순한문(1883)
    ㉡ 독립신문: 최초 민간, 본격 신문의 시초(1896)
    ㉢ 매일신문: 최초 일간
    ㉣ 제국신문: 대중 및 부녀자 대상 최초
    ㉤ 황성신문: 장지연의 「시일야방성대곡」 실림
    ㉥ 만세보: 이인직의 「혈의 누」 연재, 대한신문으로 개칭
⑤ 국어 문법서
    ㉠ 이봉운의 『국문정리』: 최초 음운 문법서
    ㉡ 지석영의 『신정국문』: 국어 전용 주장, 상소문
    ㉢ 주시경
      • 『국어문전음학』, 『국어문법』, 『말의 소리』, 『말모이』, 『대한국어문법』 등을 쓴 어문 민족주의자
      • 기난갈(품사론), 짬듬갈(문장론) 등의 용어 사용
      • 9품사(임-체언, 엇-형용사, 움-동사, 겻-조사, 잇-접속 조사, 언-관형사, 억-부사, 놀-감탄사, 끗-종결 어미) 설정
      • 호는 한힌샘, 일백천, 태백산

03 1910년대(1908~1919): 2인 문단 시대

① 2인: (육당) 최남선, (춘원) 이광수
② 신체시
    ㉠ 최초 작품: 최남선의 「해에게서 소년에게」
    ㉡ 이광수의 신체시 「우리 영웅」
③ 근대 **최초** 장편 소설: 이광수의 「무정」(1917)
④ 근대 최초 단편 소설: 이광수의 「어린 희생」(1910), 김동인의 「약한 자의 슬픔」(1919)
⑤ 최초의 근대 자유시: 주요한의 「불놀이」(1919)
⑥ 최초의 순 문예 동인지: 『창조』(1919)
⑦ 최초의 시 전문 동인지: 『장미촌』(1921)
⑧ 최초의 월간 종합지: 『소년』(1908)
⑨ 김억이 최초로 서구의 상징시를 수용한 잡지: 『태서문예신보』(1918)

① 1920년대 3대 동인지: 『창조』, 『폐허』, 『백조』
② 낭만주의 3대 동인지: 『백조』, 『폐허』, 『장미촌』
③ 시
   ㉠ 민요시 운동: 홍사용, 이상화, 김억, 김소월
   ㉡ 시조부흥운동을 주도한 단체: 국민문학파
   ㉢ 낭만적·감상적 경향 위주: 홍사용, 이상화, 황석우, 박종화
④ 소설: 사실주의 유행(김동인, 현진건, 이효석 등 3대 단편 작가)
⑤ 문단의 대립기: 절충 - 『문예공론』

경향파(KAPF, 좌익, 계급진영) 『개벽』	↔	국민문학파(우익, 민족진영) 『조선문단』

   ▶ 동반자 작가: 좌익 노선에 동조하는 힘없는 지식인(이효석, 유진오, 채만식, 박화성)
⑥ 신경향파 그룹

염군사(1922, 이념 위주) + 파스큘라(1923, 예술 위주)

⬇

KAPF(1925)

⑦ 작가와 작품

구분	호	이름	작품
시	송아	주요한	불놀이, 아름다운 새벽
	안서	김억	오다가다, 비, 봄은 간다
	상아탑	황석우	벽모(碧毛)의 묘(猫)
	상화	이상화	나의 침실로, 빼앗긴 들에도 봄은 오는가
	소월	김정식	진달래꽃
	만해	한용운	님의 침묵
소설	금동	김동인	감자, 약한 자의 슬픔, 배따라기
	빙허	현진건	운수 좋은 날, 빈처
	횡보	염상섭	표본실의 청개구리, 삼대, 만세전
	도향	나빈	물레방아, 벙어리 삼룡이, 뽕
	늘봄	전영택	화수분, 소
	여심	주요섭	사랑손님과 어머니

시	순수시파(1930)	주지시파(1934)	생명파(1936)	자연파(1939)
	시문학	자오선	시인부락, 생리	문장
	김영랑, 박용철	김광균, 김기림	서정주, 유치환	박목월, 박두진, 조지훈
	음악성, 치밀한 기교, 언어 조탁	이미지, 지성, 회화성	생명 의식	자연 회귀
소설	• 장편 소설: 염상섭의 「삼대」, 「만세전」(발표 당시 제목은 「묘지」), 「두 파산」 • 역사 소설: 김동인의 「운현궁의 봄」, 「젊은 그들」, 현진건의 「무영탑」, 박종화의 「금삼의 피」 • 풍자 소설: 채만식의 「태평천하」, 「레디메이드 인생」, 「탁류」, 「치숙」, 「소년은 자란다」 • 해학 소설: 김유정의 「동백꽃」, 「봄봄」, 「만무방」, 「따라지」, 「땡볕」, 「소낙비」, 「금 따는 콩밭」 • 농촌계몽소설: 브나로드(Vnarod) 운동과 관련 예 심훈의 「상록수」, 박화성의 「한귀」, 이무영의 「제1과 제1장」, 박영준의 「모범경작생」, 김정한의 「사하촌」			
수필	전문 수필가의 등장(김진섭, 이하윤)			
희곡	극예술 연구회(1931) 창립			
평론	순수비평(김환태)과 주지비평(최재서)			

① 문학의 공백기: 창작, 출판의 부재(不在)
② 저항 시인(앙가주망, 참여시인)
 ㉠ 이육사(남성적, 의지적, 대륙적, 선비 정신): 「절정」, 「청포도」, 「광야」, 「교목」, 「꽃」
 ㉡ 윤동주(자아 성찰, 순수): 「자화상」, 「참회록」, 「십자가」, 「간」, 「또 다른 고향」, 「서시」, 「별 헤는 밤」, 유고 시집 『하늘과 바람과 별과 시』

① 시
- ㉠ 김수영(모더니즘에서 1960년대 이후 참여시로 전환): 「풀」, 「폭포」, 「눈」
- ㉡ 송욱: 「하여지향」
- ㉢ 김춘수('존재와 본질 탐구'에서 '무의미 시'로 전환): 「꽃」, 「꽃을 위한 서시」, 「처용단장」

② 소설
- ㉠ 동시 묘사법: 김성한의 「5분간」
- ㉡ 광복 당시 분열상의 비극적 국면 묘파: 선우휘의 「불꽃」
- ㉢ 한 인격적 주체가 겪는 도덕적 갈등: 장용학의 「요한시집」
- ㉣ 소외된 인간상을 피학적 어조로 묘사: 손창섭의 「잉여인간」
- ㉤ 당시 빈곤상과 삶의 관계: 이범선의 「오발탄」
- ㉥ 농어촌 서민의 애환: 오영수의 「갯마을」
- ㉦ 삶의 부조리를 인식하고 극복함: 유주현의 「장씨 일가」, 「신의 눈초리」
- ㉧ 민족의 기개 형상화: 정한숙의 「금당벽화」
- ㉨ 토속적 삶의 간고함: 전광용의 「흑산도」
- ㉩ 지식인의 변절적 순응주의: 전광용의 「꺼삐딴 리」
- ㉺ 세속적 삶의 모순을 소설화: 박경리의 「암흑시대」

사자성어 150

- 가담항설(街談巷說) 거리나 항간에 떠도는 소문
- 각주구검(刻舟求劍) 융통성 없이 현실에 맞지 않는 낡은 생각을 고집하는 어리석음을 이르는 말 (㊠ 수주대토)
- 간난신고(艱難辛苦) 몹시 힘들고 어려우며 고생스러움
- 간담상조(肝膽相照) 서로 속마음을 털어놓고 친하게 사귐
- 갈이천정(渴而穿井) 미리 준비하지 않고 있다가 일이 지나간 뒤에는 아무리 서둘러 봐도 아무 소용이 없음 (㊠ 목이 말라야 비로소 샘을 판다)
- 감언이설(甘言利說) 귀가 솔깃하도록 남의 비위를 맞추거나 이로운 조건을 내세워 꾀는 말
- 감탄고토(甘呑苦吐) 달면 삼키고 쓰면 뱉는다는 뜻으로, 자신의 비위에 따라서 사리의 옳고 그름을 판단함
- 갑론을박(甲論乙駁) 여러 사람이 서로 자신의 주장을 내세우며 상대편의 주장을 반박함
- 개세지재(蓋世之才) 세상을 뒤덮을 만큼 뛰어난 재주. 또는 그 재주를 가진 사람
- 거두절미(去頭截尾) ① 머리와 꼬리를 잘라 버림
  ② 어떤 일의 요점만 간단히 말함
- 거안사위(居安思危) 편안할 때에도 위험과 곤란이 닥칠 것을 생각하며 잊지 말고 미리 대비해야 함
- 건곤일척(乾坤一擲) 주사위를 던져 승패를 건다는 뜻으로, 운명을 걸고 단판걸이로 승부를 겨룸
- 격화소양(隔靴搔癢) 신을 신고 발바닥을 긁는다는 뜻으로, 성에 차지 않거나 철저하지 못한 안타까움을 이르는 말
- 견강부회(牽强附會) 이치에 맞지 않는 말을 억지로 끌어 붙여 자기에게 유리하게 함
- 견문발검(見蚊拔劍) 모기를 보고 칼을 뺀다는 뜻으로, 사소한 일에 크게 성내어 덤빔
- 결자해지(結者解之) 맺은 사람이 풀어야 한다는 뜻으로, 자기가 저지른 일은 자기가 해결하여야 함

- 결초보은(結草報恩) 죽은 뒤에라도 은혜를 잊지 않고 갚음
- 계란유골(鷄卵有骨) 달걀에도 뼈가 있다는 뜻으로, 운수가 나쁜 사람은 모처럼 좋은 기회를 만나도 역시 일이 잘 안됨
- 계명구도(鷄鳴狗盜) 비굴하게 남을 속이는 하찮은 재주 또는 그런 재주를 가진 사람
- 고립무원(孤立無援) 고립되어 구원받을 데가 없음
- 고복격양(鼓腹擊壤) 태평한 세월을 즐김
- 고식지계(姑息之計) 우선 당장 편한 것만을 택하는 꾀나 방법 (⟨유⟩ 미봉책, 동족방뇨)
- 고육지계(苦肉之計) 자기 몸을 상해 가면서까지 꾸며 내는 계책이라는 뜻으로, 어려운 상태를 벗어나기 위해 어쩔 수 없이 꾸며 내는 계책
- 고장난명(孤掌難鳴) ① 외손뼉만으로는 소리가 울리지 아니한다는 뜻으로, 혼자의 힘만으로 어떤 일을 이루기 어려움
  ② 맞서는 사람이 없으면 싸움이 일어나지 않음
- 과유불급(過猶不及) 정도를 지나침은 미치지 못함과 같음 (⟨유⟩ 과여불급)
- 괄목상대(刮目相對) 눈을 비비고 상대편을 본다는 뜻으로, 남의 학식이나 재주가 놀랄 만큼 부쩍 늚
- 교각살우(矯角殺牛) 소의 뿔을 바로잡으려다가 소를 죽인다는 뜻으로, 잘못된 점을 고치려다가 그 방법이나 정도가 지나쳐 오히려 일을 그르침
- 교언영색(巧言令色) 아첨하는 말과 알랑거리는 태도 (⟨유⟩ 감언이설)
- 구밀복검(口蜜腹劍) 입에는 꿀이 있고 배 속에는 칼이 있다는 뜻으로, 말로는 친한 듯하나 속으로는 해칠 생각이 있음 (⟨유⟩ 면종복배, 표리부동)
- 구상유취(口尙乳臭) 입에서 아직 젖내가 난다는 뜻으로, 말과 행동이 매우 유치함
- 귤화위지(橘化爲枳) 회남의 귤을 회북에 옮겨 심으면 탱자가 된다는 뜻으로, 환경에 따라 사람이나 사물의 성질이 변함
- 근묵자흑(近墨者黑) 먹을 가까이하는 사람은 검어진다는 뜻으로, 나쁜 사람과 가까이 지내면 나쁜 버릇에 물들기 쉬움 (⟨유⟩ 근주자적)
- 금의야행(錦衣夜行) ① 비단 옷을 입고 밤길을 다닌다는 뜻으로, 자랑삼아 하지 않으면 생색이 나지 않음
  ② 아무 보람이 없는 일을 함
- 금의환향(錦衣還鄕) 비단옷을 입고 고향에 돌아온다는 뜻으로, 출세하여 고향에 돌아가거나 돌아옴

8

- 난형난제(難兄難弟) 누구를 형이라 하고 누구를 아우라 하기 어렵다는 뜻으로, 두 사물이 비슷하여 낫고 못함을 정하기 어려움 (㊌ 난백난중, 막상막하, 백중지간)

- 낭중지추(囊中之錐) 주머니 속의 송곳이라는 뜻으로, 재능이 뛰어난 사람은 숨어 있어도 저절로 사람들에게 알려짐

- 낭중취물(囊中取物) 주머니 속에서 물건을 꺼내듯이 아주 손쉽게 얻을 수 있음

- 노마지지(老馬之智) ① 연륜이 깊으면 나름의 장점과 특기가 있음
  ② 저마다 한 가지 재주는 지녔다는 말

- 누란지세(累卵之勢) 층층이 쌓아 놓은 알의 형세라는 뜻으로, 몹시 위태로운 형세

- 능소능대(能小能大) 모든 일에 두루 능함

- 단기지계(斷機之戒) 학문을 중도에서 그만두면 짜던 베의 날을 끊는 것처럼 아무 쓸모 없음을 경계한 말

- 단사표음(簞食瓢飮) 대나무로 만든 밥그릇에 담은 밥과 표주박에 든 물이라는 뜻으로, 청빈하고 소박한 생활을 이르는 말

- 당구풍월(堂狗風月) 서당에서 기르는 개가 풍월을 읊는다는 뜻으로, 그 분야에 대하여 경험과 지식이 전혀 없는 사람이라도 오래 있으면 얼마간의 경험과 지식을 가짐

- 당랑거철(螳螂拒轍) 제 역량을 생각하지 않고, 강한 상대나 되지 않을 일에 덤벼드는 무모한 행동거지를 비유

- 도탄지고(塗炭之苦) 진구렁에 빠지고 숯불에 타는 괴로움이라는 뜻으로, 백성이 가혹한 정치로 심한 고통을 겪음을 비유

- 동량지재(棟梁之材) 기둥과 들보로 쓸 만한 재목이라는 뜻으로, 한 집안이나 한 나라를 떠받치는 중대한 일을 맡을 만한 인재

- 득롱망촉(得隴望蜀) 농(隴)을 얻고서 촉(蜀)까지 취하고자 한다는 뜻으로, 만족할 줄을 모르고 계속 욕심을 부리는 경우를 비유

- 등고자비(登高自卑) ① 높은 곳에 오르려면 낮은 곳에서부터 오른다는 뜻으로, 일을 순서대로 하여야 함
  ② 지위가 높아질수록 자신을 낮춤

- 등하불명(燈下不明) 등잔 밑이 어둡다는 뜻으로, 가까이에 있는 물건이나 사람을 잘 찾지 못함

- 마부위침(磨斧爲針) 도끼를 갈아서 바늘을 만든다는 뜻으로, 아무리 이루기 힘든 일이라도 끊임없이 노력하면 반드시 이룰 수 있음
- 막역지우(莫逆之友) 서로 거스름이 없는 친구라는 뜻으로, 허물이 없이 아주 친한 친구 (⑨ 막역지간)
- 망년지교(忘年之交) 나이에 거리끼지 않고 허물없이 사귄 벗
- 망양보뢰(亡羊補牢) 양을 잃고 우리를 고친다는 뜻으로, 이미 어떤 일을 실패한 뒤에 뉘우쳐도 아무 소용이 없음
- 망운지정(望雲之情) 자식이 객지에서 고향에 계신 어버이를 생각하는 마음
- 맥수지탄(麥秀之嘆) 기자(箕子)가 은나라가 망한 뒤에도 보리만은 잘 자라는 것을 보고 한탄하였다는 데서 유래한 것으로, 고국의 멸망을 한탄함
- 면종복배(面從腹背) 겉으로는 복종하는 체하면서 내심으로는 배반함
- 멸사봉공(滅私奉公) 사욕을 버리고 공익을 위하여 힘씀
- 명경지수(明鏡止水) ① 맑은 거울과 고요한 물
  ② 잡념과 가식과 헛된 욕심 없이 맑고 깨끗한 마음
- 명실상부(名實相符) 이름과 실상이 서로 꼭 맞음
- 명약관화(明若觀火) 불을 보듯 분명하고 뻔함
- 명재경각(命在頃刻) 거의 죽게 되어 곧 숨이 끊어질 지경에 이름 (⑨ 풍전등화, 일촉즉발, 초미지급, 위기일발)
- 목불식정(目不識丁) 아주 간단한 글자인 '丁' 자를 보고도 그것이 '고무래'인 줄을 알지 못한다는 뜻으로, 아주 까막눈임 (⑨ 낫 놓고 기역자도 모른다)
- 목불인견(目不忍見) 눈앞에 벌어진 상황 따위를 눈 뜨고는 차마 볼 수 없음
- 묘두현령(猫頭懸鈴) 쥐가 고양이 목에 방울을 단다는 뜻으로, 실행할 수 없는 헛된 논의
- 무불통지(無不通知) 무슨 일이든지 환히 통하여 모르는 것이 없음 (⑨ 무소부지)
- 무소불위(無所不爲) 하지 못하는 일이 없음
- 무위도식(無爲徒食) 하는 일 없이 놀고먹음
- 문일지십(聞一知十) 하나를 듣고 열 가지를 미루어 안다는 뜻으로, 지극히 총명함
- 박이부정(博而不精) 널리 알지만 정밀하지는 못함
- 반목질시(反目嫉視) 서로 미워하고 질투하는 눈으로 봄 (⑨ 백안시)

10

- 반포보은(反哺報恩) 까마귀 새끼가 자라서 늙은 어미 까마귀에게 먹이를 물어다 주어 보답한다는 뜻으로, 자식이 자라서 어버이의 은혜에 보답함으로써 효를 행함 (㉠ 반포지효)
- 발본색원(拔本塞源) 좋지 않은 일의 근본 원인이 되는 요소를 완전히 없애 버려서 다시는 그러한 일이 생길 수 없도록 함
- 방약무인(傍若無人) 곁에 사람이 없는 것처럼 아무 거리낌 없이 함부로 말하고 행동하는 태도
- 백골난망(白骨難忘) 죽어서 백골이 되어도 잊을 수 없다는 뜻으로, 남에게 큰 은덕을 입었을 때의 고마움
- 백년하청(百年河淸) 중국의 황허강(黃河江)이 늘 흐려 맑을 때가 없다는 뜻으로, 아무리 오랜 시일이 지나도 어떤 일이 이루어지기 어려움
- 백중지세(伯仲之勢) 서로 우열을 가리기 힘든 형세 (㉠ 난형난제, 막상막하, 백중지간)
- 부화뇌동(附和雷同) 줏대 없이 남의 의견에 따라 움직임
- 불립문자(不立文字) 불도의 깨달음은 마음에서 마음으로 전하는 것이므로 말이나 글에 의지하지 않는다는 말 (㉠ 이심전심)
- 불문가지(不問可知) 묻지 않아도 알 수 있음
- 불치하문(不恥下問) 손아랫사람이나 지위나 학식이 자기만 못한 사람에게 모르는 것을 묻는 일을 부끄러워하지 않음
- 빙탄지간(氷炭之間) 얼음과 숯의 사이라는 뜻으로, 서로 맞지 않아 화합하지 못하는 관계
- 사면초가(四面楚歌) 아무에게도 도움을 받지 못하는, 외롭고 곤란한 지경에 빠진 형편
- 사상누각(沙上樓閣) 모래 위에 세운 누각이라는 뜻으로, 기초가 튼튼하지 못하여 오래 견디지 못할 일이나 물건
- 사필귀정(事必歸正) 모든 일은 반드시 바른길로 돌아감
- 상산구어(上山求魚) 산 위에 올라가 물고기를 구한다는 뜻으로, 도저히 불가능한 일을 굳이 하려 함을 비유 (㉠ 연목구어)
- 상전벽해(桑田碧海) 뽕나무밭이 변하여 푸른 바다가 된다는 뜻으로, 세상일의 변천이 심함을 비유
- 새옹지마(塞翁之馬) 인생의 길흉화복은 일정하지 않아 예측할 수 없음
- 설망어검(舌芒於劍) 혀가 칼보다 날카롭다는 뜻으로, 말로 남을 해칠 수 있음

■ 수구초심(首丘初心) 여우가 죽을 때 머리를 자기가 살던 굴 쪽으로 둔다는 뜻으로, 고향을 그리워하는 마음

■ 수불석권(手不釋卷) 손에서 책을 놓지 아니하고 늘 글을 읽음

■ 수어지교(水魚之交) 물이 없으면 살 수 없는 물고기와 물의 관계라는 뜻으로, 아주 친밀하여 떨어질 수 없는 사이를 비유

■ 숙맥불변(菽麥不辨) 콩인지 보리인지를 구별하지 못한다는 뜻으로, 사리 분별을 못 하고 세상 물정을 잘 모름

■ 순망치한(脣亡齒寒) 입술이 없으면 이가 시리다는 뜻으로, 서로 이해관계가 밀접한 사이에 어느 한쪽이 망하면 다른 한쪽도 그 영향을 받아 온전하기 어려움

■ 식소사번(食少事煩) 먹을 것은 적은데 할 일은 많음

■ 십벌지목(十伐之木) 열 번 찍어 베는 나무라는 뜻으로, 열 번 찍어 안 넘어가는 나무가 없음

■ 십시일반(十匙一飯) 밥 열 술이 한 그릇이 된다는 뜻으로, 여러 사람이 조금씩 힘을 합하면 한 사람을 돕기 쉬움

■ 아전인수(我田引水) 자기 논에 물 대기라는 뜻으로, 자기에게만 이롭게 되도록 생각하거나 행동함

■ 애이불비(哀而不悲) ① 슬프지만 겉으로는 슬픔을 나타내지 않음
② 슬프기는 하나 비참하지는 않음

■ 양두구육(羊頭狗肉) 양 머리를 걸어 놓고 개고기를 판다는 뜻으로, 겉보기만 그럴듯하게 보이고 속은 변변하지 않음

■ 언중유골(言中有骨) 말 속에 뼈가 있다는 뜻으로, 예사로운 말 속에 단단한 속뜻이 들어 있음

■ 염량세태(炎凉世態) 세력이 있을 때는 아첨하여 따르고 세력이 없어지면 푸대접하는 세상인심을 비유

■ 오매불망(寤寐不忘) 자나 깨나 잊지 못함

■ 오월동주(吳越同舟) 서로 적의를 품은 사람들이 한자리에 있게 된 경우나 서로 협력하여야 하는 상황을 비유적으로 이르는 말. 중국 춘추 전국 시대에, 서로 적대시하는 오나라 사람과 월나라 사람이 같은 배를 탔으나 풍랑을 만나서 서로 단합하여야 했다는 데에서 유래

■ 온고지신(溫故知新) 옛것을 익혀서 그것을 미루어 새것을 앎 (⊕ 법고창신)

- 우공이산(愚公移山) 어떤 일이든 끊임없이 노력하면 반드시 이루어짐 (㊛ 마부작침, 적소성대, 적토성산)
- 유비무환(有備無患) 미리 준비가 되어 있으면 걱정할 것이 없음
- 이구동성(異口同聲) 입은 다르나 목소리는 같다는 뜻으로, 여러 사람의 말이 한결같음
- 인과응보(因果應報) 전생에 지은 선악에 따라 현재의 행과 불행이 있고, 현세에서의 선악의 결과에 따라 내세에서 행과 불행이 있는 일
- 인지상정(人之常情) 사람이면 누구나 가지는 보통의 마음
- 일어탁수(一魚濁水) 한 마리의 물고기가 물을 흐린다는 뜻으로, 한 사람의 잘못으로 여러 사람이 피해를 입게 됨
- 임갈굴정(臨渴掘井) 목이 말라야 우물을 판다는 뜻으로, 평소에 준비 없이 있다가 일을 당하여 허둥지둥 서두름
- 자가당착(自家撞着) 같은 사람의 말이나 행동이 앞뒤가 서로 맞지 아니하고 모순됨
- 자강불식(自强不息) 스스로 몸과 마음을 가다듬어 쉬지 않음
- 적수공권(赤手空拳) 맨손과 맨주먹이라는 뜻으로, 아무것도 가진 것이 없음
- 전전반측(輾轉反側) 누워서 몸을 이리저리 뒤척이며 잠을 이루지 못함
- 전화위복(轉禍爲福) 재앙과 근심, 걱정이 바뀌어 오히려 복이 됨
- 정문일침(頂門一鍼) 정수리에 침을 꽂는다는 뜻으로, 따끔한 충고나 교훈을 이름
- 조령모개(朝令暮改) 아침에 명령을 내렸다가 저녁에 다시 고친다는 뜻으로, 법령을 자꾸 고쳐서 갈피를 잡기가 어려움
- 조삼모사(朝三暮四) 간사한 꾀로 남을 속이거나, 눈앞에 보이는 차이만 아는 어리석음
- 좌정관천(坐井觀天) 우물 속에 앉아서 하늘을 본다는 뜻으로, 사람의 견문(見聞)이 매우 좁음 (㊛ 정중관천, 정저지와)
- 주마가편(走馬加鞭) 달리는 말에 채찍질한다는 뜻으로, 잘하는 사람을 더욱 장려함
- 주마간산(走馬看山) 말을 타고 달리며 산천을 구경한다는 뜻으로, 자세히 살피지 아니하고 대충대충 보고 지나감
- 중구난방(衆口難防) 뭇사람의 말을 막기가 어렵다는 뜻으로, 막기 어려울 정도로 여럿이 마구 지껄임
- 지기지우(知己之友) 자기의 속마음을 참되게 알아주는 친구

- **지록위마(指鹿爲馬)** ① 사슴을 가리켜 말이라고 한다는 뜻으로, 윗사람을 농락하여 권세를 마음대로 함
  ② 모순된 것을 끝까지 우겨서 남을 속이려는 짓을 비유
- **창해일속(滄海一粟)** 넓고 큰 바닷속의 좁쌀 한 알이라는 뜻으로, 아주 많거나 넓은 것 가운데 있는 매우 하찮고 작은 것 (㊌ 구우일모)
- **천우신조(天佑神助)** 하늘이 돕고 신령이 도움. 또는 그런 일
- **천재일우(千載一遇)** 천 년 동안 단 한 번 만난다는 뜻으로, 좀처럼 만나기 어려운 좋은 기회
- **청출어람(靑出於藍)** 쪽에서 뽑아낸 푸른 물감이 쪽보다 더 푸르다는 뜻으로, 제자나 후배가 스승이나 선배보다 나음을 비유 (㊌ 후생가외)
- **초미지급(焦眉之急)** 눈썹에 불이 붙었다는 뜻으로, 매우 급함
- **촌철살인(寸鐵殺人)** 한 치의 쇠붙이로도 사람을 죽일 수 있다는 뜻으로, 간단한 말로도 남을 감동하게 하거나 남의 약점을 찌를 수 있음
- **침소봉대(針小棒大)** 작은 일을 크게 불리어 떠벌림
- **타산지석(他山之石)** 다른 산의 나쁜 돌이라도 자신의 산의 옥돌을 가는 데에 쓸 수 있다는 뜻으로, 본이 되지 않은 남의 말이나 행동도 자신의 지식과 인격을 수양하는 데에 도움이 될 수 있음을 비유
- **토사구팽(兎死狗烹)** 토끼가 죽으면 토끼를 잡던 사냥개도 필요 없게 되어 주인에게 삶아 먹히게 된다는 뜻으로, 필요할 때는 쓰고 필요 없을 때는 야박하게 버리는 경우
- **평지풍파(平地風波)** 평온한 자리에서 일어나는 풍파라는 뜻으로, 뜻밖에 분쟁이 일어남을 비유
- **풍수지탄(風樹之歎)** 효도를 다하지 못한 채 어버이를 여읜 자식의 슬픔
- **하로동선(夏爐冬扇)** 여름의 화로와 겨울의 부채라는 뜻으로, 격이나 철에 맞지 않음
- **하석상대(下石上臺)** 아랫돌 빼서 윗돌 괴고 윗돌 빼서 아랫돌 괸다는 뜻으로, 임시변통으로 이리저리 둘러맞춤
- **학수고대(鶴首苦待)** 학처럼 목을 길게 빼고 간절히 기다림
- **한우충동(汗牛充棟)** 짐으로 실으면 소가 땀을 흘리고, 쌓으면 들보에까지 찬다는 뜻으로, 가지고 있는 책이 매우 많음
- **해로동혈(偕老同穴)** 살아서는 같이 늙고 죽어서는 한 무덤에 묻힌다는 뜻으로, 생사를 같이하자는 부부의 굳은 맹세

- 허심탄회(虛心坦懷) 품은 생각을 터놓고 말할 만큼 아무 거리낌이 없고 솔직함
- 형창설안(螢窓雪案) 반딧불이 비치는 창과 눈에 비치는 책상이라는 뜻으로, 어려운 가운데서도 학문에 힘씀을 비유 (⑪ 형설지공)
- 호가호위(狐假虎威) 남의 권세를 빌려 위세를 부림. 여우가 호랑이의 위세를 빌려 호기를 부린다는 데에서 유래
- 호구지책(糊口之策) 가난한 살림에서 그저 겨우 먹고 살아가는 방책
- 호사유피(虎死留皮) 호랑이는 죽어서 가죽을 남긴다는 뜻으로, 사람은 죽어서 명예를 남겨야 함
- 호사토읍(狐死兔泣) 여우의 죽음에 토끼가 슬피 운다는 뜻으로, 같은 무리의 불행을 슬퍼함을 비유
- 화룡점정(畵龍點睛) 무슨 일을 하는 데에 가장 중요한 부분을 완성함을 비유적으로 이르는 말. 용을 그리고 난 후에 마지막으로 눈동자를 그려 넣었더니 그 용이 실제 용이 되어 홀연히 구름을 타고 하늘로 날아 올라갔다는 고사에서 유래
- 혼정신성(昏定晨省) 밤에는 부모의 잠자리를 보아 드리고 이른 아침에는 부모의 밤새 안부를 묻는다는 뜻으로, 부모를 잘 섬기고 효성을 다함
- 흥진비래(興盡悲來) 즐거운 일이 지나가면 슬픈 일이 닥쳐온다는 뜻으로, 세상일은 순환됨 (⑪ 고진감래)

현재 나의 실력을 객관적으로 파악해 보자!

모바일 OMR
답안분석 서비스

도서에 수록된 모의고사에 대한 객관적인 결과(정답률, 순위)를 종합적으로 분석하여 제공합니다.

OMR 입력

성적분석

채점결과

※OMR 답안분석 서비스는 등록 후 30일간 사용 가능합니다.

참여
방법

 → LOG IN → → → ① ② ③ ④ ⑤
① ② ③ ④ ⑤
① ② ③ ④ ⑤
→ →

도서 내 모의고사
우측 상단에 위치한
QR코드 찍기

로그인
하기

'시작하기'
클릭

'응시하기'
클릭

나의 답안을
모바일 OMR
카드에 입력

'성적분석 &
채점결과'
클릭

현재 내 실력
확인하기

군무원 전기직
FINAL 실전
봉투모의고사

Contents

Guidance notes for parents

What your child will need to sit these papers

- A quiet place to sit the exam
- A clock which is visible to your child
- A way to play the audio download
- A pencil and an eraser
- A piece of paper

Your child should not use a calculator for any of these papers.

How to invigilate the test papers

Your child should sit Test A, Paper 1 then have a 15-minute break. They should then sit Paper 2. Don't help your child or allow any talking. Review the answers with your child and help improve their weaker areas. At a later date, your child should sit Test B, Papers 1 and 2 in a two-hour session.

Step 1: Remove the answers and keep them hidden from your child.

Step 2: Remove the answer sheet section. Your child should write their full name on top of the first answer sheet. Give them the question paper booklet. They must not open the paper until they are told to do so by the audio instructions.

Step 3: Start the audio.

Step 4: Ask your child to work through the practice questions before the time starts for each section. An example is already marked on each section of the answer sheet. Your child should mark the answer sheet clearly and check that the practice questions are correctly marked.

Step 5: Mark the answer sheet. Then, together with your child, work through the questions that were answered incorrectly. When working through the Non-verbal Reasoning sections, ensure you have the question papers open to help explain the answers to your child.

How your child should complete the answer sheet

Your child MUST NOT write their answers on the question paper, they must use the answer sheet. They should put a horizontal line through the boxes on the answer sheet. To change an answer, your child should fully erase the incorrect answer and then clearly select a new answer. Any rough workings should be done on a separate piece of paper.

The audio instructions

Both papers have audio instructions to allow your child to learn, listen and act upon audio instructions.

Audio instructions are at the start, during and at the end of the sections. Audio warnings on the time remaining will be given at varying intervals. Your child should listen out for these warnings.

The symbols at the foot of the page

Written instructions are at the foot of the page. Your child MUST follow these instructions:

Continue working

Stop and wait for instructions

Your child can review questions within the allocated time, but must not move onto the next section until they are allowed to do so.

The instructions and examples at the beginning of the section

In the instructions, your child should look for: the time allowed; how many questions there are; and how to complete the answers.

Examples are at the beginning of every section to show the type of question included in a particular section. The example questions will be worked through as part of the audio instructions.

Developing time-management skills and working at speed

These test papers have been used with previous pupils of the CEM exam in various counties. They provide essential practice of the types of questions which could arise, in addition to the strictly timed conditions, which will help your child practise their time-management skills.

Marking the papers

Each question is worth one mark.

Scores

Overall scores your child should be aiming for:

- 75% or more on the first pack of 2 papers if taken in the weeks leading up to the exam
- 70% or more on the second pack of 2 papers if taken in the weeks leading up to the exam.

A weighted score attaches a certain amount of weight to each section in the exam.

How to work out your child's score:

Add together the scores for Non-verbal Reasoning and Maths sections (both Numeracy and Problem Solving). This will give you score A. This relates to both sections in all papers.

Then add together the remaining scores for all English sections, which will give you score B.

Then add scores A and B together and divide them by 2.

This will give you an average weighted score across the 2 packs.

To calculate your child's weighted score as a percentage, divide your child's score by the maximum score, and multiply it by 100.

Once you have completed this, you will have two percentages and the combined weighted score across the two papers is the middle of these two percentages.

For example: If your child scores 46 out of 92 for English, this equals 50%.

If your child scores 62 out of 82, this equals approximately 76%. So the combined weighted score across the two papers is 50% + 76%, which equals 126%. If you divide this by 2, this equals 63%. This is your child's weighted score.

The maximum scores:

Test A Paper 1 English – 49

Test A Paper 1 Maths and Non-verbal Reasoning – 36

Test A Paper 2 English – 43

Test A Paper 2 Maths and Non-verbal Reasoning – 43

Test B Paper 1 English – 48

Test B Paper 1 Maths and Non-verbal Reasoning – 37

Test B Paper 2 English – 35

Test B Paper 2 Maths and Non-verbal Reasoning – 41

English maximum scores, Test A Papers 1 and 2 – 92

Maths and Non-verbal Reasoning maximum scores, Test A Papers 1 and 2 – 79

English maximum scores, Test B Papers 1 and 2 – 83

Maths and Non-verbal Reasoning maximum scores, Test B Papers 1 and 2 – 78

Please note the following:

As the content varies from year to year in CEM exams, a good score in this paper does not guarantee a pass, and a lower score may not always suggest a fail!

What happens if your child does not score a good mark?

Identify strengths and weaknesses

Continue to provide a wide variety of questions to build your child's knowledge. Focus on the areas in which your child did not perform as well.

Timings

Allow your child to continue practising working under timed conditions.

Test A Paper 1

Instructions

1. Ensure you have pencils and an eraser with you.

2. Make sure you are able to see a clock or watch.

3. Write your name on the answer sheet.

4. Do not open the question booklet until you are told to do so by the audio instructions.

5. Listen carefully to the audio instructions given.

6. Mark your answers on the answer sheet only.

7. All workings must be completed on a separate piece of paper.

8. You should not use a calculator, dictionary or thesaurus at any point in this paper.

9. Move through the papers as quickly as possible and with care.

10. Follow the instructions at the foot of each page.

11. You should mark your answers with a horizontal strike, as shown on the answer sheet.

12. If you want to change your answer, ensure that you rub out your first answer and that your second answer is clearly more visible.

13. You can go back and review any questions that are within the section you are working on only. You must await further instructions before moving onto another section.

Symbols and Phrases used in the Tests

 Instructions  Time allowed for this section   Stop and wait for further instructions   Continue working

Comprehension

INSTRUCTIONS

 YOU HAVE 9 MINUTES TO COMPLETE THE FOLLOWING SECTION.

YOU HAVE 10 QUESTIONS TO COMPLETE WITHIN THE TIME GIVEN.

EXAMPLES

Comprehension Example

Some people choose to start their Christmas shopping early in October. It has been reported that some people even buy their Christmas presents in the sales in August. In recent years, people have had the option of purchasing their Christmas presents online.

Example 1

According to the passage, what is the earliest that people start their Christmas shopping?

A   In the preceding summer
B   In the preceding October
C   In the preceding November
D   Christmas Eve
E   In early December

The correct answer is A. This has already been marked in Example 1 in the Comprehension section of your answer sheet.

Practice Question 1

In recent years, what has caused a change in how people shop?

A   There are more shops.
B   Shops are more crowded.
C   You can easily organise your journey to the shops.
D   New products are available.
E   There has been a rise in use of the Internet.

The correct answer is E. Please mark this in Practice Question 1 in the Comprehension section of your answer sheet.

STOP AND WAIT FOR FURTHER INSTRUCTIONS

Read the following passage and then answer the questions below.

The History of Art

Art has always been part of society. Even as far back as prehistoric times, early modern humans (Homo sapiens) were expressing their thoughts, beliefs and feelings by producing cave art. There are many examples of Palaeolithic cave art. The finest known example can be found in a cave in Lascaux, in South West France. The vast network of caves is believed to be just under 18,000 years old. The drawings and paintings mainly include the animals which lived in the area at that time. Human figures and other abstract images are also depicted. Visitors are now unable to see the real examples, as the cave is closed to allow the cave art to be preserved. Since 2001, visitors have only been able to visit a replica of the caves.

Other civilisations have expressed their art in different mediums. We have many fragmented examples of hand-crafted sculptures from the Ancient Greeks, Romans and Egyptians. These civilisations also expressed themselves through their monumental architecture. Their public buildings were built on a huge scale and were originally beautifully embellished. Much of this embellishment has now vanished. However, the beauty of these buildings can still be seen, both in the design of the building, and in some small remaining fragments of the decoration.

Much later during the Renaissance period, a new artistic movement, originating in Italy, swept through Western Europe. One characteristic of this movement was the introduction of perspective into works of art. However, the key feature of this new style was 'chiaroscuro', which means 'light' and 'dark'. This gave new emphasis to the illusion of three-dimensional figures, in contrast to the two-dimensional figures that had preceded this period. Figures were more realistic, making them almost lifelike.

Art attracts the interest of communities and individuals. Many wealthy individuals have extensive art collections, which are an expression of their passion for art. Many also buy art as an investment, in the hope that the value of their purchase will rise.

Over the past 30 years, there has been a gradual realisation that art can be beneficial to the community as a whole. In some cases, redevelopment projects now include a piece of 'public art'. This is often a large sculpture, sited in a prominent position to enhance the environment.

Modern art attracts much controversy. Some hold the view that the art of the 21st century should not be viewed as art. Many commentators say that the installations are merely there to attract the attention of the media. Many sculptures are also considered grotesque and in bad taste. However, many of the most successful artists over the centuries have been those who pushed the boundaries, and who initially attracted controversy.

(1) How old is the cave at Lascaux?

A   Less than 10,000 years old
B   Over 20,000 years old
C   Less than 20,000 years old
D   More than 30,000 years old
E   Less than 8,000 years old

CONTINUE WORKING

2 Which phrase best describes the art at Lascaux?

    A   Many sculptures of human figures are found at the site
    B   There are no paintings of animals
    C   The vast majority are paintings of caves
    D   There are many sculptures of animals
    E   The vast majority of the paintings are of animals

3 Why are the caves now closed to the public?

    A   To allow the caves to be preserved
    B   To allow for more visitors to attend
    C   To allow for restoration of the area
    D   To allow for more time to visit the caves
    E   To allow for more replicas to be made

4 What evidence remains of the art from the ancient civilisations of Rome, Egypt and Greece?

    A   Decorations from small sculptures
    B   Small buildings and paintings
    C   Large sculptures only
    D   Fragments of sculptures and large buildings
    E   Beautifully embellished clothing

5 Where did the Renaissance start?

    A   In Italy
    B   In Rome
    C   In England
    D   In Egypt
    E   In Eastern Europe

6 Why did the Renaissance have such an impact on painting techniques?

    A   Paintings emphasised two-dimensional figures
    B   Paintings looked more realistic
    C   Portraits of people were no longer painted
    D   Paintings were now only produced in colour
    E   Paintings were only produced in black and white

CONTINUE WORKING

(7) Which of the following is given in the passage as a reason for individuals buying art?

A   To give a piece of art to a community
B   To help the artist
C   To be controversial
D   To place it in their garden
E   To make an investment

(8) What is 'public art'?

A   Art placed in a person's house
B   Art placed in an area to benefit a community, or newly developed area
C   Art created in the 20th century
D   Art creating media attention
E   Art created to be controversial

(9) What is the meaning of the word 'prominent' in the context of the passage?

A   Realistic
B   Worthwhile
C   Egotistical
D   Hidden
E   Noticeable

(10) Which is the phrase that best summarises the final paragraph?

A   Modern art is always liked by people
B   Modern art is only produced to be installed near the boundaries of communities
C   Modern art is traditional
D   Modern art is often controversial
E   Modern art makes artists wealthy

STOP AND WAIT FOR FURTHER INSTRUCTIONS ⊗

Shuffled Sentences

INSTRUCTIONS

 YOU HAVE 8 MINUTES TO COMPLETE THE FOLLOWING SECTION.

YOU HAVE 15 QUESTIONS TO COMPLETE WITHIN THE TIME GIVEN.

EXAMPLES

Example 1

The following sentence is shuffled and also contains one unnecessary word. Rearrange the sentence correctly in order to identify the unnecessary word.

dog the ran fetch the to stick gluing.

A	B	C	D	E
gluing	dog	ran	the	stick

The correct answer is A. This has already been marked in Example 1 in the Shuffled Sentences section of your answer sheet.

Practice Question 1

The following sentence is shuffled and also contains one unnecessary word. Rearrange the sentence correctly in order to identify the unnecessary word.

pushed Emma stood up and closed the table under the chairs.

A	B	C	D	E
chairs	stood	under	closed	Emma

The correct answer is D. Please mark this in Practice Question 1 in the Shuffled Sentences section of your answer sheet.

STOP AND WAIT FOR FURTHER INSTRUCTIONS

Each sentence below is shuffled and also contains one unnecessary word.
Rearrange each sentence correctly in order to identify the unnecessary word.

1 book the reserve is I think film better than the.

A	B	C	D	E
I	better	reserve	film	book

---

2 curtains to paint she drew warmth in the keep the.

A	B	C	D	E
paint	curtains	warmth	to	the

---

3 play the firm record number of insurance kept the claims busy.

A	B	C	D	E
play	record	claims	busy	insurance

---

4 up the down pillows are more duck comfortable.

A	B	C	D	E
duck	are	up	comfortable	pillows

---

5 quick you need dough to question the be to answer.

A	B	C	D	E
answer	need	quick	dough	question

---

6 barbecue since the despite went weather the ahead.

A	B	C	D	E
went	despite	weather	ahead	since

---

7 was not stable horse the building earthquake the following.

A	B	C	D	E
earthquake	building	following	horse	was

CONTINUE WORKING

(8) her up stair to at continued the girl stare.

A	B	C	D	E
stair	continued	girl	her	stare

(9) beginning breath she drew a blind before deep her speech.

A	B	C	D	E
before	drew	blind	speech	her

(10) tried use the sofa after looking was a years of number tired of.

A	B	C	D	E
sofa	tried	years	use	was

(11) the current rain was coming to an end monarch reign the of.

A	B	C	D	E
was	reign	current	monarch	rain

(12) kicked small the Roger window through the ball.

A	B	C	D	E
Roger	small	window	ball	through

(13) the on the motorway caused in heavy traffic accident.

A	B	C	D	E
on	caused	in	motorway	accident

(14) Eva at noon Jon due is to meet earlier.

A	B	C	D	E
earlier	Jon	Eva	noon	at

(15) dinner light the rather substantial guests felt bloated after their.

A	B	C	D	E
dinner	the	bloated	light	felt

STOP AND WAIT FOR FURTHER INSTRUCTIONS ✖

Numeracy

INSTRUCTIONS

 YOU HAVE 6 MINUTES TO COMPLETE THE FOLLOWING SECTION.

YOU HAVE 13 QUESTIONS TO COMPLETE WITHIN THE TIME GIVEN.

EXAMPLES

The questions within this section are not multiple choice. Write the answer to each question on the answer sheet by selecting the correct digits from the columns provided.

Example 1

Calculate 14 + 23

The correct answer is 37. This has already been marked in Example 1 in the Numeracy section of your answer sheet.

Practice Question 1

Calculate 83 – 75

The correct answer is 8. Please mark this in Practice Question 1 in the Numeracy section of your answer sheet. Note that a single-digit answer should be marked with a 0 in the left-hand column, so mark 08 on your answer sheet.

STOP AND WAIT FOR FURTHER INSTRUCTIONS

① Calculate the answer to the following:

$3 \times 5 - 4$

CONTINUE WORKING

(2) Calculate the answer to the following:

24 − 4 ÷ 2

(3) Calculate the answer to the following:

18 − 6 ÷ 3

(4) Select the appropriate number or numbers to complete the sequence in place of the ?

0, 1, 1, 2, ?, 5, 8

(5) Calculate the range of the following data:

4, 2, 5, 8, 2, 11, 14, 1, 5, 3, 7, 8, 9, 10

(6) Which of these is not exactly divisible by 7?

17, 49, 28, 56, 70

(7) Which of these is not a factor of 63?

1, 19, 21, 63, 3

(8) Which of these is a common factor of both 18 and 48?

4, 24, 12, 6, 7

(9) In three years' time, I will be twice as old as I am now. How old am I now?

(10) Alan was 9, two years ago. How old will he be in one year's time?

(11) How many months are there from 30 April to 30 November?

(12) How many weeks are there in the 9 months from the start of a non-leap year to the end of September?

(13) Calculate what number between 40 and 50 has a remainder of 7 when divided by 9.

STOP AND WAIT FOR FURTHER INSTRUCTIONS

Problem Solving

INSTRUCTIONS

 YOU HAVE 8 MINUTES TO COMPLETE THE FOLLOWING SECTION.

YOU HAVE 10 QUESTIONS TO COMPLETE WITHIN THE TIME GIVEN.

EXAMPLES

Example 1

Calculate the following:

If I buy five apples at 20p each and four bananas at 35p each, how much change will I receive if I pay with a £5 note?

A   £2.60
B   £3.40
C   £2.40
D   £3.60
E   £1.35

The correct answer is A. This has already been marked in Example 1 in the Problem Solving section of your answer sheet.

Practice Question 1

Calculate the following: There are 17 people on a bus when it arrives at a bus stop. Eleven people get on the bus, and three get off. How many people are then left on the bus?

A   28
B   31
C   34
D   25
E   14

The correct answer is D. Please mark this in Practice Question 1 in the Problem Solving section of your answer sheet.

STOP AND WAIT FOR FURTHER INSTRUCTIONS

Calculate the following.

(1) If a bag of 50 marbles is shared between friends so that the friends have 10 marbles, 15 marbles and 25 marbles, in what ratio have they been shared?

A	1 : 2	**B**	1 : 2 : 5	**C**	2 : 4 : 8
D	2 : 3 : 5	**E**	10 : 10 : 20		

(2) I am unaware that my watch stopped at 7:15 a.m. I check my watch on the way to the station. The correct time then is 7:30 a.m. Thinking I am early, I then buy a cup of coffee taking 10 minutes. My train is due to depart at 7:35 a.m. How late does the train need to be in order for me to catch it?

A	3 minutes	**B**	6 minutes	**C**	2 minutes
D	1 minutes	**E**	4 minutes		

Questions 3, 4 and 5 are linked so that questions 4 and 5 follow on from question 3.

(3) A class has 30 children in it. 60% of the children in the class are girls. How many boys are in the class?

A	16	**B**	18	**C**	15
D	14	**E**	12		

(4) If five new children join the class at the start of the next year, how many girls are there in the larger class if there are still 60% girls in the larger class?

A	21	**B**	14	**C**	12
D	15	**E**	18		

(5) What is the ratio of boys to girls in the larger class in its simplest form?

A	12 : 18	**B**	5 : 3	**C**	10 : 6
D	2 : 3	**E**	21 : 14		

(6) There are three buses every hour from Gerrards Cross to Beaconsfield, with buses departing at regular, equally spaced intervals. If the buses are always on time, what is the longest I would have to wait at the bus stop?

A	Just under 20 minutes
B	Just over 20 minutes
C	Just under 5 minutes
D	Just over 5 minutes
E	10 minutes

CONTINUE WORKING ⬛➡

(7) What is the average time I would have to wait for a bus if I arrived at the bus stop in Gerrards Cross at random times, during which there were buses every 20 minutes (three buses per hour)?

A	20 minutes	**B**	6 minutes	**C**	10 minutes
D	15 minutes	**E**	7 minutes		

(8) If the bus travels a three-mile journey in 20 minutes, what is its average speed for the journey in mph?

A	0 mph	**B**	60 mph	**C**	30 mph
D	9 mph	**E**	3 mph		

(9) What is the length of time between:

10 past nine in the morning and a quarter to 4 in the afternoon?

A	6 hours 35 minutes
B	5 hours 35 minutes
C	6 hours 25 minutes
D	7 hours 25 minutes
E	8 hours

(10) There are 2847 people in a large secondary school. 1527 are girls and teachers. 2649 are girls or boys.

Use the information above to calculate the number of girls, boys and teachers.

A	1450 girls, 1120 boys, 150 teachers
B	1320 girls, 1329 boys, 198 teachers
C	1239 girls, 1230 boys, 198 teachers
D	769 girls, 1820 boys, 168 teachers
E	1329 girls, 1320 boys, 198 teachers

STOP AND WAIT FOR FURTHER INSTRUCTIONS ⊗

Synonyms

INSTRUCTIONS

 YOU HAVE 7 MINUTES TO COMPLETE THE FOLLOWING SECTION.

YOU HAVE 24 QUESTIONS TO COMPLETE WITHIN THE TIME GIVEN.

EXAMPLES

Example 1

Select the word that is most similar in meaning to the following word:

cold

A	B	C	D	E
collect	fence	foggy	windy	chilly

The correct answer is E. This has already been marked in Example 1 in the Synonyms section of your answer sheet.

Practice Question 1

Select the word that is most similar in meaning to the following word:

start

A	B	C	D	E
cramped	begin	free	without	change

The correct answer is B. Please mark this in Practice Question 1 in the Synonyms section of your answer sheet.

STOP AND WAIT FOR FURTHER INSTRUCTIONS

For each row, select the word from the table that is most similar in meaning to the word above the table.

1 abundance

A	B	C	D	E
jumping	squeeze	exclusion	scarcity	plenty

2 tranquil

A	B	C	D	E
agitate	calm	pointless	tame	trite

3 obstinate

A	B	C	D	E
economy	inspiring	inflexible	forgiving	pleasant

4 erratic

A	B	C	D	E
coy	succinct	affable	volatile	serene

5 melancholy

A	B	C	D	E
crude	suitable	automatic	multitude	sad

6 helix

A	B	C	D	E
spiral	rebuke	barbaric	helicopter	submarine

7 obtuse

A	B	C	D	E
angle	unintelligent	bright	devout	triumphant

8 adequate

A	B	C	D	E
exercise	unfit	suitable	earthquake	complex

CONTINUE WORKING ⏵

9 tenacity

A	B	C	D	E
incite	evade	evaluate	scarcity	resoluteness

10 insolent

A	B	C	D	E
confess	solemn	multitude	rude	solvent

11 enchanted

A	B	C	D	E
delighted	deplorable	egotistic	impertinent	insolent

12 affable

A	B	C	D	E
affected	majestic	resourceful	fallible	amiable

13 contingent

A	B	C	D	E
contain	dependent	subtract	greet	astonish

14 bulging

A	B	C	D	E
injure	flaw	forehead	convex	wound

15 uninterested

A	B	C	D	E
apathetic	intended	overseas	anger	serene

16 box

A	B	C	D	E
din	lucid	advance	crate	distinctive

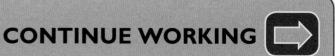

CONTINUE WORKING

17 twisted

A	B	C	D	E
respond	attire	mystify	gnarled	inflexible

18 wound

A	B	C	D	E
flustered	coy	injure	motion	part

19 hopeful

A	B	C	D	E
doctor	berate	optimistic	subsequent	congregate

20 importance

A	B	C	D	E
significance	naïve	distinctive	madness	litter

21 proof

A	B	C	D	E
vital	derivative	evidence	necessary	select

22 adapt

A	B	C	D	E
mimic	homicide	acclimatise	liable	culprit

23 stroll

A	B	C	D	E
bogus	saunter	moreover	icon	velocity

24 copy

A	B	C	D	E
transcribe	dogma	cautious	malevolent	ruffian

STOP AND WAIT FOR FURTHER INSTRUCTIONS ⬡✕

Non-Verbal Reasoning

INSTRUCTIONS

 YOU HAVE 7 MINUTES TO COMPLETE THE FOLLOWING SECTION.

YOU HAVE 13 QUESTIONS TO COMPLETE WITHIN THE TIME GIVEN.

EXAMPLES

REFLECTION Example 1

Select how the following shape or pattern would appear when reflected in the dashed line:

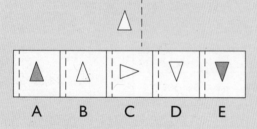

The correct answer is B. This has already been marked in Example 1 in the Non-Verbal Reasoning section of your answer sheet.

REFLECTION Practice Question 1

Select how the following shape or pattern would appear when reflected in the dashed line:

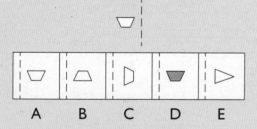

The correct answer is A. Please mark this in Practice Question 1 in the Non-Verbal Reasoning section of your answer sheet.

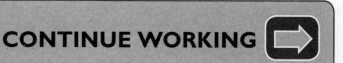

CONTINUE WORKING

CONNECTION Example 2

Look at the two shapes on the left immediately below. Find the connection between them.

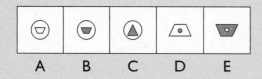

Select the shape that is related to the third shape above by applying the same connection.

The correct answer is B. This has already been marked in Example 2 in the Non-Verbal Reasoning section of your answer sheet.

CONNECTION Practice Question 2

Look at the two shapes on the left immediately below. Find the connection between them.

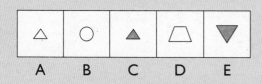

Select the shape that is related to the third shape above by applying the same connection.

The correct answer is E. Please mark this in Practice Question 2 in the Non-Verbal Reasoning section of your answer sheet.

STOP AND WAIT FOR FURTHER INSTRUCTIONS ⮾

1 Look at the two shapes on the left immediately below.
Find the connection between them and apply it to the third shape.

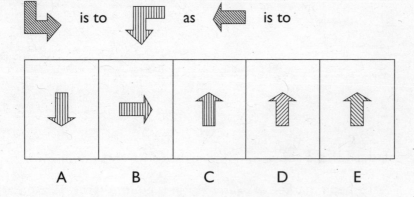

A   B   C   D   E

2 Look at the two shapes on the left immediately below.
Find the connection between them and apply it to the third shape.

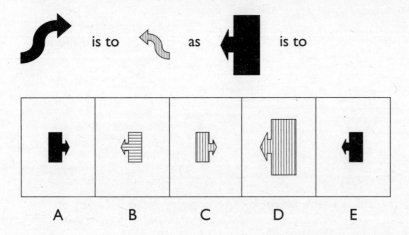

A   B   C   D   E

3 Select the correct picture from the row on the right in order to finish the incomplete sequence on the left.

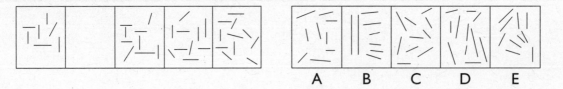

A   B   C   D   E

4 Select the correct picture from the row on the right in order to finish the incomplete sequence on the left.

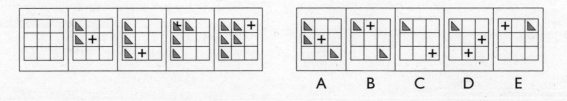

A   B   C   D   E

CONTINUE WORKING

(5) Which shape or pattern completes the larger square?

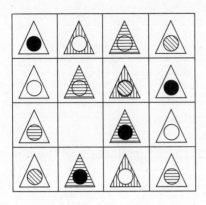

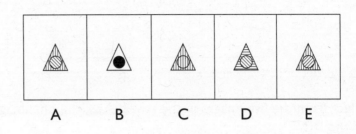

A   B   C   D   E

(6) Which shape or pattern completes the larger square in the place of the?

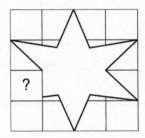

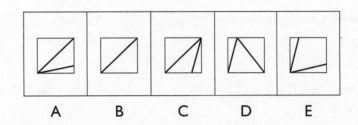

A   B   C   D   E

(7) Select how the following shape or pattern would appear when reflected in the dashed line.

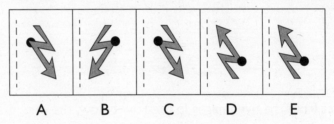

A   B   C   D   E

(8) Select how the following shape or pattern would appear when reflected in the dashed line.

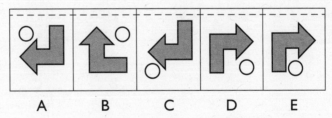

A   B   C   D   E

CONTINUE WORKING ➡

(9) Select from the five images in the row below, the one image that is a reflection of the image on the left.

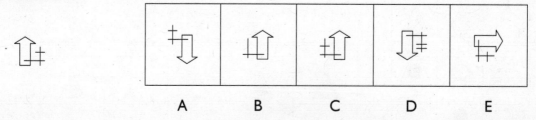

A   B   C   D   E

(10) Select from the five images in the row below, the one image that is a reflection of the image on the left.

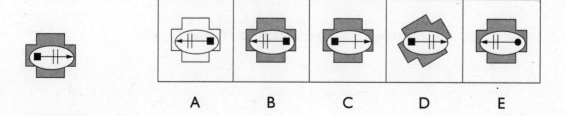

A   B   C   D   E

(11) Select from the five images in the row below, the one image that is a reflection of the image on the left.

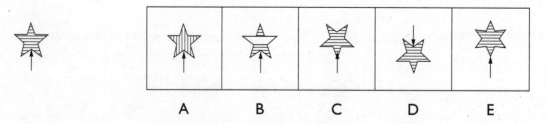

A   B   C   D   E

(12) Select from the five images in the row below, the one image that is a reflection of the image on the left.

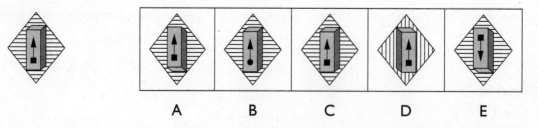

A   B   C   D   E

(13) Select from the five images in the row below, the one image that is a reflection of the image on the left.

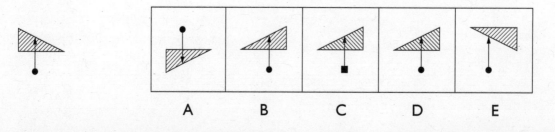

A   B   C   D   E

END OF PAPER

Test A Paper 2

Instructions

1. Ensure you have pencils and an eraser with you.
2. Make sure you are able to see a clock or watch.
3. Write your name on the answer sheet.
4. Do not open the question booklet until you are told to do so by the audio instructions.
5. Listen carefully to the audio instructions given.
6. Mark your answers on the answer sheet only.
7. All workings must be completed on a separate piece of paper.
8. You should not use a calculator, dictionary or thesaurus at any point in this paper.
9. Move through the papers as quickly as possible and with care.
10. Follow the instructions at the foot of each page.
11. You should mark your answers with a horizontal strike, as shown on the answer sheet.
12. If you want to change your answer, ensure that you rub out your first answer and that your second answer is clearly more visible.
13. You can go back and review any questions that are within the section you are working on only. You must await further instructions before moving onto another section.

Symbols and Phrases used in the Tests

 Instructions    Time allowed for this section   Stop and wait for further instructions   Continue working

Problem Solving

 YOU HAVE 8 MINUTES TO COMPLETE THE FOLLOWING SECTION.

YOU HAVE 10 QUESTIONS TO COMPLETE WITHIN THE TIME GIVEN.

EXAMPLES

A £2.60	B £3.40	C £2.40	D 25	E £1.35
F £3.60	G 14	H 31	I 28	J 34

Example 1

Calculate the following:

If I buy five apples at 20p each, and four bananas at 35p each, how much change will I receive if I pay with a £5 note.

The correct answer is A. This has already been marked in Example 1 in the Problem Solving section of your answer sheet.

Practice Question 1

Calculate the following:

There are 17 people on a bus when it arrives at a bus stop. Eleven people get on the bus, and three get off. How many people are then left on the bus?

The correct answer is D. Please mark this in Practice Question 1 in the Problem Solving section of your answer sheet.

STOP AND WAIT FOR FURTHER INSTRUCTIONS

A 40p	B 20p	C 100	D 45 minutes	E 19,200
F 240	G 50 minutes	H 30p	I £6.80	J £3.20

Several questions will follow for you to answer. Select an answer to each question from the 10 different possible answers in the table above. You may use an answer for more than one question.

1. Harji is in a supermarket and buys the following:

   Four pears at 40p each and twice as many apples, which cost half the price of the pears. How much change should Harji receive if she pays with a £10 note?

2. Harji also buys the following to make a fruit salad:

   Bananas (B) and Kiwis (K)

   Use the following information to work out the price in pence of one banana:

   4B + 6K = 260 pence

   5B + 6K = 280 pence

3. Harji notices a special offer on yoghurt. The normal price (without the offer) is £1.20 per pot of yoghurt.

   The offer is 'Buy 3 for the price of 2'.

   How much less would each pot of yoghurt cost under the offer, if three pots are bought?

4. Harji entered the supermarket at quarter to 11 that morning. She is due to meet her friend for a coffee in the supermarket at half-past 12 in the afternoon. Her shopping in the supermarket takes 55 minutes. How long does Harji have to wait to meet her friend after completing her shopping (her friend arrives five minutes early)?

5. Harji buys some frozen food as part of her shopping and wants to get home before it defrosts. She places the frozen food in her trolley at 12.20 (5 minutes before she meets her friend). She is with her friend for 15 minutes.

   Her drive home is 20 km, and she drives at an average speed of 40 km/h.

   When Harji arrives home, how long has the frozen food been out of the freezer?

CONTINUE WORKING

(6) The supermarket serves free coffee to its customers. If the supermarket has served 180 coffees between opening time (8 a.m.) and noon, and for the entire day (until 8 p.m.) there were 420 coffees served, how many coffees were served between noon and closing time?

(7) The dimensions of the supermarket floor are 80 m long by 60 m wide.

The entire floor is covered by square tiles with the following dimensions:

50 cm by 50 cm

How many tiles are required to cover the entire floor area?

(8) If seven lemons cost £1.40, how much do 16 lemons cost?

(9) There are seven women working at the supermarket for every five men. If there are 140 women working at the supermarket, how many men work at the supermarket?

(10) The total cost of the shopping is £123.27. Harji hands over £130 to the man at the checkout. Harji realises that the man on the checkout has not given her enough change when she counts the change of £6.43. How much additional change should Harji have received?

STOP AND WAIT FOR FURTHER INSTRUCTIONS ⊗

Cloze

 YOU HAVE 10 MINUTES TO COMPLETE THE FOLLOWING SECTION.

YOU HAVE 20 QUESTIONS TO COMPLETE WITHIN THE TIME GIVEN.

EXAMPLES

Example 1

Read the sentence below and select the most appropriate word from the table.

A	B	C	D	E
backdrop	carefully	drawer	disadvantage	dilution

The undulating hills were the perfect Q1 _____ for the watercolour painting.

Please select your answer to go in the place of (Q1) in the above sentence.

The correct answer is A. This has already been marked in Example 1 in the Cloze section of your answer sheet.

Practice Question 1

Read the sentence below and select the most appropriate word from the table.

A	B	C	D	E
had	interior	success	attend	absent

The girl decided she would like to Q2 _____ the party.

Please select your answer to go in the place of (Q2) in the above sentence.

The correct answer is D. Please mark the answer D in Practice Question 1 in the Cloze section of your answer sheet.

STOP AND WAIT FOR FURTHER INSTRUCTIONS

Read the passage and select the most appropriate word from the table below.

A	B	C	D	E
parking	properties	competitive	multitude	aspire

F	G	H	I	J
description	extended	stylish	external	exemplified

The UK Housing Market

Most young people (Q1) _____ to own their own home. Low interest rates have allowed people to afford monthly mortgage payments. However, after a long period of interest rates remaining at an all time low, interest rates are set to rise.

Since the housing market boom of the 1980s, estate agency has been a profitable, but (Q2) _____ marketplace.

Many estate agents now advertise on the Internet, using well-established websites to market their (Q3) _____. A typical house will be advertised with a (Q4) _____ of internal and (Q5) _____ photographs. There is usually a (Q6) _____ of the property, as well as floor plans which show the layout and room sizes. A typical description includes details, such as those (Q7) _____ in the following passage:

'A well proportioned and (Q8) _____ four bedroom end of terrace family house, in a highly sought-after residential area, within easy reach of good local schools and shops. The accommodation has been (Q9) _____ by the current owners and comprises in brief: a storm porch, entrance hall, living room with double doors leading to a dining room, a modern fitted kitchen/breakfast room, an orangery, downstairs cloakroom, four bedrooms, two en-suite shower rooms and a bathroom. Further benefits include gas fired central heating, double glazing, a rear garden laid mostly to lawn and off road (Q10) _____.'

CONTINUE WORKING

Read the passage and select the most appropriate word from the table below.

A	B	C	D	E
empire	ancient	turbulent	theatre	collapsed

F	G	H	I	J
understood	spectators	survive	buildings	Italy

The Origins Of Theatre

In the early 3rd century BC, life in (Q11)_____ Greece changed.
Alexander the Great died and his (Q12)_____ fragmented. These became
(Q13)_____ times and it was at this time that the (Q14)_____
played a central role in the daily lives of Ancient Greeks.

Theatres could hold tens of thousands of (Q15)_____ .

The comedies which were shown, were so popular that they spread to other areas of the ancient
world, even as far as (Q16)_____ . Comedy is understood by all and is
(Q17)_____ by people from all walks of life.

The Romans attacked Greece from 282 BC onwards, and eventually the Greek empire
(Q18)_____ . The Romans embraced Greek culture and the
(Q19)_____ that still (Q20)_____ today in Ancient
Rome, allude to the Greek culture that the Romans wanted to replicate.

STOP AND WAIT FOR FURTHER INSTRUCTIONS ⊗

Non-Verbal Reasoning

 YOU HAVE 8 MINUTES TO COMPLETE THE FOLLOWING SECTION.

YOU HAVE 15 QUESTIONS TO COMPLETE WITHIN THE TIME GIVEN.

EXAMPLES

CUBES Example 1

Look at the cube net below. Select the only cube that could be formed from the net below.

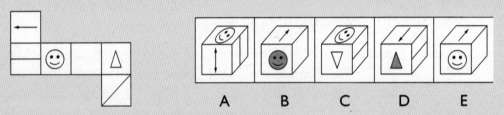

The correct answer is E. This has already been marked in Example 1 in the Non-Verbal Reasoning section of your answer sheet.

CUBES Practice Question 1

Look at the cube net below. Select the only cube that could be formed from the net below.

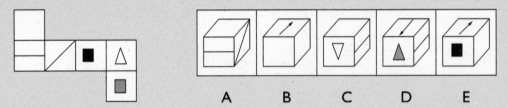

The correct answer is A. Please mark this in Practice Question 1 in the Non-Verbal Reasoning section of your answer sheet.

CONTINUE WORKING ➡

BELONGS TO GROUP Example 2

Which of the patterns in the row below belongs in the group within the oval?

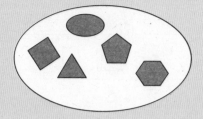
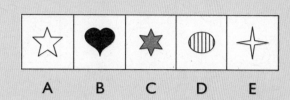

A   B   C   D   E

The correct answer is C. This has already been marked in Example 2 in the Non-Verbal Reasoning section of your answer sheet.

BELONGS TO GROUP Practice Question 2

Which of the patterns in the row below belongs in the group within the oval?

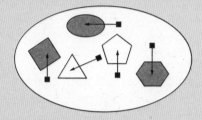
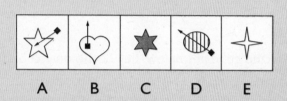

A   B   C   D   E

The correct answer is A. Please mark this in Practice Question 2 in the Non-Verbal Reasoning section of your answer sheet.

STOP AND WAIT FOR FURTHER INSTRUCTIONS

1 Which of the patterns in the row below belongs in the group within the oval?

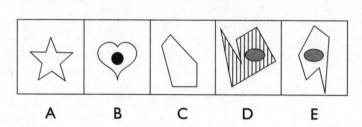

A   B   C   D   E

CONTINUE WORKING

(2) Which of the patterns in the row below belongs in the group within the oval?

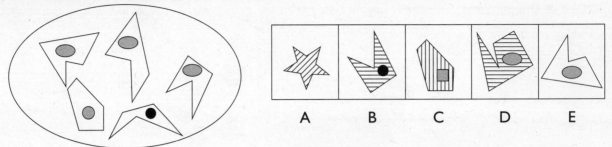

A B C D E

(3) Which of the patterns in the row below belongs in the group within the oval?

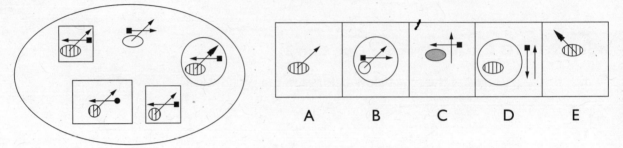

A B C D E

(4) Look at the cube net below. Select the only cube that could be formed from the net.

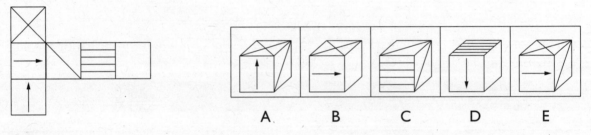

A B C D E

(5) Look at the cube net below. Select the only cube that could be formed from the net.

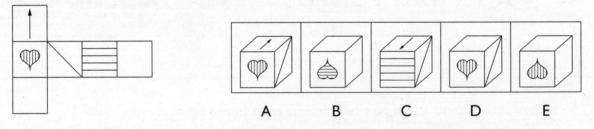

A B C D E

(6) Look at the cube net below. Select the only cube that could be formed from the net.

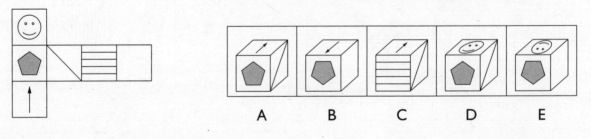

A B C D E

CONTINUE WORKING ⏵

7 Look at the cube net below. Select the only cube that could be formed from the net.

A   B   C   D   E

8 Look at the cube net below. Select the only cube that could be formed from the net.

A   B   C   D   E

9 Look at the codes for the following patterns and identify the missing code for the pattern on the far right.

CD   AE   BF   AD

A	AF
B	AE
C	BD
D	AC
E	CE

10 Look at the codes for the following patterns and identify the missing code for the pattern on the far right.

CF   AE   BD   AD

A	BE
B	AE
C	BD
D	BF
E	CE

11 Look at the codes for the following patterns and identify the missing code for the pattern on the far right.

BZ   AX   BX   AY

A	AX
B	AZ
C	BZ
D	BY
E	BX

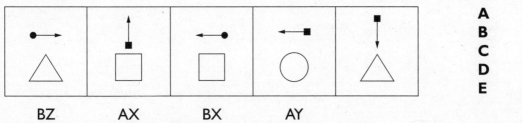

CONTINUE WORKING

12 Look at the codes for the following patterns and identify the missing code for the pattern on the far right.

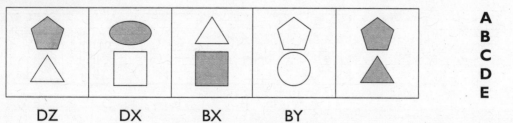

DZ	DX	BX	BY	

A   DY
B   DX
C   BZ
D   BY
E   DZ

13 Look at the codes for the following patterns and identify the missing code for the pattern on the far right.

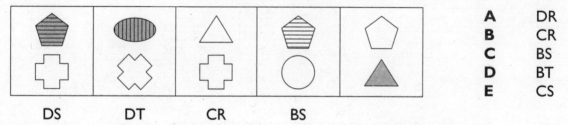

DS	DT	CR	BS	

A   DR
B   CR
C   BS
D   BT
E   CS

14 Look at the codes for the following patterns and identify the missing code for the pattern on the far right.

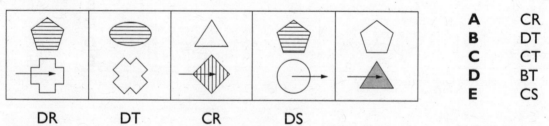

DR	DT	CR	DS	

A   CR
B   DT
C   CT
D   BT
E   CS

15 Look at the codes for the following patterns and identify the missing code for the pattern on the far right.

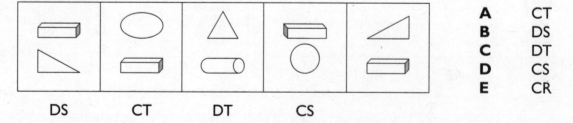

DS	CT	DT	CS	

A   CT
B   DS
C   DT
D   CS
E   CR

STOP AND WAIT FOR FURTHER INSTRUCTIONS ⬡✖

Grammar

INSTRUCTIONS

YOU HAVE 5 MINUTES TO COMPLETE THE FOLLOWING SECTION.

YOU HAVE 8 QUESTIONS TO COMPLETE WITHIN THE TIME GIVEN.

EXAMPLES

Example 1

Select the word below that is misspelt.

A	B	C	D	E
cinema	while	repeet	home	open

The correct answer is C. This has already been marked in Example 1 in the Grammar section of your answer sheet.

Practice Question 1

Select the correct prefix or suffix below to give the opposite to the word 'legal':

A	B	C	D	E
in	im	un	il	non

The correct answer is D. Please mark the answer D in Practice Question 1 in the Grammar section of your answer sheet.

STOP AND WAIT FOR FURTHER INSTRUCTIONS

1 Identify a homophone of the word 'sew' from the words below.

A	B	C	D	E
seen	pig	piglet	sewn	sow

2 Identify the homograph of the word 'bow' from the words below.

A	B	C	D	E
tie	bow	head	royal	boat

3 Select the correct prefix or suffix below to give the opposite to the word 'probable'.

A	B	C	D	E
in	im	dis	un	de

4 Select the word below that is misspelt.

A	B	C	D	E
comittee	whom	once	home	since

5 Select the word below that is misspelt.

A	B	C	D	E
beret	embark	curiousity	apex	appalled

6 Select the word below that is misspelt.

A	B	C	D	E
dilemna	client	burn	bedroom	appalled

7 Select the word below that is misspelt.

A	B	C	D	E
acquire	abate	abstain	adept	existance

8 Select the word below that is misspelt.

A	B	C	D	E
futher	simile	sly	sham	sty

STOP AND WAIT FOR FURTHER INSTRUCTIONS

Antonyms

 INSTRUCTIONS

 YOU HAVE 5 MINUTES TO COMPLETE THE FOLLOWING SECTION.

YOU HAVE 15 QUESTIONS TO COMPLETE WITHIN THE TIME GIVEN.

EXAMPLE I

Which word is least similar to the following word:

light

A	B	C	D	E
dark	water	feather	bright	hill

The correct answer is A. This has already been marked in Example 1 in the Antonyms section of your answer sheet.

Practice Question 1

Which word is least similar to the following word:

smooth

A	B	C	D	E
allow	beneath	rough	whilst	shade

The correct answer is C. Please mark the answer C in Practice Question 1 in the Antonyms section of your answer sheet.

STOP AND WAIT FOR FURTHER INSTRUCTIONS

Which word is least similar to the following word:

① audible

A	B	C	D	E
inaudible	common	thrive	reaction	unfriendly

② immense

A	B	C	D	E
advance	selfish	success	tiny	narrow

③ just

A	B	C	D	E
simple	hinder	unjust	absurd	disadvantage

④ condone

A	B	C	D	E
condemn	loose	keep	common	victory

⑤ lazy

A	B	C	D	E
free	industrious	unwise	right	frank

⑥ essential

A	B	C	D	E
inessential	public	polite	encouraged	disobedient

⑦ leader

A	B	C	D	E
lazy	loose	deter	follower	dissuade

CONTINUE WORKING ⮕

8 disdain

A	B	C	D	E
success	failure	admiration	aggressive	awkward

9 prohibit

A	B	C	D	E
allow	valley	victory	dissuade	narrow

10 obedient

A	B	C	D	E
maintain	presence	extract	disobedient	preserve

11 prudent

A	B	C	D	E
imprudent	calm	dense	shallow	encouraged

12 inconspicuous

A	B	C	D	E
maintain	allow	thrive	lever	noticeable

13 wisdom

A	B	C	D	E
clear	silence	folly	maximum	find

14 ominous

A	B	C	D	E
auspicious	fright	repulsive	deceitful	reaction

15 abstain

A	B	C	D	E
frank	immigration	abundant	use	smart

STOP AND WAIT FOR FURTHER INSTRUCTIONS ⊗

Numeracy

INSTRUCTIONS

 YOU HAVE 9 MINUTES TO COMPLETE THE FOLLOWING SECTION.

YOU HAVE 18 QUESTIONS TO COMPLETE WITHIN THE TIME GIVEN.

EXAMPLES

Some of the questions within this section are not multiple choice. For these questions, write the answer to each question on the answer sheet by selecting the correct digits from the columns provided.

Example 1

Calculate 14 + 23

The correct answer is 37. This has already been marked in Example 1 in the Numeracy section of your answer sheet.

Practice Question 1

Calculate 83 – 75

The correct answer is 8. Please mark the answer in Practice Question 1 in the Numeracy section of your answer sheet. Note that a single-digit answer should be marked with a 0 in the left-hand column. So mark 08 on your answer sheet.

STOP AND WAIT FOR FURTHER INSTRUCTIONS

For the questions in this section that are not multiple choice, you should write the answer to the question on the answer sheet by selecting the digits from the columns of brackets.

(1) How many weeks are there in half of a non-leap year?

CONTINUE WORKING

② Calculate 60 + 2 × 2

③ Select the appropriate number or numbers to complete the sequence in place of the ? in the brackets below:

169, 15, 144, 14, 121, ?

④ Which of these is not divisible by 5?

20, 65, 95, 48, 100

⑤ Calculate how many sixths there are in the answer to the following:

$\frac{2}{3} + \frac{1}{6}$

⑥ If 0.2 were written as a fraction, with the numerator being 1, what would the denominator be?

⑦ If 0.585 were rounded to 2 significant figures, the answer would contain how many hundredths?

⑧ If 9.95 was rounded to 1 decimal place, and then the answer subtracted from 10, how many tenths would be in the answer?

⑨ Which of these is not divisible by 50?

200, 360, 150, 400, 50

| A | 200 | B | 360 | C | 150 |
| D | 400 | E | 50 | | |

⑩ Calculate the radius of the circle below, which has a diameter of 10 cm.

10 cm

| A | 10 | B | 31.4 | C | 3.14 |
| D | 25 | E | 5 | | |

CONTINUE WORKING

(11) Calculate the following:

The perimeter of a semi-circle with the straight edge measuring 10 cm.

A	20 cm		**B**	5 cm		**C**	31.4 cm
D	25.7 cm		**E**	15.7 cm			

(12) Calculate the mean value of the following data:

5, 3, 6, 8, 3, 6, 5, 6, 2, 5

A	36		**B**	49		**C**	4.9
D	5		**E**	4			

(13) Select an expression which describes the following:

The remainder of a cake, after 2 people have eaten some. The first person eats twice the amount of cake that the second person eats. The second person eats 1 slice. The cake is cut into 6 equal slices. The size of the whole cake is P. Both people eat all the cake they are served.

A	$\dfrac{3}{8}$		**B**	3		**C**	P
D	0.5P		**E**	3P			

(14) Consider the probability of the following situation:
If I roll a dice and it shows a 3, and then roll a second dice, what is the probability that the total of the dice will be higher than 3?

A	1 in 6		**B**	2 in 6		**C**	4 in 6
D	6 in 6		**E**	3 in 6			

(15) There are two parallel lines of equal length on a graph. The first line has coordinates starting at (0, 3) and ending at (4, 9). The second line starts at coordinates (3, 0). Find the coordinates of the end of the second line, if the second point of each line is the same direction from the first point.

A	(7, 6)		**B**	(6, 7)		**C**	(5, 4)
D	(−7, 6)		**E**	(7, −6)			

CONTINUE WORKING

(16) Calculate the following:

$\frac{1}{2} \times \frac{2}{7}$

A $\frac{1}{7}$ **B** $\frac{1}{14}$ **C** $\frac{2}{4}$

D $\frac{14}{2}$ **E** $\frac{2}{3}$

(17) Calculate the following:

$\frac{3}{4} \times \frac{8}{12}$

A $\frac{2}{5}$ **B** $\frac{1}{3}$ **C** $\frac{1}{2}$

D $\frac{12}{48}$ **E** $\frac{11}{16}$

(18) Calculate the following:

$\frac{3}{9} \div \frac{1}{3}$

A 1 **B** $\frac{1}{9}$ **C** $\frac{3}{9}$

D $\frac{4}{12}$ **E** $\frac{3}{24}$

END OF PAPER

Test B Paper 1

Instructions

1. Ensure you have pencils and an eraser with you.
2. Make sure you are able to see a clock or watch.
3. Write your name on the answer sheet.
4. Do not open the question booklet until you are told to do so by the audio instructions.
5. Listen carefully to the audio instructions given.
6. Mark your answers on the answer sheet only.
7. All workings must be completed on a separate piece of paper.
8. You should not use a calculator, dictionary or thesaurus at any point in this paper.
9. Move through the papers as quickly as possible and with care.
10. Follow the instructions at the foot of each page.
11. You should mark your answers with a horizontal strike, as shown on the answer sheet.
12. If you want to change your answer, ensure that you rub out your first answer and that your second answer is clearly more visible.
13. You can go back and review any questions that are within the section you are working on only. You must await further instructions before moving onto another section.

Symbols and Phrases used in the Tests

 Instructions    Time allowed for this section   Stop and wait for further instructions   Continue working

Comprehension

 YOU HAVE 8 MINUTES TO COMPLETE THE FOLLOWING SECTION.

YOU HAVE 10 QUESTIONS TO COMPLETE WITHIN THE TIME GIVEN.

EXAMPLES

Comprehension Example

Some people choose to start their Christmas shopping early in October. It has been reported that some people even buy their Christmas presents in the sales in August. In recent years, people have the option of purchasing their Christmas presents online.

Example 1

According to the passage, what is the earliest that people start their Christmas shopping?

A   In the preceding summer
B   In the preceding October
C   In the preceding November
D   Christmas Eve
E   In early December

The correct answer is A. This has already been marked in Example 1 in the Comprehension section of your answer sheet.

Practice Question 1

In recent years, what has caused a change in how people shop?

A   There are more shops
B   Shops are more crowded
C   You can easily organise your journey to the shops
D   New products are available
E   There has been a rise in use of the Internet

The correct answer is E. Please mark this in Practice Question 1 in the Comprehension section of your answer sheet.

STOP AND WAIT FOR FURTHER INSTRUCTIONS

Read the following passage, then answer the questions below.

The Georgian House

While sitting in their lounge, Helen and John both realised that their once beautifully decorated home had become uninspiring, tired and unfashionable.

"Are you thinking what I am thinking John?" Helen asked tentatively. "Yes, the lounge looks shabby and I am not sure that it looks special anymore," said John. The lounge had been designed with exquisite taste, and represented the pinnacle of Helen's talents, but it was now a shadow of its former self.

Helen had always been artistically minded and had initially wanted to be an interior designer. However, she had never managed to realise her dream. She loved colour and texture, and often changed the interior of her home according to the passing whims of fashion. She enjoyed redecorating her lounge walls in a more fashionable colour scheme. She was generally inspired by different, and often unusual influences. Sometimes, it would be the colour of an outfit which her friend was wearing, or the colour scheme featured in a magazine advertisement. On occasions, Helen had stayed in five-star hotels, which had so inspired her that she wanted to replicate the ambience in her home. However, she had recently been too busy to notice, as her elderly uncle had been suffering with a chronic illness, and she had been busy tending to his needs. The room which she had previously been so proud of, had now deteriorated.

Helen set to work to rejuvenate her lounge. The room continued to be important as her family spent most of their recreational time there. She decided that she would remove the existing colour scheme of red and gold, and would replace it with soft blue and grey hues that had become fashionable in recent years. The problem that she now faced was the carpet, which was coral in colour, and the rug which was gold and brown.

The next morning she rolled up the rug and placed it outside her front door with a note saying, "Please take!"

She then single-handedly pulled up the carpet. Instantly, the lounge appeared fresher. She realised that the room now looked much larger, and that the coral carpet had been quite oppressive.

Helen was now unsure as to how she should tackle what had become a rather large project. She thought how lucky it was that she did not have to remove any wallpaper.

Helen then bought some small samples of paint at her local ironmongers. The shopkeeper had seen the extensive collection of paint samples and had given her some good advice.

"Here is a little secret that only the best designers know." Helen was sure that she would know his secret. However, she was surprised when she learnt something new. "When deciding on the shade of paint, the only way you really and truly get an idea of how it is going to look, is by painting sample areas in the corners of the room".

CONTINUE WORKING

Helen was amazed that she had never thought of this! As she wandered home, happily swinging her hessian bag, she listened to the clattering of the paint pots. She relished the thought of removing the faded grandeur of her lounge and replacing it with exquisite colours which would highlight the traditional features of her rather wonderful Georgian house.

1 What does 'a shadow of its former self' mean?

A   More selfless
B   Less impressive
C   More showing
D   Less tasteful
E   Less oppressive

2 What is Helen's job?

A   Interior designer
B   Fashion designer
C   Advertising executive
D   Doctor
E   Passage does not say

3 Which of these phrases is mentioned as having inspired Helen in the past?

A   A hospital in which her uncle had been recovering
B   Advertisements on the television
C   Restaurants which she had visited
D   Colourful clothes and luxurious hotels
E   Photographs in shop windows

4 What did Helen do with the carpet?

A   She wrote a note and attached it to the carpet
B   She rolled it up and put it outside
C   She removed it on her own
D   It was left 'in situ'
E   It was replaced with a new carpet

5 What is the meaning of the word 'chronic'?

A   Occurring in later life
B   Occurring on the weekend
C   Occurring at intermittent intervals
D   Occurring for a short period
E   Occurring for a long period

CONTINUE WORKING

6 What type of word is 'pinnacle'?

A Verb
B Noun
C Adjective
D Adverb
E Pronoun

7 Why had Helen not noticed that her lounge had become shabby?

A Because she had been busy with recreational activities
B Because she had been on holiday
C Because she had been designing advertisements
D Because she had been staying in five-star hotels
E Because a family member had been ill

8 Why was Helen's lounge so important?

A Because the wallpaper was nice
B Because her elderly uncle was coming to stay
C Because it was close to the kitchen
D Because it was the place where her family spent their time
E Because Helen had deteriorated

9 What did Helen learn from the shopkeeper?

A A tradition
B A design secret
C Some upsetting news
D A new piece of fabric
E A new carpet

10 What colours did Helen want to use in her rejuvenated lounge?

A Grey and red tones
B Coral and grey tones
C Blue and coral tones
D Red and gold tones
E Grey and blue tones

STOP AND WAIT FOR FURTHER INSTRUCTIONS

Shuffled Sentences

INSTRUCTIONS

 YOU HAVE 10 MINUTES TO COMPLETE THE FOLLOWING SECTION.

YOU HAVE 15 QUESTIONS TO COMPLETE WITHIN THE TIME GIVEN.

EXAMPLES

Example 1

The following sentence is shuffled and also contains one unnecessary word. Rearrange the sentence correctly, in order to identify the unnecessary word.

dog the ran fetch the to stick gluing.

A	B	C	D	E
gluing	dog	ran	the	stick

The correct answer is A. This has already been marked in Example 1 in the Shuffled Sentences section of your answer sheet.

Practice Question 1

The following sentence is shuffled and also contains one unnecessary word. Rearrange the sentence correctly, in order to identify the unnecessary word.

pushed Emma stood up and closed the table under the chair.

A	B	C	D	E
chair	stood	under	closed	Emma

The correct answer is D. Please mark this in Practice Question 1 in the Shuffled Sentences section of your answer sheet.

STOP AND WAIT FOR FURTHER INSTRUCTIONS

Each sentence below is shuffled and also contains one unnecessary word.
Rearrange each sentence correctly, in order to identify the unnecessary word.

(1) he sitting in his bought morning that the engine enjoyed boy car which had.

A	B	C	D	E
the	in	engine	car	boy

(2) biscuit despite awful hungry was still girl eating her the last.

A	B	C	D	E
biscuit	the	her	awful	last

(3) like which brand music we listening to show radio classical the plays.

A	B	C	D	E
show	brand	listening	which	plays

(4) a dancer young became talented the a man training result as extend of his.

A	B	C	D	E
dancer	became	of	result	extend

(5) gardening courageous most according people to is exercise good.

A	B	C	D	E
courageous	to	is	gardening	exercise

(6) promptly overhead the started competition despite o' clock ten at quietly thunderstorm the.

A	B	C	D	E
the	at	quietly	overhead	despite

(7) house lengthy reading completed he finally novel the.

A	B	C	D	E
he	and	completed	novel	house

CONTINUE WORKING

8 ways according many you in scientists for eggs good are some to severe.

A	B	C	D	E
some	severe	good	for	ways

9 day dentists teeth flossed recommend brushing a twice your all.

A	B	C	D	E
all	a	day	flossed	twice

10 electric and singers chargeable was atmosphere the the amazing were.

A	B	C	D	E
chargeable	singers	and	the	electric

11 milk I out still although heavily have supermarket the I been run today to have of.

A	B	C	D	E
I	today	heavily	out	still

12 attractive arranged designer the sketch interior an has produced.

A	B	C	D	E
arranged	designer	of	the	house

13 forward wonderful standard we looking had time we our to not were party aunt's a but.

A	B	C	D	E
looking	a	to	our	standard

14 barking awoken most neighbours threw the the by of were dog.

A	B	C	D	E
barking	by	the	threw	most

15 calm needs overgrown the mowing grass garden the in.

A	B	C	D	E
calm	needs	for	garden	in

STOP AND WAIT FOR FURTHER INSTRUCTIONS

Numeracy

 YOU HAVE 6 MINUTES TO COMPLETE THE FOLLOWING SECTION.

YOU HAVE 13 QUESTIONS TO COMPLETE WITHIN THE TIME GIVEN.

EXAMPLES

The questions within this section are not multiple choice. Write the answer to each question on the answer sheet by selecting the correct digits from the columns provided.

Example 1

Calculate 14 + 23

The correct answer is 37. This has already been marked in Example 1 in the Numeracy section of your answer sheet.

Practice Question 1

Calculate 83 – 75

The correct answer is 8. Please mark this in Practice Question 1 in the Numeracy section of your answer sheet. Note that a single-digit answer should be marked with a 0 in the left-hand column, so mark 08 on your answer sheet.

STOP AND WAIT FOR FURTHER INSTRUCTIONS

(1) How many days are there between the following 2 dates (inclusive):

3rd February 2015 to 2nd March 2015

(2) How many weeks in 56 days?

(3) Look at the picture of the triangle.

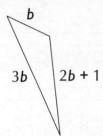

b

$3b$ $2b + 1$

If $b = 3$, calculate the length of the perimeter in centimetres.

(4) I walk at 2.5 mph. The bus stop is 0.5 miles away from home. How long in minutes is the walk from home to the bus stop?

(5) Two years ago Jenny was two years younger than Kate. If Kate is now 12, how old is Jenny?

(6) Select the appropriate number or numbers to complete the sequence in place of the ? in the brackets below.

(36, 20, 12, 8, ?, 5)

(7) What is the 18th term in the following series:

105, 100, 95, 90, 85...

(8) The petrol tank in my car is currently $\frac{2}{3}$ full. The capacity of the tank is

84 litres. How many more litres will it hold?

(9) Calculate the number of 200 ml cups I can fill from a 1.5 litre bottle of water.

(10) How many quarters of an hour are there in 180 minutes?

(11) How many vertices are there on a triangular prism?

(12) Calculate the following:

$8 + (2 \times 13)$

(13) Calculate the following:

$583 - 495$

STOP AND WAIT FOR FURTHER INSTRUCTIONS ⊗

Problem Solving

INSTRUCTIONS

 YOU HAVE 10 MINUTES TO COMPLETE THE FOLLOWING SECTION.

YOU HAVE 10 QUESTIONS TO COMPLETE WITHIN THE TIME GIVEN.

EXAMPLES

A £2.60	B £3.40	C £2.40	D 25	E £1.35
F £3.60	G 14	H 31	I 28	J 34

Example 1

Calculate the following:

If I buy five apples at 20p each, and four bananas at 35p each, how much change will I receive if I pay with a £5 note.

The correct answer is A. This has already been marked in Example 1 in the Problem Solving section of your answer sheet.

Practice Question 1

Calculate the following:

There are 17 people on a bus when it arrives at a bus stop. Eleven people get on the bus, and three get off. How many people are then left on the bus?

The correct answer is D. Please mark this in Practice Question 1 in the Problem Solving section of your answer sheet.

STOP AND WAIT FOR FURTHER INSTRUCTIONS

A £450	B 3	C 24	D £28,900	E £25,000
F £1,200	G 12	H £1,100	I £150	J 13

Select an answer to each question from the 10 different possible answers in the table above. You may use an answer for more than one question.

1. Alison is having a new kitchen put into her house. The kitchen is supposed to be fitted by 4 men who will complete the kitchen in 6 days. However, only 2 of the men are available to fit the kitchen. If all of the men work at the same speed, how many days will it take the 2 men to fit the kitchen?

2. The floor is slightly larger than before as the kitchen has been extended. The floor now measures 6 m in length by 4 m in width. How many metres squared is the area of the floor now?

3. The floor is to be covered with large square tiles. Each edge of a tile measures 50 cm. How many boxes of tiles are required, if each box contains 40 tiles?

4. The new oven has a discount of 25% as it is in the sale. The original price was £600. What is the discount on the oven?

5. Alison borrowed £20,000 from the bank to pay for the new kitchen extension. The bank charges Alison interest of 6% each year on the amount that she borrowed. How much interest does the bank charge each year?

6. The fridge has $\frac{1}{3}$ off the original price, as it too is in the sale. If the sale price is £300, what was the original price?

7. The planning and building of the kitchen extension took three months in total. How many weeks was this?

8. When completed, the new extended kitchen cost £21,100 in total. How much more was this than the amount Alison first borrowed from the bank?

9. Alison is planning to sell her house. Before the kitchen extension, she had her house valued. It was valued then at £200,000. The house was valued again after the extension at £250,000. Taking into account how much Alison spent on her new kitchen, how much will Alison gain from the new kitchen extension, if she sells the house for the new value?

10. The new value of Alison's house after the extension is 10 times the price paid when she bought the house 34 years ago. How much did Alison pay for the house 34 years ago?

STOP AND WAIT FOR FURTHER INSTRUCTIONS

Synonyms

 YOU HAVE 5 MINUTES TO COMPLETE THE FOLLOWING SECTION.

YOU HAVE 23 QUESTIONS TO COMPLETE WITHIN THE TIME GIVEN.

EXAMPLES

Example 1

Select the word that is most similar in meaning to the following word:

cold

A	B	C	D	E
collect	fence	foggy	windy	chilly

The correct answer is E. This has already been marked in Example 1 in the Synonyms section of your answer sheet.

Practice Question 1

Select the word that is most similar in meaning to the following word:

start

A	B	C	D	E
cramped	begin	free	without	change

The correct answer is B. Please mark this in Practice Question 1 in the Synonyms section of your answer sheet.

STOP AND WAIT FOR FURTHER INSTRUCTIONS

Select the word from each table that is most similar in meaning to the word above the table.

(1) pitiful

A	B	C	D	E
deep	fanciful	insignificant	gleeful	serene

(2) curvature

A	B	C	D	E
straight	arc	duplicate	certain	treasured

(3) misfortune

A	B	C	D	E
tiresome	carefully	transfer	setback	boast

(4) futile

A	B	C	D	E
lush	assess	determined	timid	ineffective

(5) escarpment

A	B	C	D	E
cliff	absurd	dip	average	mandatory

(6) woe

A	B	C	D	E
courage	triumph	boredom	civility	anguish

(7) perpendicular

A	B	C	D	E
familiar	violet	upright	aspect	decline

CONTINUE WORKING ➡

8 outside

A	B	C	D	E
unravel	ending	exterior	core	revolve

9 slight

A	B	C	D	E
traitor	grand	scent	observe	slender

10 void

A	B	C	D	E
prevent	gap	foil	lavish	equilibrium

11 peculiar

A	B	C	D	E
loyal	spectacular	curious	frantic	eruption

12 talented

A	B	C	D	E
passage	ordinary	distorted	accomplished	incompetent

13 union

A	B	C	D	E
alliance	resolve	ambition	distraction	repetition

14 particulars

A	B	C	D	E
role	resumption	details	senses	revolutions

15 quirky

A	B	C	D	E
menace	unconventional	liable	agility	smirk

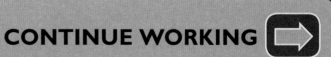

CONTINUE WORKING

16 sour

A	B	C	D	E
charming	ponder	acrimonious	trusted	delightful

17 compound

A	B	C	D	E
blend	conquer	rise	beaming	inscription

18 utmost

A	B	C	D	E
utter	lest	exterior	moisten	ultimate

19 flourish

A	B	C	D	E
thrive	wither	fragment	imitate	flawed

20 neutral

A	B	C	D	E
indifferent	navigation	drab	deduct	sift

21 type

A	B	C	D	E
embed	ability	attire	contact	mode

22 spectacle

A	B	C	D	E
spiritual	pound	parade	improvise	analysis

23 estimate

A	B	C	D	E
projection	quarrel	engagement	supple	deterioration

STOP AND WAIT FOR FURTHER INSTRUCTIONS

Non-Verbal Reasoning

 ## INSTRUCTIONS

 YOU HAVE 6 MINUTES TO COMPLETE THE FOLLOWING SECTION.

YOU HAVE 14 QUESTIONS TO COMPLETE WITHIN THE TIME GIVEN.

EXAMPLES

COMPLETE THE SEQUENCE Example 1

Select the picture from the bottom row that will complete the sequence in place of the ? in the top row.

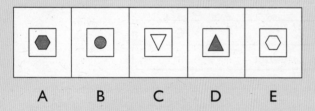

A   B   C   D   E

The correct answer is C. This has already been marked in Example 1 in the Non-Verbal Reasoning section of your answer sheet.

CONTINUE WORKING

COMPLETE THE SEQUENCE Practice Question 1

Select the picture from the bottom row that will complete the sequence in place of the ? in the top row.

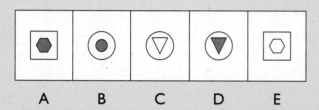

A   B   C   D   E

The correct answer is D. Please mark this in Practice Question 1 in the Non-Verbal Reasoning section of your answer sheet.

STOP AND WAIT FOR FURTHER INSTRUCTIONS

Select the correct pictures from the bottom row in order to finish the incomplete sequence on the top row. One picture should be chosen for Q1 and another picture for Q2.

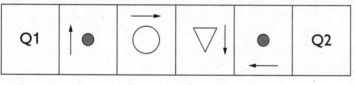

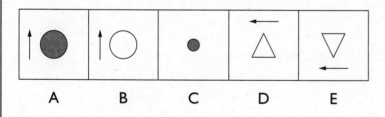

A   B   C   D   E

CONTINUE WORKING

Select the correct pictures from the bottom row in order to finish the incomplete sequence on the top row. One picture should be chosen for Q3 and another picture for Q4.

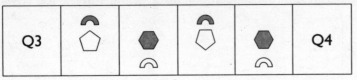

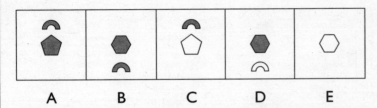

A   B   C   D   E

Select the correct pictures from the bottom row in order to finish the incomplete sequence on the top row. One picture should be chosen for Q5 and another picture for Q6.

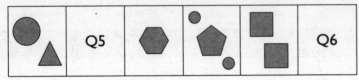

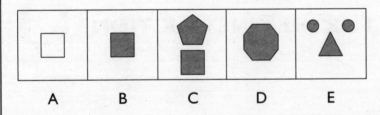

A   B   C   D   E

Select the correct pictures from the bottom row in order to finish the incomplete sequence on the top row. One picture should be chosen for Q7 and another picture for Q8.

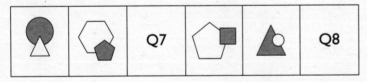

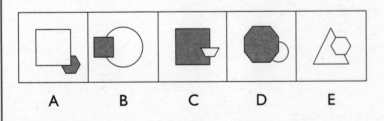

A   B   C   D   E

CONTINUE WORKING

Select the correct pictures from the bottom row in order to finish the incomplete sequence on the top row. One picture should be chosen for Q9 and another picture for Q10.

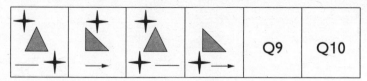

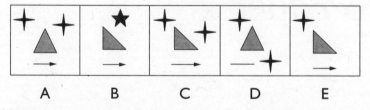

A   B   C   D   E

Select the correct pictures from the bottom row in order to finish the incomplete sequence on the top row. One picture should be chosen for Q11 and another picture for Q12.

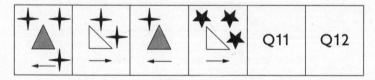

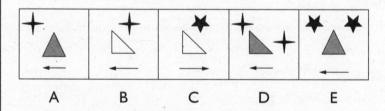

A   B   C   D   E

Select the correct pictures from the bottom row in order to finish the incomplete sequence on the top row. One picture should be chosen for Q13 and another picture for Q14.

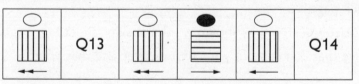

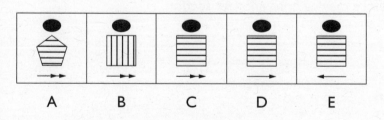

A   B   C   D   E

END OF PAPER

Test B Paper 2

Instructions

1. Ensure you have pencils and an eraser with you.

2. Make sure you are able to see a clock or watch.

3. Write your name on the answer sheet.

4. Do not open the question booklet until you are told to do so by the audio instructions.

5. Listen carefully to the audio instructions given.

6. Mark your answers on the answer sheet only.

7. All workings must be completed on a separate piece of paper.

8. You should not use a calculator, dictionary or thesaurus at any point in this paper.

9. Move through the paper as quickly as possible and with care.

10. Follow the instructions at the foot of each page.

11. You should mark your answers with a horizontal strike, as shown on the answer sheet.

12. If you want to change your answer, ensure that you rub out your first answer and that your second answer is clearly more visible.

13. You can go back and review any questions that are within the section you are working on only. You must await further instructions before moving onto another section.

Symbols and Phrases used in the Tests

 Instructions  Time allowed for this section Stop and wait for further instructions Continue working

Problem Solving

 INSTRUCTIONS

 YOU HAVE 12 MINUTES TO COMPLETE THE FOLLOWING SECTION.

YOU HAVE 10 QUESTIONS TO COMPLETE WITHIN THE TIME GIVEN.

EXAMPLES

A	B	C	D	E	F	G	H	I	J
£2.60	£3.40	£2.40	25	£1.35	£3.60	14	31	28	34

Example 1

Calculate the following:

If I buy 5 apples at 20p each and 4 bananas at 35p each, how much change will I receive if I pay with a £5 note?

The correct answer is A. This has been marked in Example 1 in the Problem Solving section of your answer sheet.

Practice Question 1

Calculate the following:

There are 17 people on a bus when it arrives at a bus stop.
11 people get on the bus and 3 get off. How many people are then left on the bus?

The correct answer is D. Please mark the answer D in the Problem Solving section of your answer sheet.

STOP AND WAIT FOR FURTHER INSTRUCTIONS

Several questions will follow for you to answer.

A	B	C	D	E	F	G	H	I	J
£500	06:00	8	17:00	9	05:00	£20	£1,100	£550	10

Select an answer to each question from the possible answers in the table above.
You may use an answer for more than one question.

(1) Sara and her family are going on a two-week holiday to Australia. Sara is married to Jack. They have two children, Greg and Horace, aged 15 and 13 respectively at the time of the holiday. The flights to Australia from their home in London cost £3,300 in total for the family of four. If the adult tickets were twice the price of the child tickets, how much did the flights for each child cost? (Child tickets are for under-16s.)

(2) The flight stops in Singapore before refuelling to continue to Sydney, Australia. The stopover time in Singapore is three hours before taking off again for Sydney. Take off is scheduled for 09:00 on 21 December 2015 from London. The flight is due to arrive in Singapore at 07:00 (Singapore time) the following day. Singapore is eight hours ahead of London. If the flight time to Sydney from Singapore is five hours, when is the flight scheduled to arrive in Sydney using Sydney time, which is two hours ahead of Singapore?

(3) How many hours ahead of London is Sydney?

(4) Passengers in London were able to check-in at the airport three hours before the scheduled take-off time. What time could passengers on the London to Sydney flight check-in from?

(5) The family organised a taxi to collect them from their London home in Putney, one hour before the earliest check-in time. The taxi collected the family on time. What time was this?

(6) The exchange rate at the time the family purchased some travellers cheques in Australian Dollars, was $1.75 (Australian Dollars):£1 (British Pounds).

Excluding any transaction fee, how much did it cost the family in pounds to buy $1,925 (Australian Dollars)?

(7) The family also changed some British pounds into Australian Dollars before they left London at the same rate ($1.75:£1). They received $875 in Australian Dollars. Excluding any transaction fee, how much did this cost them in pounds?

CONTINUE WORKING

(8) Horace bought some surf shorts in Sydney out of the money changed before they left London. The shorts were originally $70. They were on sale with a discount on the original price of 50%. How much did the surf shorts cost Horace in British Pounds?

(9) On the flight from London bound for Sydney, there were 468 passengers who boarded the flight in London. Fifteen of these passengers only had tickets to Singapore, as this was their final destination. If 461 passengers arrived in Sydney, how many passengers boarded the plane for the first leg of their journey in Singapore?

(10) Whilst queuing for the Sydney Aquarium, Greg saw one of his old school friends, Ian Baldwin, who he had not seen since Christmas in 2005. Approximately how many years is it since Greg last saw Ian Baldwin?

STOP AND WAIT FOR FURTHER INSTRUCTIONS ⬡✕

Cloze

 YOU HAVE 10 MINUTES TO COMPLETE THE FOLLOWING SECTION.

YOU HAVE 20 QUESTIONS TO COMPLETE WITHIN THE TIME GIVEN.

EXAMPLES

Example 1

Read the sentence below and select the most appropriate word from the table.

A	B	C	D	E
backdrop	carefully	drawer	disadvantage	dilution

The undulating hills were the perfect Q1 _____ for the watercolour painting.

Please select your answer to go in the place of Q1 in the sentence above.

The correct answer is A. This has already been marked in Example 1 in the Cloze section of your answer sheet.

Practice Question 1

Read the sentence below and select the most appropriate word from the table.

A	B	C	D	E
had	interior	success	attend	absent

The girl decided she would like to Q2 _____ the party.

Please select your answer to go in the place of Q2 in the sentence above.

The correct answer is D. Please mark the answer D in Practice Question 1 in the Cloze section of your answer sheet.

STOP AND WAIT FOR FURTHER INSTRUCTIONS

Read the following passage and select the most appropriate word from the table below by choosing the letter above the word. There are 10 questions. For example, Q1 is where you should put your answer to Question 1 on your answer sheet.

A	B	C	D	E
forming	unearthed	technical	visiting	carefully
F	**G**	**H**	**I**	**J**
apparent	advertisement	graveyard	guided	remote

An Archaeologist's Response

Dear Mrs Bates,

I would like to confirm my interest in your Q1 _____ for an archaeologist working on the site in Northamptonshire.

As stated in the job description, I would be happy to work on a contract basis with the hope of eventually Q2 _____ part of your core team of archaeologists.

I have previous experience on archaeological digs around the UK and also overseas. I am skilled in the necessary Q3 _____ knowledge required when on site.

I worked for a number of weeks on a project where Roman remains were found in a Q4 _____ field in Worcestershire. Once we had started the dig, it became Q5 _____ that the site was of great interest and importance. In the last few weeks of the dig, we Q6 _____ a previously undiscovered mosaic. The tesserae were Q7 _____ removed and were then placed in a local museum.

I then worked on a project in a Q8 _____ in London. I was a member of a team who were part of a 'rescue archaeology' project. We had no longer than four weeks to excavate and record the findings within the graveyard, before the developers built a teashop on the site. I learned a great deal from this project and was pleased to have been chosen to work on such a prestigious project of national importance.

I would also like to state that at various points in time, I have been asked to provide Q9 _____ tours for amateur archaeologists Q10 _____ the sites. I would be very happy to provide this service, should you wish me to assist in this way.

Yours sincerely,

Max Granger

CONTINUE WORKING

Read the following passage and select the most appropriate word from the table below, by selecting the letter above the word. There are 10 questions. For example, Q11 is where you should put your answer to Question 11 on your answer sheet.

A	B	C	D	E
provisions	treacherous	necessary	working	reputable
F	G	H	I	J
tow	breakdown	estimated	travelling	motorists

Instructions for the Winter Months

Q11 _____ by car in the winter months is a concern for many
Q12 _____ and can add to the statistics for weather-related deaths. Here are some guidelines for consideration when driving in sub-zero conditions.

- What should you take with you on a long journey?

  You should take a shovel in case you are stuck in a snowdrift.

  Take blankets and enough clothing layers to keep you warm in the event of a
  Q13 _____.

  Take some food and drinks with you. It is not uncommon for traffic to be at a standstill for many hours and so you should have Q14 _____ with you for that occurrence.

- What happens if you breakdown?

  Do you have cover from a Q15 _____ company which you can contact in the event of a breakdown? Would you want them to Q16 _____ your car to the nearest garage or would you want them to take you to your home? How much will this cost?

- Is there anything else you can do to prepare for your journey?

  If you know that the conditions are Q17 _____ then snow chains for your wheels are recommended.

  Contact the person who you are travelling to see, and tell them your
  Q18 _____ time of arrival.

- Is your car in good Q19 _____ order?

  Check your oil levels and make sure you have more than enough fuel to reach your destination.

  Avoid travelling unless it is absolutely Q20 _____.

STOP AND WAIT FOR FURTHER INSTRUCTIONS

Non-Verbal Reasoning

 YOU HAVE 8 MINUTES TO COMPLETE THE FOLLOWING SECTION.

YOU HAVE 13 QUESTIONS TO COMPLETE WITHIN THE TIME GIVEN.

EXAMPLES

CUBE NET Example 1

Look at the cube net. Select the only cube that could be formed from the net below.

The correct answer is E. This has already been marked in Example 1 in the Non-Verbal Reasoning section of your answer sheet.

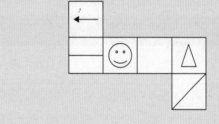

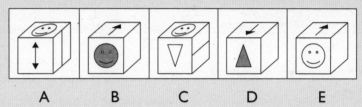

A   B   C   D   E

CUBE NET Practice Question 1

Look at the cube net. Select the only cube that could be formed from the net below.

The correct answer is A. Please mark this in Practice Question 1 in the Non-Verbal Reasoning section of your answer sheet.

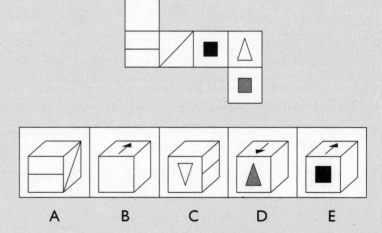

A   B   C   D   E

CONTINUE WORKING

LEAST SIMILAR Example 2

Select the image that is least similar to the other images.

The correct answer is B. This has already been marked in Example 2 in the Non-Verbal Reasoning section of your answer sheet.

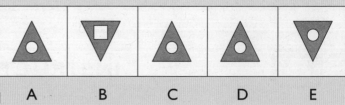

A   B   C   D   E

LEAST SIMILAR Practice Question 2

Select the image that is least similar to the other images.

The correct answer is E. Please mark this in Practice Question 2 in the Non-Verbal Reasoning section of your answer sheet.

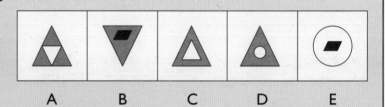

A   B   C   D   E

STOP AND WAIT FOR FURTHER INSTRUCTIONS

(1) Select the image that is least similar to the other images.

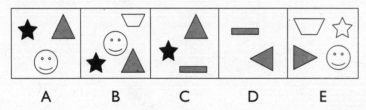

A   B   C   D   E

(2) Select the image that is least similar to the other images.

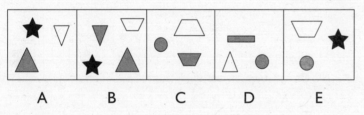

A   B   C   D   E

CONTINUE WORKING

(3) Select the image that is least similar to the other images.

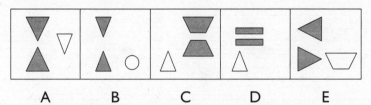

A   B   C   D   E

(4) Select the image that is least similar to the other images.

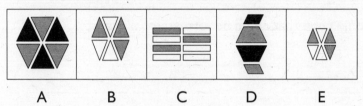

A   B   C   D   E

(5) Select the image that is least similar to the other images.

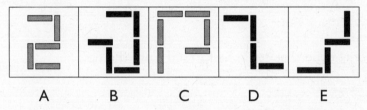

A   B   C   D   E

(6) Select the image that is least similar to the other images.

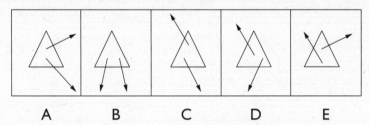

A   B   C   D   E

(7) Look at the cube net. Select the only cube that could be formed from the net.

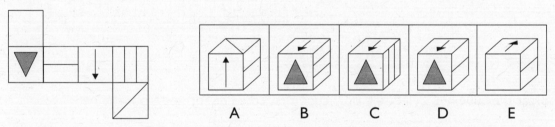

A   B   C   D   E

(8) Look at the cube net. Select the only cube that could be formed from the net.

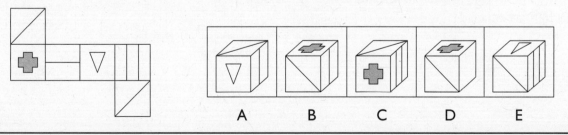

A   B   C   D   E

CONTINUE WORKING

9 Look at the cube net. Select the only cube that could be formed from the net.

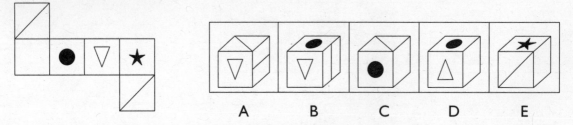

A   B   C   D   E

10 Look at the cube net. Select the only cube that could be formed from the net.

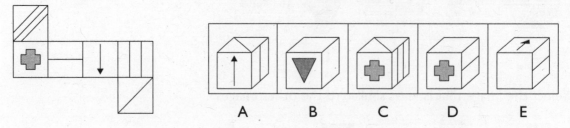

A   B   C   D   E

11 Look at the cube net. Select the only cube that could be formed from the net.

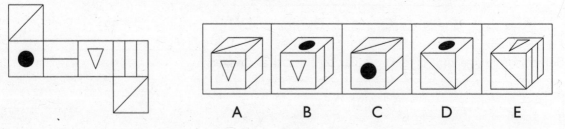

A   B   C   D   E

12 Look at the cube net. Select the only cube that could be formed from the net.

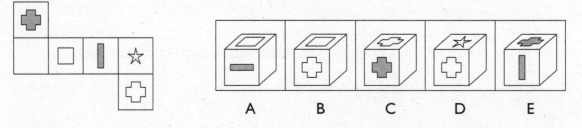

A   B   C   D   E

13 Look at the cube net. Select the only cube that could be formed from the net.

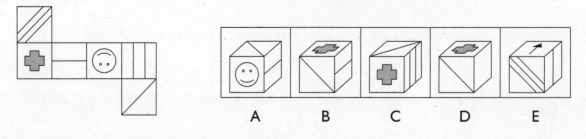

A   B   C   D   E

STOP AND WAIT FOR FURTHER INSTRUCTIONS ⊗

Antonyms

INSTRUCTIONS

 YOU HAVE 5 MINUTES TO COMPLETE THE FOLLOWING SECTION.

YOU HAVE 15 QUESTIONS TO COMPLETE WITHIN THE TIME GIVEN.

EXAMPLES

Example 1

Select the word that is least similar to the following word:

light

A	B	C	D	E
dark	water	feather	bright	hill

The correct answer is A dark. This has already been marked in Example 1 in the Antonyms section of your answer sheet.

Practice Question 1

Select the word that is least similar to the following word:

smooth

A	B	C	D	E
allow	beneath	rough	whilst	shade

The correct answer is C rough. Please mark the answer C in Practice Question 1 in the Antonyms section of your answer sheet.

STOP AND WAIT FOR FURTHER INSTRUCTIONS

In each row, select the word from the table that is least similar to the word above the table.

(1) interested

A	B	C	D	E
straight	animated	apathetic	vivid	decent

(2) lush

A	B	C	D	E
barren	just	reliable	frank	jovial

(3) durable

A	B	C	D	E
irritable	unreliable	upbeat	agitated	bustling

(4) detect

A	B	C	D	E
delicate	slight	find	flaw	hide

(5) eschew

A	B	C	D	E
shun	dodge	embrace	avoid	order

(6) agreement

A	B	C	D	E
harmony	dispute	unison	chorus	compatible

CONTINUE WORKING ⏵

(7) accumulate

A	B	C	D	E
hoard	divide	regime	readiness	vague

(8) arid

A	B	C	D	E
serene	barren	fertile	review	design

(9) replica

A	B	C	D	E
regain	original	defence	greet	inhabitant

(10) solo

A	B	C	D	E
isolation	typhoon	titan	refuge	combined

(11) sorrow

A	B	C	D	E
obnoxious	cheer	externally	dissect	grief

(12) dirty

A	B	C	D	E
intensive	apparent	purify	vivid	gaudy

CONTINUE WORKING ▶

13 delicious

A	B	C	D	E
precedence	quibble	variable	appetising	bland

14 naïve

A	B	C	D	E
revive	experienced	tactful	uphold	headway

15 demote

A	B	C	D	E
distinctly	upgrade	impulse	elevate	contort

STOP AND WAIT FOR FURTHER INSTRUCTIONS ✖

Numeracy

 YOU HAVE 10 MINUTES TO COMPLETE THE FOLLOWING SECTION.

YOU HAVE 18 QUESTIONS TO COMPLETE WITHIN THE TIME GIVEN.

EXAMPLES

The questions within this section are not multiple-choice. Write the answer to each question on the answer sheet by selecting the correct digits from the columns provided.

Example 1

Calculate 14 + 23

The correct answer is 37. This has already been marked in Example 1 in the Numeracy section of your answer sheet.

Practice Question 1

Calculate 83 – 75

The correct answer is 8. Write the answer in Practice Question 1 in the Numeracy section of the answer sheet. Note that a single-digit answer should be marked with a 0 in the left-hand column, so mark 08 on your answer sheet.

STOP AND WAIT FOR FURTHER INSTRUCTIONS

(1) Calculate the following:

274 − 175

(2) Find the missing number to replace ? to make the equation correct:

47 − 14 = 3 × ?

(3) Calculate the next number in the following sequence:

7, 8, 10, 13, 17, ?

(4) What is the number if 61 is 3 less than 8 times the number?

(5) Look at the Venn Diagram showing information about children in a class.

Children

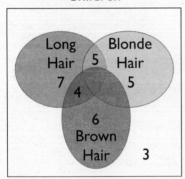

How many of the children had long hair, blonde hair or brown hair?

(6) How many days are in September?

(7) Calculate the following:

−12 + 19

(8) What is the range of the following shoe sizes:

3, 5, 7, 2, 8, 6, 3, 4, 5, 7, 4, 1, 6, 9, 4

CONTINUE WORKING ▷

(9) Jackie paid £64 for a bike after a 20% discount. What was the original price in £ of the bike?

(10) Find the value of y if:

$21 - y = 2y$

(11) Jay has three times as many cards as Judy. Judy has twice as many as Martin. There are 252 cards in total. How many cards does Judy have?

(12) Calculate:

91 divided by 7

(13) How many sixths of a cake are there in three whole cakes?

(14) What is the smallest number of coins from which I could make £2.89 exactly?

(15) If eight children have each received seven Christmas cards, how many Christmas cards have the eight children received in total?

(16) If the temperature on 2 January was −3°C, and the temperature on 7 January was −11°C, by how many °C had the temperature dropped between these two dates?

(17) There are twice as many teachers in Woodchurch Primary School as there were 20 years ago. There are 14 teachers currently. How many teachers were there 20 years ago?

(18) In five years' time, I will be nine years younger than my older sister and my older sister will be a third of my mother's age. My mother is 40 now. How old am I now?

END OF PAPER

THIS PAGE HAS DELIBERATELY BEEN LEFT BLANK

Answers to Test A Paper 1

Comprehension

Q1 *C*
The caves are just under 18,000 years old, so the correct option is less than 20,000 years old

Q2 *E*
The vast majority of the paintings are of animals

Q3 *A*
To allow the caves to be preserved

Q4 *D*
Fragments of sculptures and large buildings

Q5 *A*
In Italy

Q6 *B*
Paintings looked more realistic

Q7 *E*
To make an investment

Q8 *B*
Art placed in an area to benefit a community, or newly developed area

Q9 *E*
Noticeable

Q10 *D*
Modern art is often controversial

Shuffled Sentences

Q1 *C*
reserve
I think the book is better than the film.

Q2 *A*
paint
She drew the curtains to keep the warmth in.

Q3 *A*
play
The record number of claims kept the insurance firm busy.

Q4 *C*
up
The duck down pillows are more comfortable.

Q5 *D*
dough
You need to be quick to answer the question.

Q6 *E since*
Despite the weather the barbecue went ahead.

Q7 *D*
horse
The building was not stable following the earthquake.

Q8 *A*
stair
The girl continued to stare up at her.

Q9 *C*
blind
She drew a deep breath before beginning her speech.

Q10 *B*
tried
The sofa was looking tired after a number of years of use.

Q11 *E*
rain
The reign of the current monarch was coming to an end.

Q12 *B*
small
Roger kicked the ball through the window.

Q13 *C*
in
The accident caused heavy traffic on the motorway.

Q14 *A*
earlier
Jon is due to meet Eva at noon.

Q15 *D*
light
The guests felt rather bloated after their substantial dinner.

Numeracy

Q1 *(11)*
$3 \times 5 = 15$, $15 - 4 = 11$ uses order of operations rules BODMAS

Q2 *(22)*
$4 \div 2 = 2$, $24 - 2 = 22$ uses order of operations rules BODMAS

Q3 (16)
$6 \div 3 = 2, 18 - 2 = 16$ uses order of operations rules BODMAS

Q4 (03)
$1 + 2 = 3$ The next number is the sum of the last 2 numbers (Fibonacci sequence).

Q5 (13)
range is highest value less the lowest value, $14 - 1 = 13$

Q6 (17)
When 17 is divided by 7 there is a remainder of 3.

Q7 (19)
This does not divide exactly into 63, as there is a remainder of 6.

Q8 (06)
This is the only factor of both 18 and 48.

Q9 (03)
$n + 3 = n + n$ (n is my age now) so $n = 3$

Q10 (12)
Alan is 11 now, so will be 12 in 1 year from now.

Q11 (07)
April is month 4, November is month 11, so $11 - 4 = 7$ months.

Q12 (39)
There are exactly 52 weeks in a non-leap year, which is 12 months long.
So in 3 months, or quarter of a year, there will be $52 \div 4 = 13$ weeks, and in 9 months there are $52 - 13 = 39$ weeks.

Q13 (43)
We are looking for a number which is 7 more than a multiple of 9, and between 40 and 50. Try these multiples of 9 : 27, 36, 45. When 7 is added to each, this gives: 34, 43 and 52, so 43 is the only answer between 40 and 50.

Problem Solving

Q1 **D**
$2 : 3 : 5$
Simplifying the ratio $10 : 15 : 25$ (by dividing by 5)

Q2 **B**
6 minutes.
I actually finish buying coffee at 7.40 am. The only answer option that means the train departs at or after 7.40 is B.

Q3 **E**
12
60% girls, so 40% must be boys; 10% of 30 is 3, so 40% of 30 is $4 \times 3 = 12$

Q4 **A**
21
60% of (30 + 5). 10% of 35 is 3.5, 60% of 35 is $6 \times 3.5 = 21$

Q5 **D**
$2 : 3$
40% boys 60% girls, 14 boys and 21 girls, simplifies to $2 : 3$ (by dividing by 7)

Q6 **A**
Just under 20 minutes
3 buses every hour or 60 minutes, means one bus every 20 minutes as they are always on time. If you just missed a bus, you would have just under 20 minutes to wait until the next bus.

Q7 **C**
10 minutes
The longest is 20 minutes and shortest is 0 minutes, so the average time is $\frac{(0 + 20)}{2} = 10$ minutes.

Q8 **D**
9 mph
3 miles in 20 minutes means the bus travels 9 miles in 60 minutes, so 9 miles per hour.

Q9 **A**
6 hrs 35 mins, 2 hours 50 plus 3 hours 45 mins, from 9:10 a.m. to 3:45 p.m.

Q10 **E**
girls 1329, boys 1320, teachers 198,
Boys = 2847 (all) − 1527(teachers and girls) = 1320

Synonyms

Q1	**E** plenty	**Q13**	**B** dependent
Q2	**B** calm	**Q14**	**D** convex
Q3	**C** inflexible	**Q15**	**A** apathetic
Q4	**D** volatile	**Q16**	**D** crate
Q5	**E** sad	**Q17**	**D** gnarled
Q6	**A** spiral	**Q18**	**C** injure
Q7	**B** unintelligent	**Q19**	**C** optimistic
Q8	**C** suitable	**Q20**	**A** significance
Q9	**E** resoluteness	**Q21**	**C** evidence
Q10	**D** rude	**Q22**	**C** acclimatise
Q11	**A** delighted	**Q23**	**B** saunter
Q12	**E** amiable	**Q24**	**A** transcribe

Non-Verbal Reasoning

Q1 C
Rotation 90 degrees clockwise, identical diagonal stripes change to vertical.

Q2 C
Reflection in vertical line, becomes smaller and colour changes to vertical stripes

Q3 B
Count increasing so missing shape must have 8 lines

Q4 C
Triangle count increases, building on last pattern, 1 + sign randomly positioned

Q5 A
Circle shading is diagonally arranged from bottom left to top right. Outer triangle shading on middle two columns is alternating between vertical and horizontal

Q6 A
Completes the star image

Q7 C
Reflection in vertical line, ensuring layering is correct with black dot on top of zigzag. Black dot should be the closest part of the image to the reflection line.

Q8 D
Arrow should be closest to the reflection line, and pointing to the right, and must ensure correct position of circle.

Q9 C
Reflection in vertical line, vertical line could be either side

Q10 B
Reflection in vertical line, vertical line could be either side

Q11 D
Reflection in horizontal line, horizontal line could be above or below

Q12 E
Reflection in horizontal line, horizontal line could be above or below

Q13 D
Reflection in vertical line, vertical line could be either side, diagonal stripes into the right angle corner of triangle; circle on base of arrow

Answers to Test A Paper 2

Problem Solving

Q1 I
£6.80
$4 \times 40 + 8 \times 20 = 320p$, so
$1000 - 320 = 680$ pence – £6.80

Q2 B
20p
As the only difference in total cost in the 2 equations is caused by the additional banana (5 up from 4) which must therefore cost 20 pence.

Q3 A
40p
3 pots would be £3.60 without the offer (so £1.20 each), but with the offer, the 3 pots cost only £2.40 (so only 80p each). So the offer saves 40p per pot.

Q4 D
45 minutes
10:45 to 12:30 is 1 hour and 45 minutes or 105 minutes. Shopping takes Harji 55 minutes which leaves 50 minutes wait, but this is reduced by 5 minutes as her friend arrives 5 minutes early.

Q5 G
50 minutes
The frozen food is in her trolley for 20 minutes (5 + 15), and the time to get home is 30 minutes, giving a total of 50 minutes. Time to get home is worked out as follows: her speed is 40 km per hour, so to travel a distance of 20 km will only take $\frac{1}{2}$ an hour or 30 minutes.

Q6 *F*
240, 420 – 180 = 240

Q7 *E*
19,200
As 4 tiles will fit in each square metre, and there are 80 × 60 square metres to cover (80 × 60 = 4800) 4 × 4800 = 19 200 tiles

Q8 *J*
£3.20
Each lemon costs 140p divided by 7 = 20p, so 16 lemons cost 16 × 20 = 320p or £3.20

Q9 *C*
100 as 140 ÷ 7 × 5 = 100

Q10 *H*
30p
As the expected change was £130.00 – £123.27 = £6.73 so Harji received 30p less than she should have received.

Cloze

Q1	*E*	aspire	**Q11**	*B*	ancient
Q2	*C*	competitive	**Q12**	*A*	empire
Q3	*B*	properties	**Q13**	*C*	turbulent
Q4	*D*	multitude	**Q14**	*D*	theatre
Q5	*I*	external	**Q15**	*G*	spectators
Q6	*F*	description	**Q16**	*J*	Italy
Q7	*J*	exemplified	**Q17**	*F*	understood
Q8	*H*	stylish	**Q18**	*E*	collapsed
Q9	*G*	extended	**Q19**	*I*	buildings
Q10	*A*	parking	**Q20**	*H*	survive

Non-Verbal Reasoning

Q1 *C*
As this is the only 5-sided shape.

Q2 *E*
As this is the only 5-sided white shape with a 1-sided shape inside.

Q3 *B*
As this is the only image with an arrow coming from within a 1-sided shape, with another arrow crossing it horizontally.

Q4 *D*
As the arrow on the bottom of the net turns upside down when the face joins the striped face.

Q5 *E*
As there is a blank face beneath the heart, and the other blank face wraps around from the left to join the right side of the heart.

Q6 *B*
As the blank face on the right wraps around to join the left of the pentagon. The net is rotated a half turn to create the pattern displayed on the cube.

Q7 *E*
As the point of the hexagon will point into the stripes when these faces join. The net is rotated a half turn to create the pattern displayed on the cube, with the blank face ending up on the right side of the cube.

Q8 *D*
As the point of the hexagon will point into the stripes when these faces join. The net is rotated a quarter turn anti-clockwise to create the pattern displayed on the cube, with the blank face ending up on the top of the cube. E is not possible because the blank face would appear on the left of the cube if the hexagon is on the front face.

Q9 *A*
AF as the first letter relates to the top shape, and the second letter relates to the direction of the stripes.

Q10 *D*
BF as the first letter relates to the bottom shape (or top shape), and the second letter relates to the boldness of the line (fine, medium or heavy bold) on the top shape.

Q11 *B*
AZ as the first letter relates to the shape on the base of the arrow, and the second letter relates to the lower shape.

Q12 *E*
DZ as the first letter relates to the colour of the top shape, and the second letter relates to the lower shape.

Q13 *E*
CS as the first letter relates to the shade and stripes on the top shape, and the second letter relates to the shape on top.

Q14 A

CR as the first letter relates to the stripes on the top shape, and the second letter relates to whether the arrow head is within or outside the lower shape (or non-existent).

Q15 C

DT as the first letter relates to the number of sides on the non 3-dimensional shape, and the second letter relates to the position of the 3-dimensional shape.

Grammar

Q1	**E** sow	**Q5**	**C** curiosity
Q2	**B** bow	**Q6**	**A** dilemma
Q3	**B** im	**Q7**	**E** existence
Q4	**A** committee	**Q8**	**A** further

Antonyms

Q1	**A** inaudible	**Q9**	**A** allow
Q2	**D** tiny	**Q10**	**D** disobedient
Q3	**C** unjust	**Q11**	**A** imprudent
Q4	**A** condemn	**Q12**	**E** noticeable
Q5	**B** industrious	**Q13**	**C** folly
Q6	**A** inessential	**Q14**	**A** auspicious
Q7	**D** follower	**Q15**	**D** use
Q8	**C** admiration		

Numeracy

Q1 26

Half of 52

Q2 64

Using BODMAS $2 \times 2 = 4$, then add 60

Q3 13

There are two alternating sequences.

Q4 48

This is not exactly divisible by 5, as it would leave a remainder of 3.

Q5 5

Convert $\frac{2}{3}$ into $\frac{4}{6}$ and add the other $\frac{1}{6}$

Q6 5

0.2 is the same as $\frac{2}{10}$ which can be simplified to $\frac{1}{5}$

Q7 59

As this is rounded to 0.59 to 2 significant figures

Q8 0 9.95 rounded to 1 decimal place is 10.0, and 10.0 − 10 = 0

Q9 B

360

This is not exactly divisible by 50, it would leave a remainder of 10

Q10 E

5

As the radius is half of the diameter of a circle (centre to edge)

Q11 D

25.7 cm

Circumference is $2 \times 3.14 \times 5 = 31.4$
Half of this is 15.7. Adding 10 (straight edge) gives 25.7

Q12 C

4.9

As mean is the average found by dividing the sum of the data by the number of pieces of data $= \frac{49}{10} = 4.9$

Q13 D

0.5P

The first person eats 2 slices, so 3 slices out of 6 will remain, or $\frac{1}{2} = 0.5$ as a decimal

Q14 D

6 in 6

As the lowest score on the second dice is 1, giving a total on the two dice of 4 or more

Q15 A

(7,6)

As the distance from the start to the end of the first line is (4,6). Add this to (3,0) to give the end coordinates of the second line.

Q16 A

$\frac{1}{7}$

Multiplying the top line gives 2, and bottom line 14, and $\frac{2}{14}$ simplifies to $\frac{1}{7}$

Q17 C

$\frac{1}{2}$

Multiplying the top line gives 24, and bottom line 48, and $\frac{24}{48}$ simplifies to $\frac{1}{2}$

Q18 A

1, as dividing by $\frac{1}{3}$ is the same as multiplying by 3. When multiplying $\frac{3}{9}$ by 3 gives $\frac{9}{9}$ which is the same as 1.

Answers to Test B Paper 1

Comprehension

1. **B**
   Less impressive
2. **E**
   Passage does not say
3. **D**
   Colourful clothes and luxurious hotels
4. **C**
   She removed it on her own.
5. **E**
   Occurring for a long period of time
6. **B**
   Noun
7. **E**
   Due to a family member being ill
8. **D**
   Due to it being the place where her family spent their time
9. **B**
   A design secret
10. **E**
    Grey and blue tones

Shuffled Sentences

1. **C**
   engine The boy enjoyed sitting in his car which he had bought that morning.
2. **D**
   awful Despite eating her last biscuit the girl was still hungry.
3. **B**
   brand We like listening to the radio show which plays classical music.
4. **E**
   extend As a result of his training the young man became a talented dancer.
5. **A**
   courageous According to most people gardening is good exercise.
6. **C**
   quietly The competition started promptly at ten o'clock despite the thunderstorm overhead.
7. **E**
   house He finally completed reading the lengthy novel.

The word 'and' does not appear in the shuffled sentence and can be eliminated immediately.

8. **B**
   severe According to some scientists eggs are good for you in many ways.
9. **D**
   flossed All dentists recommend brushing your teeth twice a day.
10. **A**
    chargeable The singers were amazing and the atmosphere was electric.
11. **C**
    heavily Although I have been to the supermarket today I have still run out of milk.
12. **A**
    arranged The interior designer has produced an attractive sketch.
    The words 'of' and 'house' do not appear in the shuffled sentence and can be eliminated immediately.
13. **E**
    standard We were not looking forward to our aunt's party but we had a wonderful time.
14. **D**
    threw Most of the neighbours were awoken by the dog barking.
15. **A**
    calm The overgrown grass in the garden needs mowing.
    The word 'for' does not appear in the shuffled sentence and can be eliminated immediately.

Numeracy

1. *28*
   2015 is not a leap year as it is odd, so 25 + 2 + 1 (includes both the 3rd Feb and 2nd March) 1 relates to the 3rd of February in addition as the question is inclusive dates.
2. *8*
   56 divided by 7
3. *19*
   b + 2b + 3b = 6b, so 6b + 1 = perimeter. As the question tells us b = 3, (6 x 3) + 1 = 19
4. *12*
   As you are walking at 2.5 miles in each hour (or 60 minutes). A distance of 0.5 miles is one fifth of 2.5 miles. So, if 2.5 miles are covered

in 60 minutes, one fifth of the distance would be covered in one fifth of the time. 60 divided by 5 is 12 minutes.

5. 10

as Jenny will always be 2 years younger than Kate.

6. 6

as the difference is halving between each consecutive pair of numbers in the sequence. Differences are 16, 8, 4 so the next difference is 2.

7. 20

as each term is 5 less than the previous term. To work out the 18th (or any term in the sequence) use 110 – 5n where n is the position of the term wanted (18 in this case). 110 – (5 × 18) = 20

8. 28

as this is 84 divided by 3 (the tank is one third empty).

9. 7

as 1.5 l equals 1,500 ml, and when this is divided by 200, the answer is 7 full cups with a remainder of 100 ml.

10. 12

180 divided by 15 (as quarter of an hour is 15 minutes).

11. 6

The vertices are the corners on this 3D shape, and there are 3 on each triangle at the ends of the prism.

12. 34

Using BODMAS to first calculate the brackets which come to 26, then add 8.

13. 88

Problem Solving

1. G

12 days as half the men will take twice as long to fit.

2. C

24 (6 × 4)

3. B

3, as 4 tiles fit into each metre squared, so 4 × 24 = 96 tiles required. 40 tiles per box (2 boxes have only 80, so 3 boxes will be required).

4. I

£150 (0.25 × £600)

5. F

£1,200 as 1% of £20,000 is £200, so 6% is 6 × 200 = £1,200

6. A

£450, as the sale price is $\frac{2}{3}$ of the original price.

7. J

52 weeks in a year divided by 4 = 13 weeks.

8. H

£1,100 (21,100 – 20,000)

9. D

£28,900 (increase in house value of £50,000 less the cost of the new kitchen of £21,100)

10. E

£25,000 (£250,000 divided by 10)

Synonyms

1. C insignificant
2. B arc
3. D setback
4. E ineffective
5. A cliff
6. E anguish
7. C upright
8. C exterior
9. E slender
10. B gap
11. C curious
12. D accomplished
13. A alliance
14. C details
15. B unconventional
16. C acrimonious
17. A blend
18. E ultimate
19. A thrive
20. A indifferent
21. E mode
22. C parade
23. A projection

Non-Verbal Reasoning

Q1. E

Sequence shapes repeat after 3 images in same order. The arrows are rotating clockwise.

Q2. B

Sequence shapes repeat after 3 images in same order. The arrows are rotating clockwise.

Q3. D

Sequence shapes alternate in both shading and number of sides. The arch switches from top to bottom and also from shaded to blank. The arch is always blank when beneath the hexagon.

Q4. C

Sequence shapes alternate in both shading and number of sides. The arch switches from top to bottom and also from shaded to blank. The pentagon also turns a half turn from one image to the next.

Q5. E

All shapes are grey and the number of sides in the sequence increases by one each time (it is necessary to add the number of sides where there is more than one shape). 3 sides on the triangle + 1 side on each of the 2 circles gives 5 sides.

Q6. *C*

All shapes are grey and the number of sides in the sequence increases by one each time (it is necessary to add the number of sides where there is more than one shape). 5 sides on the pentagon + 4 sides on square gives 9 sides.

Q7. *C*

Background shapes large, whilst foreground shape smaller. Also both large and small shapes switch shading as the sequence continues. The number of sides of the shapes is irrelevant.

Q8. *B*

Background shapes large, whilst foreground shape smaller. Also both large and small shapes switch shading as the sequence continues. The number of sides of the shapes is irrelevant.

Q9. *D*

Triangles swap from equilateral (having two, four point stars and a horizontal line underneath), to right angled (having an arrow underneath and one black, four-point star).

Q10. *E*

Triangles swap from equilateral (having two, four point stars and a horizontal line underneath), to right angled (having an arrow underneath and one black, four-point star).

Q11. *E*

Triangles swap from grey equilateral (having a left facing arrow underneath), to white right angled (having a right facing arrow underneath). Number of stars decrease from 3 to 2 to 1 but with 5-point stars for second half of sequence.

Q12. *C*

Triangles swap from grey equilateral (having a left facing arrow underneath), to white right angled (having a right facing arrow underneath). Number of stars decrease from 3 to 2 to 1 but with 5-point stars for second half of sequence.

Q13. *C*

Circles on top alternate black and white, whilst arrows switch direction beneath and stripes change from vertical to horizontal. First 3 arrows are double headed, second 3 are single headed.

Q14. *D*

Circles on top alternate black and white, whilst arrows switch direction beneath and stripes change from vertical to horizontal. First 3 arrows are double headed, second 3 are single headed.

Answers to Test B Paper 2

Problem Solving

1. *I*

   £550 for each of the child tickets. The adult tickets were £1,100 each. Effectively, the two child tickets cost the same as one adult flight. £3,300 ÷ 3 = £1,100 per adult, and half of this for each child.

2. *D*

   17:00 Flight leaves Singapore 3 hours later at 10:00. Add 5 hours flight time to Sydney, and add 2 hours to reflect the time difference.

3. *J*

   10 : 8 + 2

4. *B*

   06:00 Flight scheduled to take off at 9 a.m. 3 hours earlier is 6 a.m.

5. *F*

   05:00 as this is 1 hour before check-in opens.

6. *H*

   £1,100 : $1,925 divided by 1.75 = 1,100. It may be easier to convert 1.75 into an improper fraction $\left(\frac{7}{4}\right)$. Dividing by $\frac{7}{4}$ is done by multiplying by $\frac{4}{7}$.

   1925 × 4 = 7,700. Divide this by 7 to give £1,100.

7. *A*

   £500 : $875 divided by $\frac{7}{4}$ (or 1.75) is the same as multiplying by 4 then dividing by 7.

   4 x 875 = 3,500

   3500 ÷ 7 = £500

8. G

£20 : 50% of $70 = $35

$35 divided by 1.75 = £20

9. C

8: 468 − 15 = 453

461 − 453 = 8 people boarded initially in Singapore.

10. J

10: 2015 − 2005 = 10 years (the flight took off in London on 21 December 2015, and the holiday was only a 2-week holiday, so the closest answer is 10 years).

Cloze

1. **G** advertisement
2. **A** forming
3. **C** technical
4. **J** remote
5. **F** apparent
6. **B** unearthed
7. **E** carefully
8. **H** graveyard
9. **I** guided
10. **D** visiting
11. **I** travelling
12. **J** motorists
13. **G** breakdown
14. **A** provisions
15. **E** reputable
16. **F** tow
17. **B** treacherous
18. **H** estimated
19. **D** working
20. **C** necessary

Non-Verbal Reasoning

1. D

Only answer without a star (all others have stars).

2. B

Only answer with 4 shapes (all others have 3).

3. E

Only answer where the grey shapes are not a reflection of each other in a horizontal line.

4. D

Only answer where the shapes are not the same.

5. A

Only answer where the number of rectangles is not even.

6. B

Only image where both arrows come from the same side.

7. A

Net requires half-turn rotation

8. B

No rotation of net required

9. E

No rotation of net required

10. C

Net requires half-turn rotation

11. C

No rotation of net required

12. D

No rotation of net required

13. A

Net requires half-turn rotation

Antonyms

1. **C** apathetic
2. **A** barren
3. **B** unreliable
4. **E** hide
5. **C** embrace
6. **B** dispute
7. **B** divide
8. **C** fertile
9. **B** original
10. **E** combined
11. **B** cheer
12. **C** purify
13. **E** bland
14. **B** experienced
15. **B** upgrade

Numeracy

1. 99
2. 11

Left-hand side equals 33, so 11 must be missing number (as 33 = 11 × 3).

3. 22

as the difference between each pair of consecutive numbers is increasing by 1. Differences are 1, 2, 3, 4 so next is 5 and 17 + 5 = 22.

4. 8

as adding 3 back on to 61 means 64 is 8 times the number, so the number must be 8.

5. 27

This is the addition of all numbers within those sets (exclude 3 outside of all sets) 7 + 5 + 4 + 5 + 6 = 27.

6. 30
7. 7
8. 8

Highest less lowest is 9 − 1 = 8.

9. £80

as £64 is now 80% of the original price. Divide this by 4 and multiply that by 5 to scale the amount back up to the original price. 64 ÷ 4 = 16, and 16 × 5 = 80.

10. *7*

Rearrange by adding y to both sides to give
21 = 3y, so y = 21 divided by 3 = 7.

11. *56*

Write all numbers of cards as an expression
of one of the other people in the question, e.g.
Say Martin has y cards, therefore Judy has 2y
cards (as she has twice as many), and Jay will
have 6y cards. Total cards could be written as 9y
and this equals 252 cards, so y = 252 ÷ 9 = 28,
and so Judy has 28 × 2 = 56 cards.

12. *13*

13. *18*

6 pieces in each of the 3 cakes.

14. *7*

Coins would be £2, 50p, 20p, 10p, 5p, 2p, 2p.

15. *56*

(8 × 7)

16. *8*

17. *7*

Half of 14

18. *1*

as in 5 years my mother will be 45, and
my older sister will be a third of 45 which
is 15. So if my sister will be 15 in 5 years'
time, that means she is 10 now. I am 9 years
younger which means I am 10 − 9 = 1
year old.

Pupil's Full Name:

Instructions:
Mark the boxes correctly like this ⬛

Please sign your name here:

Comprehension

Example 1

| ✦ | B | C | D | E |

Practice Question 1

| A | B | C | D | E |

1	A	B	C	D	E
2	A	B	C	D	E
3	A	B	C	D	E
4	A	B	C	D	E
5	A	B	C	D	E
6	A	B	C	D	E
7	A	B	C	D	E
8	A	B	C	D	E
9	A	B	C	D	E
10	A	B	C	D	E

Shuffled Sentences

Example 1

| ✦ | B | C | D | E |

Practice Question 1

| A | B | C | D | E |

1	A	B	C	D	E
2	A	B	C	D	E
3	A	B	C	D	E
4	A	B	C	D	E
5	A	B	C	D	E
6	A	B	C	D	E
7	A	B	C	D	E
8	A	B	C	D	E
9	A	B	C	D	E
10	A	B	C	D	E
11	A	B	C	D	E
12	A	B	C	D	E
13	A	B	C	D	E
14	A	B	C	D	E
15	A	B	C	D	E

Numeracy

Example: 3 7

Practice Question 1

1   2

3   4   5   6

7   8   9   10

11   12   13

(Each numeracy answer consists of two columns of boxes numbered 0–9.)

Problem Solving

Example 1

~~A~~	B	C	D	E

Practice Question 1

A	B	C	D	E
1	A	B	C	D	E
2	A	B	C	D	E
3	A	B	C	D	E
4	A	B	C	D	E
5	A	B	C	D	E
6	A	B	C	D	E
7	A	B	C	D	E
8	A	B	C	D	E
9	A	B	C	D	E
10	A	B	C	D	E

Synonyms

Example 1

A	B	C	D	~~E~~

Practice Question 1

A	B	C	D	E
1	A	B	C	D	E
2	A	B	C	D	E
3	A	B	C	D	E
4	A	B	C	D	E
5	A	B	C	D	E
6	A	B	C	D	E
7	A	B	C	D	E
8	A	B	C	D	E
9	A	B	C	D	E
10	A	B	C	D	E
11	A	B	C	D	E
12	A	B	C	D	E
13	A	B	C	D	E
14	A	B	C	D	E
15	A	B	C	D	E
16	A	B	C	D	E
17	A	B	C	D	E
18	A	B	C	D	E
19	A	B	C	D	E
20	A	B	C	D	E
21	A	B	C	D	E

22	A	B	C	D	E
23	A	B	C	D	E
24	A	B	C	D	E

Non-Verbal Reasoning

REFLECTION Example 1

A	~~B~~	C	D	E

REFLECTION Practice Question 1

A	B	C	D	E

CONNECTION Example 2

A	~~B~~	C	D	E

CONNECTION Practice Question 2

A	B	C	D	E
1	A	B	C	D	E
2	A	B	C	D	E
3	A	B	C	D	E
4	A	B	C	D	E
5	A	B	C	D	E
6	A	B	C	D	E
7	A	B	C	D	E
8	A	B	C	D	E
9	A	B	C	D	E
10	A	B	C	D	E
11	A	B	C	D	E
12	A	B	C	D	E
13	A	B	C	D	E

Pupil's Full Name:

2

Instructions:
Mark the boxes correctly like this 🖝

Please sign your name here:

Problem Solving

Example 1

🖝 B C D E F G H I J

Practice Question 1

A B C D E F G H I J

1 A B C D E F G H I J
2 A B C D E F G H I J
3 A B C D E F G H I J
4 A B C D E F G H I J
5 A B C D E F G H I J
6 A B C D E F G H I J
7 A B C D E F G H I J
8 A B C D E F G H I J
9 A B C D E F G H I J
10 A B C D E F G H I J

Cloze

Example 1

🖝 B C D E

Practice Question 1

A B C D E

1 A B C D E F G H I J
2 A B C D E F G H I J
3 A B C D E F G H I J
4 A B C D E F G H I J
5 A B C D E F G H I J
6 A B C D E F G H I J
7 A B C D E F G H I J
8 A B C D E F G H I J
9 A B C D E F G H I J
10 A B C D E F G H I J
11 A B C D E F G H I J
12 A B C D E F G H I J
13 A B C D E F G H I J
14 A B C D E F G H I J

15 A B C D E F G H I J
16 A B C D E F G H I J
17 A B C D E F G H I J
18 A B C D E F G H I J
19 A B C D E F G H I J
20 A B C D E F G H I J

Non-Verbal Reasoning

CUBES Example 1

A B C D E

CUBES Practice Question 1

A B C D E

BELONGS TO GROUP Example 2

A B C D E

BELONGS TO GROUP
Practice Question 2

A B C D E

1 A B C D E
2 A B C D E
3 A B C D E
4 A B C D E
5 A B C D E
6 A B C D E
7 A B C D E
8 A B C D E
9 A B C D E
10 A B C D E
11 A B C D E
12 A B C D E
13 A B C D E
14 A B C D E
15 A B C D E

Grammar

Example 1

	A	B	C	D	E

Practice Question 1

	A	B	C	D	E
1	A	B	C	D	E
2	A	B	C	D	E
3	A	B	C	D	E
4	A	B	C	D	E
5	A	B	C	D	E
6	A	B	C	D	E
7	A	B	C	D	E
8	A	B	C	D	E

Antonyms

Example 1

	A	B	C	D	E

Practice Question 1

	A	B	C	D	E
1	A	B	C	D	E
2	A	B	C	D	E
3	A	B	C	D	E
4	A	B	C	D	E
5	A	B	C	D	E
6	A	B	C	D	E
7	A	B	C	D	E
8	A	B	C	D	E
9	A	B	C	D	E
10	A	B	C	D	E
11	A	B	C	D	E
12	A	B	C	D	E
13	A	B	C	D	E
14	A	B	C	D	E
15	A	B	C	D	E

Numeracy

Example: 3 7

Practice Question 1

(number grid bubbles 0–9)

1, 2

(number grid bubbles 0–9)

3, 4, 5, 6

(number grid bubbles 0–9)

7, 8

(number grid bubbles 0–9)

	A	B	C	D	E
9	A	B	C	D	E
10	A	B	C	D	E
11	A	B	C	D	E
12	A	B	C	D	E
13	A	B	C	D	E
14	A	B	C	D	E
15	A	B	C	D	E
16	A	B	C	D	E
17	A	B	C	D	E
18	A	B	C	D	E

Pupil's Full Name:

Instructions:
Mark the boxes correctly like this ▅

Please sign your name here:

Comprehension

Example 1

| A̶ | B | C | D | E |

Practice Question 1

| A | B | C | D | E |

	A	B	C	D	E
1	A	B	C	D	E
2	A	B	C	D	E
3	A	B	C	D	E
4	A	B	C	D	E
5	A	B	C	D	E
6	A	B	C	D	E
7	A	B	C	D	E
8	A	B	C	D	E
9	A	B	C	D	E
10	A	B	C	D	E

Shuffled Sentences

Example 1

| A̶ | B | C | D | E |

Practice Question 1

| A | B | C | D |

	A	B	C	D	E
1	A	B	C	D	E
2	A	B	C	D	E
3	A	B	C	D	E
4	A	B	C	D	E
5	A	B	C	D	E
6	A	B	C	D	E
7	A	B	C	D	E
8	A	B	C	D	E
9	A	B	C	D	E
10	A	B	C	D	E
11	A	B	C	D	E
12	A	B	C	D	E
13	A	B	C	D	E
14	A	B	C	D	E
15	A	B	C	D	E

Numeracy

Example 3 7   **Practice** Question 1   **1**   **2**

(Numeracy answer grids with digits 0–9 in columns for Example, Practice Question 1, and questions 1–13.)

3   **4**   **5**   **6**

7   **8**   **9**   **10**

11   **12**   **13**

Problem Solving

Example 1

~~A~~ B C D E F G H ┼ ┬

Practice Question 1

A B C D E F G H ┼ ┬

1	A	B	C	D	E	F	G	H	┼	┬
2	A	B	C	D	E	F	G	H	┼	┬
3	A	B	C	D	E	F	G	H	┼	┬
4	A	B	C	D	E	F	G	H	┼	┬
5	A	B	C	D	E	F	G	H	┼	┬
6	A	B	C	D	E	F	G	H	┼	┬
7	A	B	C	D	E	F	G	H	┼	┬
8	A	B	C	D	E	F	G	H	┼	┬
9	A	B	C	D	E	F	G	H	┼	┬
10	A	B	C	D	E	F	G	H	┼	┬

Synonyms

Example 1

A B C D ~~E~~

Practice Question 1

A B C D E

1	A	B	C	D	E
2	A	B	C	D	E
3	A	B	C	D	E
4	A	B	C	D	E
5	A	B	C	D	E
6	A	B	C	D	E
7	A	B	C	D	E
8	A	B	C	D	E
9	A	B	C	D	E
10	A	B	C	D	E
11	A	B	C	D	E
12	A	B	C	D	E
13	A	B	C	D	E
14	A	B	C	D	E
15	A	B	C	D	E
16	A	B	C	D	E
17	A	B	C	D	E
18	A	B	C	D	E
19	A	B	C	D	E
20	A	B	C	D	E
21	A	B	C	D	E

22	A	B	C	D	E
23	A	B	C	D	E

Non-Verbal Reasoning

COMPLETE THE SEQUENCE
Example 1

A B ~~C~~ D E

COMPLETE THE SEQUENCE
Practice Question 1

A B C D E

1	A	B	C	D	E
2	A	B	C	D	E
3	A	B	C	D	E
4	A	B	C	D	E
5	A	B	C	D	E
6	A	B	C	D	E
7	A	B	C	D	E
8	A	B	C	D	E
9	A	B	C	D	E
10	A	B	C	D	E
11	A	B	C	D	E
12	A	B	C	D	E
13	A	B	C	D	E
14	A	B	C	D	E

Pupil's Full Name:

2

Instructions:
Mark the boxes correctly like this ⬛

Please sign your name here:

Problem Solving

Example 1
Ⓐ B C D E F G H ╪ ╪

Practice Question 1
A B C D E F G H ╪ ╪

1	A	B	C	D	E	F	G	H	╪	╪
2	A	B	C	D	E	F	G	H	╪	╪
3	A	B	C	D	E	F	G	H	╪	╪
4	A	B	C	D	E	F	G	H	╪	╪
5	A	B	C	D	E	F	G	H	╪	╪
6	A	B	C	D	E	F	G	H	╪	╪
7	A	B	C	D	E	F	G	H	╪	╪
8	A	B	C	D	E	F	G	H	╪	╪
9	A	B	C	D	E	F	G	H	╪	╪
10	A	B	C	D	E	F	G	H	╪	╪

Cloze

Example 1
Ⓐ B C D E

Practice Question 1
A B C D E

1	A	B	C	D	E	F	G	H	╪	╪
2	A	B	C	D	E	F	G	H	╪	╪
3	A	B	C	D	E	F	G	H	╪	╪
4	A	B	C	D	E	F	G	H	╪	╪
5	A	B	C	D	E	F	G	H	╪	╪
6	A	B	C	D	E	F	G	H	╪	╪
7	A	B	C	D	E	F	G	H	╪	╪
8	A	B	C	D	E	F	G	H	╪	╪
9	A	B	C	D	E	F	G	H	╪	╪
10	A	B	C	D	E	F	G	H	╪	╪
11	A	B	C	D	E	F	G	H	╪	╪
12	A	B	C	D	E	F	G	H	╪	╪
13	A	B	C	D	E	F	G	H	╪	╪
14	A	B	C	D	E	F	G	H	╪	╪

15	A	B	C	D	E	F	G	H	╪	╪
16	A	B	C	D	E	F	G	H	╪	╪
17	A	B	C	D	E	F	G	H	╪	╪
18	A	B	C	D	E	F	G	H	╪	╪
19	A	B	C	D	E	F	G	H	╪	╪
20	A	B	C	D	E	F	G	H	╪	╪

Non-Verbal Reasoning

CUBE NET Example 1
A B C D ⊟

CUBE NET Practice Question 1
A B C D E

LEAST SIMILAR Example 2
A ⊟ C D E

LEAST SIMILAR Practice Question 2
A B C D E

1	A	B	C	D	E
2	A	B	C	D	E
3	A	B	C	D	E
4	A	B	C	D	E
5	A	B	C	D	E
6	A	B	C	D	E
7	A	B	C	D	E
8	A	B	C	D	E
9	A	B	C	D	E
10	A	B	C	D	E
11	A	B	C	D	E
12	A	B	C	D	E
13	A	B	C	D	E

Antonyms

Example 1

~~A~~   B   C   D   E

Practice Question 1

A   B   C   D   E

1 A B C D E
2 A B C D E
3 A B C D E
4 A B C D E
5 A B C D E
6 A B C D E
7 A B C D E
8 A B C D E
9 A B C D E
10 A B C D E
11 A B C D E
12 A B C D E
13 A B C D E
14 A B C D E
15 A B C D E

Numeracy

Example	Practice	1	2
3 7	Question 1		

7 8 9 10 11 12 13 14 15 16 17 18

3 4 5 6

Collins

11+ Practice Papers

Part 2

In partnership with 11+ TUTORING ACADEMY

Philip McMahon

Contents

Guidance notes for parents

What your child will need to sit these papers

- A quiet place to sit the exam
- A clock which is visible to your child
- A way to play the audio download
- A pencil and an eraser
- A piece of paper

Your child should not use a calculator for any of these papers.

How to invigilate the test papers

Your child should sit Test C, Paper 1 then have a 15-minute break. They should then sit Paper 2. Don't help your child or allow any talking. Review the answers with your child and help improve their weaker areas. At a later date, your child should sit Test D, Papers 1 and 2 in a two-hour session.

Step 1: Remove the answers and keep them hidden from your child.

Step 2: Remove the answer sheet section. Your child should write their full name on top of the first answer sheet. Give them the question paper booklet. They must not open the paper until they are told to do so by the audio instructions.

Step 3: Start the audio.

Step 4: Ask your child to work through the practice questions before the time starts for each section. An example is already marked on each section of the answer sheet. Your child should mark the answer sheet clearly and check that the practice questions are correctly marked.

Step 5: Mark the answer sheet. Then, together with your child, work through the questions that were answered incorrectly. When working through the Non-verbal Reasoning sections, ensure you have the question papers open to help explain the answers to your child.

How your child should complete the answer sheet

Your child MUST NOT write their answers on the question paper, they must use the answer sheet. They should put a horizontal line through the boxes on the answer sheet. To change an answer, your child should fully erase the incorrect answer and then clearly select a new answer. Any rough workings should be done on a separate piece of paper.

The audio instructions

Both papers have audio instructions to allow your child to learn, listen and act upon audio instructions. Audio instructions are at the start, during and at the end of the sections. Audio warnings on the time remaining will be given at varying intervals. Your child should listen out for these warnings.

The symbols at the foot of the page

Written instructions are at the foot of the page. Your child MUST follow these instructions:

Continue working

Stop and wait for instructions

Your child can review questions within the allocated time, but must not move onto the next section until they are allowed to do so.

The instructions and examples at the beginning of the section

In the instructions, your child should look for: the time allowed; how many questions there are; and how to complete the answers.

Examples are at the beginning of every section to show the type of question included in a particular section. The example questions will be worked through as part of the audio instructions.

Developing time-management skills and working at speed

These test papers have been used with previous pupils of the CEM exam in various counties. They provide essential practice of the types of questions which could arise, in addition to the strictly timed conditions, which will help your child practise their time-management skills.

Marking the papers

Each question is worth one mark.

Scores

Overall scores your child should be aiming for:

- 75% or more on the first pack of 2 papers if taken in the weeks leading up to the exam
- 70% or more on the second pack of 2 papers if taken in the weeks leading up to the exam.

A weighted score attaches a certain amount of weight to each section in the exam.

How to work out your child's score:

Add together the scores for Non-verbal Reasoning and Maths sections (both Numeracy and Problem Solving). This will give you score A. This relates to both sections in all papers.

Then add together the remaining scores for all English sections, which will give you score B.

Then add scores A and B together and divide them by 2.

This will give you an average weighted score across the 2 packs.

To calculate your child's weighted score as a percentage, divide your child's score by the maximum score, and multiply it by 100.

Once you have completed this, you will have two percentages and the combined weighted score across the two papers is the middle of these two percentages.

For example: If your child scores 46 out of 92 for English, this equals 50%.

If your child scores 62 out of 82, this equals approximately 76%. So the combined weighted score across the two papers is 50% + 76%, which equals 126%. If you divide this by 2, this equals 63%. This is your child's weighted score.

The maximum scores:

Test C Paper 1 English – 39

Test C Paper 1 Maths and Non-verbal Reasoning – 48

Test C Paper 2 English – 57

Test C Paper 2 Maths and Non-verbal Reasoning – 25

Test D Paper 1 English – 30

Test D Paper 1 Maths and Non-verbal Reasoning – 43

Test D Paper 2 English – 57

Test D Paper 2 Maths and Non-verbal Reasoning – 25

English maximum scores, Test C Papers 1 and 2 – 96

Maths and Non-verbal Reasoning maximum scores, Test C Papers 1 and 2 – 73

English maximum scores, Test D Papers 1 and 2 – 87

Maths and Non-verbal Reasoning maximum scores, Test D Papers 1 and 2 – 68

Please note the following:

As the content varies from year to year in CEM exams, a good score in this paper does not guarantee a pass, and a lower score may not always suggest a fail!

What happens if your child does not score a good mark?

Identify strengths and weaknesses

Continue to provide a wide variety of questions to build your child's knowledge. Focus on the areas in which your child did not perform as well.

Timings

Allow your child to continue practising working under timed conditions.

Test C Paper 1

Instructions

1. Ensure you have pencils and an eraser with you.
2. Make sure you are able to see a clock or watch.
3. Write your name on the answer sheet.
4. Do not open the question booklet until you are told to do so by the audio instructions.
5. Listen carefully to the audio instructions given.
6. Mark your answers on the answer sheet only.
7. All workings must be completed on a separate piece of paper.
8. You should not use a calculator, dictionary or thesaurus at any point in this paper.
9. Move through the papers as quickly as possible and with care.
10. Follow the instructions at the foot of each page.
11. You should mark your answers with a horizontal strike, as shown on the answer sheet.
12. If you want to change your answer, ensure that you rub out your first answer and that your second answer is clearly more visible.
13. You can go back and review any questions that are within the section you are working on only. You must await further instructions before moving onto another section.

Symbols and Phrases used in the Tests

 Instructions Time allowed for this section Stop and wait for further instructions Continue working

Comprehension

INSTRUCTIONS

 YOU HAVE 8 MINUTES TO COMPLETE THE FOLLOWING SECTION.

YOU HAVE 10 QUESTIONS TO COMPLETE WITHIN THE TIME GIVEN.

EXAMPLES

Comprehension Example

Some people choose to start their Christmas shopping early in October. It has been reported that some people even buy their Christmas presents in the sales in August. In recent years, people have the option of purchasing their Christmas presents online.

Example 1

According to the passage, what is the earliest that people start their Christmas shopping?

A   In the preceding summer
B   In the preceding October
C   In the preceding November
D   Christmas Eve
E   In early December

The correct answer is A. This has already been marked in Example 1 in the Comprehension section of your answer sheet.

Practice Question 1

What has caused a change in how people shop, in recent years?

A   There are more shops.
B   Shops are more crowded.
C   You can easily organise your journey to the shops.
D   New products are available
E   There has been a rise in use of the Internet

The correct answer is E. Please mark this in Practice Question 1 in the Comprehension section of your answer sheet.

STOP AND WAIT FOR FURTHER INSTRUCTIONS

The Popularity of Allotments

The changing of the seasons can be clearly seen in allotments, which are often located on the periphery of residential areas in Britain. Allotments are pieces of land divided into plots and then allocated to families or individuals. Allotments, which were once left barren, have once again

Line 5 become popular with young people wanting to be self-sufficient, providing the majority of their food for themselves and their young families. They do however, require a significant investment of time and energy.

The winter months are often a period of inactivity. The ground is too hard for much work to happen, and the weather too cold for many crops to grow.

Line 10 Once spring has sprung, the allotments become a hive of activity with everyone attending their plots at least once a fortnight. At this stage in the year, the work is ploughing and sowing the vegetables, which the allotment holders hope will grow in abundance from that point onwards. In a good year, when the conditions are right, there should be a plentiful harvest.

Line 15 With the onset of summer, the work changes. Regular watering is needed to ensure that the crops do not wilt and die. There is often an additional peril in the form of insects, which can engulf and devastate the crops. The treatment of these pests depends on the allotment holders' beliefs, as to whether they want to use pesticides or natural, environmentally-friendly

Line 20 alternatives, to defeat an infestation. Traditional methods, such as nets placed over brassicas (purple sprouting broccoli) can ward off butterflies from laying their eggs. If one butterfly lays its eggs here, an entire crop can be destroyed as a result. When the sun is shining the weeds also grow and this means that hoeing is required on a weekly basis.

Line 25 In the autumn months, most of the crops are harvested and enjoyed. Many are cut down in preparation for the following year. Expertise and knowledge of the individual varieties of all the crops are required. An amateur allotment holder needs to learn about sowing, growing and harvesting to ensure a plentiful yield.

Line 30 The waiting lists for allotments are growing year by year as their popularity increases. Allotments are normally held for a generation, resulting in long waiting lists of many years in some places.

(1) Read the passage above and answer the following questions.

In the context of the passage, what type of word is the word 'allocated'?

A   Metaphor
B   Noun
C   Verb
D   Homophone
E   Adjective

CONTINUE WORKING ⏵

2 According to the passage, which phrase best describes the current situation with allotments?

A   Allotments are very popular
B   Nobody wants an allotment
C   Allotments are very expensive to buy
D   Allotments are mainly held by older people
E   Allotments are reversing

3 According to the passage, which of the following best describes the following phrase:

'a significant investment of time and energy'?

A   Allotments need power
B   Allotments are very expensive
C   Allotments need expertise
D   Allotments can be bought and sold
E   Allotments require people to spend time and effort

4 According to the passage, which phrase best describes what happens in the winter months?

A   People attend every two weeks
B   People attend every week
C   Crops grow well in the winter
D   Nothing happens
E   Allotment holders harvest their crops

5 In the context of the passage, what is the meaning of 'a hive of activity'?

A   A place where bees live
B   A busy place
C   A place which is extremely quiet
D   A place where people go to be active
E   A place to have some time alone

6 What is the meaning of 'abundance'?

A   A large quantity
B   A small quantity
C   A straight line
D   A regular pattern
E   A haphazard way

(7) Which word is the most similar to 'engulf'?

A   Formulate
B   Harden
C   Arrange
D   Envelop
E   Be aware of

(8) According to the passage, how often should 'hoeing' be completed?

A   Every three weeks
B   Every ten days
C   Once a fortnight
D   Every five days
E   Every seven days

(9) Which word is the most similar to the phrase 'ward off'?

A   Worshipful
B   General
C   Aggregate
D   Repel
E   Trustworthy

(10) According to the passage, describe the grammatical term for 'yield' within the context of the sentence, 'a plentiful yield'.

A   Verb
B   Noun
C   Adjective
D   Metaphor
E   Simile

STOP AND WAIT FOR FURTHER INSTRUCTIONS ⊗

Grammar

INSTRUCTIONS

 YOU HAVE 5 MINUTES TO COMPLETE THE FOLLOWING SECTION.

YOU HAVE 9 QUESTIONS TO COMPLETE WITHIN THE TIME GIVEN.

EXAMPLES

Read the passage below and answer the 9 questions that follow. There are some mistakes in the use of capital letters and punctuation. In some questions there may be no errors.

> The dogs were running in the garden. As the postman opened the gate, the dogs started biting the postman's leg.

Example 1

Look at the following options taken from the above passage. Select the option that contains a punctuation or grammar error, if any.

A	B	C	D	E
The dogs	were	in the	garden	No errors

The correct answer is E. This has already been marked in Example 1 in the Grammar section of your answer sheet.

Practice Question 1

Look at the following options taken from the above passage. Select the option that contains a punctuation or grammar error, if any.

A	B	C	D	E
As the postman	the dogs	biting	the postmans	No errors

The correct answer is D. Please mark the answer D in Practice Question 1 in the Grammar section of your answer sheet.

STOP AND WAIT FOR FURTHER INSTRUCTIONS ⊗

Read the passage below and answer the 9 questions that follow. There are some mistakes in the use of capital letters and punctuation. In some questions there may be no errors.

Emily and Laura were sisters. Laura was the elder of the two sisters. They were heading out to drop of some clothes at the local jumble sale. Laura carried a large bag of clothes to the village hall jumble sale. she could not see in front of herself and tripped on the uneven pavement. She nearly got a bad accident. Luckily Emily caught her as she fell. After dropping off the bag of clothes, they had a quick browse at what was on offer.

"This jacket of mine is wore out," remarked Emily. "I'll see if I can get a new one here."

Whilst perusing the clothes, Laura realised she hurted her leg when she nearly fell over earlier. They decided to head home after emily realised there were no suitable jackets to buy. "Lets run home together," said Emily, but after a while Laura said, "I cannot run no further."

Look at the following sentences from the above passage and select the answer from below that has a grammatical or punctuation error, if any.

(1) Laura was the elder of the two sisters.

A	B	C	D	E
Laura	was	elder	sisters	No errors

(2) she could not see in front of herself and tripped on the uneven pavement.

A	B	C	D	E
in front	could not	she	pavement.	No errors

(3) She nearly got a bad accident.

A	B	C	D	E
She	nearly	got	a bad	No errors

(4) "This jacket of mine is wore out," remarked Emily.

A	B	C	D	E
"This	jacket of	out," remarked	is wore out,"	No errors

CONTINUE WORKING ⇨

5. "I'll see if I can get a new one here."

A	B	C	D	E
"I'll	see if	I can get	a new one here."	No errors

6. Whilst perusing the clothes, Laura realised she hurted her leg when she nearly fell over earlier.

A	B	C	D	E
Whilst perusing	the clothes,	she hurted her leg	when she nearly	No errors

7. They decided to head home after emily realised there were no suitable jackets to buy.

A	B	C	D	E
They decided to	head home after	emily realised	jackets to buy	No errors

8. "Lets run home together," said Emily, but after a while Laura said, "I cannot run no further."

A	B	C	D	E
"Lets run	home together,"	said Emily,	but after	No errors

9. "Lets run home together," said Emily, but after a while Laura said, "I cannot run no further."

A	B	C	D	E
said Emily,	while Laura said,	"I cannot run	no further	No errors

STOP AND WAIT FOR FURTHER INSTRUCTIONS ⊗

Numeracy

 YOU HAVE 19 MINUTES TO COMPLETE THE FOLLOWING SECTION.

YOU HAVE 39 QUESTIONS TO COMPLETE WITHIN THE TIME GIVEN.

EXAMPLES

Example 1

Calculate 53 – 42

| **A** | 12 | **B** | 1 | **C** | 4 | **D** | 5 | **E** | 11 |

The correct answer is E. This has already been marked in Example 1 in the Numeracy section of your answer sheet.

Practice Question 1

Calculate 95 – 75

| **A** | 21 | **B** | 20 | **C** | 19 | **D** | 18 | **E** | 13 |

The correct answer is B. Please mark this in Practice Question 1 in the Numeracy section of your answer sheet.

STOP AND WAIT FOR FURTHER INSTRUCTIONS ⊗

(1) What is the number if 21 is three times more than half of this number?

A   36   **B**   48   **C**   126   **D**   7   **E**   14

(2) Select the appropriate number or numbers to complete the sequence in place of the ? in the sequence below.

31, 32, 34, ?, 41

A   35   **B**   36   **C**   37   **D**   38   **E**   39

(3) Select the appropriate numbers to complete the subtraction in place of the ? in the incomplete calculation below.

Your choice of answers is written as the missing numbers should appear in the question from left to right.

```
  ? 9 ? 4
-   7 8 ?
---------
  4 ? 3 3
```

A   4, 1, 1, 1   **B**   4, 1, 2, 1   **C**   3, 9, 8, 7
D   3, 1, 1, 1   **E**   4, 1, 2, 2

(4) My journey by car across London in the rush hour averages 8 mph. The distance of the journey is 1.6 miles. How long does the journey take?

A   4 minutes   **B**   5 minutes   **C**   16 minutes
D   15 minutes   **E**   12 minutes

(5) Susan works in a café and gets a staff discount of 20% on all food and drink that she purchases there. She has lunch in the café every weekday. She spends £24 each week in the café on her lunch. What is the value of the discount on her food purchased in the café each week?

A   £8   **B**   £4   **C**   £5   **D**   £6   **E**   £4.80

(6) Mohammed is 4 years older than Emily's brother, William. Emily and William are twins. If Emily is 7, how old is Mohammed?

A   3   **B**   11   **C**   9   **D**   12   **E**   4

CONTINUE WORKING

7 Arrange the following in order of size, from smallest to largest.

101 mm, 10.11 cm, $\frac{1}{10}$ m, 10 km, 11 cm

A $\frac{1}{10}$ m, 101 mm, 10.11 cm, 11 cm, 10 km

B 101 mm, $\frac{1}{10}$ m, 10.11 cm, 11 cm, 10 km

C $\frac{1}{10}$ m, 10.11 cm, 101 mm, 11 cm, 10 km

D $\frac{1}{10}$ m, 101 mm, 11 cm, 10.11 cm, 10 km

E $\frac{1}{10}$ m, 10km, 101 mm, 10.11 cm, 11 cm

8 Select the only equation that is incorrect.

A $453 - 2 = 452 - 0$
B $5,868 - 1,869 = 3,999$
C $901 = 1001 - 10 \times 10$
D $65 = 3 \times 21 + 2$
E $86 = 50 + 2 \times 18$

9 Calculate 26^2.

A   767   B   520   C   176   D   576   E   676

10 Identify the number that the vertical arrow is pointing to on the number line.

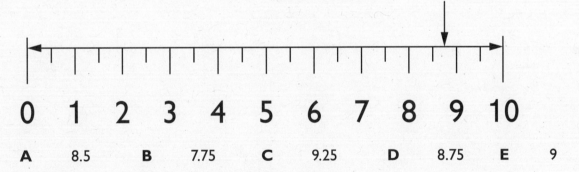

A   8.5   B   7.75   C   9.25   D   8.75   E   9

11 Calculate 3 hours and 55 minutes on from 9:25 a.m.

A   12:20 p.m.   B   1:20 p.m.   C   1 p.m.
D   10:25 a.m.   E   11:25 a.m.

CONTINUE WORKING ⇨

(12) Calculate $\frac{1}{3} \div 3$

    A $\frac{3}{9}$ **B**   2   **C** $\frac{1}{9}$ **D** $\frac{1}{8}$ **E** $\frac{4}{6}$

(13) Which number is half way between 23 and 7?

    A   15   **B**   16   **C**   25   **D**   15.5   **E**   14.5

(14) A map has a scale of 1 : 500,000. If two churches are 5 mm apart on the map, how far apart are they in real life?

    A   10,000 m   **B**   6,500 m   **C**   125 km
    D   100 km   **E**   2,500 m

(15) How many grams are there in 0.52 kg?

    A   250   **B**   52   **C**   5,200
    D   520   **E**   7

(16) Calculate 1.1% of 70.

    A   0.77   **B**   0.66   **C**   0.55   **D**   0.5   **E**   0.4

(17) Select the number to go in place of the question mark.

    $? \times 15 = 75$

    A   5   **B**   4   **C**   3   **D**   6   **E**   7

CONTINUE WORKING ⇨

18 Look at the chart below and answer the question that follows.

The chart shows the favourite hobby of each child in a class.

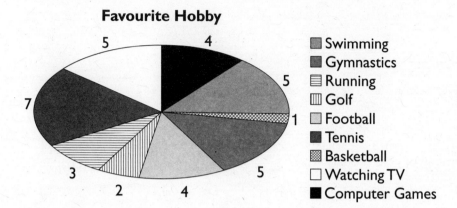

Favourite Hobby

Swimming
Gymnastics
Running
Golf
Football
Tennis
Basketball
Watching TV
Computer Games

Which is the least favourite hobby of the children in the class?

A　　Tennis　　　　　　**B**　　Gymnastics　　　　　**C**　　Watching TV
D　　Basketball　　　　 **E**　　Swimming

Look at the chart below and answer the questions that follow.

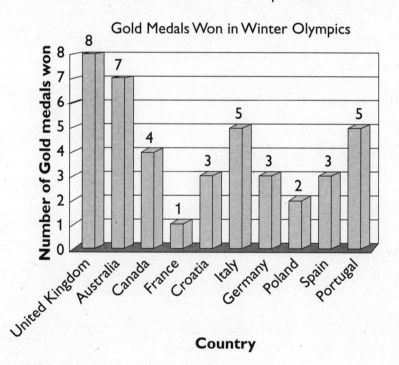

Gold Medals Won in Winter Olympics

19 What is the mode number of gold medals won?

A　　3　　　　**B**　　4　　　　**C**　　5　　　　**D**　　6　　　　**E**　　7

CONTINUE WORKING

⃝20 Which country won the second most gold medals?

A United Kingdom   **B** Australia   **C** Portugal
D Spain   **E** Germany

⃝21 What is the median number of medals won?

A 3.5   **B** 3   **C** 4   **D** 5   **E** 6

⃝22 What is the mean number of gold medals won?

A 4   **B** 4.5   **C** 3.1   **D** 4.1   **E** 10

Look at the Venn diagram below, which shows the number of children that like certain types of cars, then answer the questions that follow.

Children

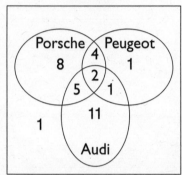

⃝23 How many children like both Audi and Peugeot cars?

A 1   **B** 3   **C** 2   **D** 5   **E** 24

⃝24 Out of all of the children asked, how many do not like Peugeots?

A 24   **B** 13   **C** 25   **D** 16   **E** 12

⃝25 How many children like Porsche cars, but do not like Audi cars?

A 12   **B** 17   **C** 23   **D** 8   **E** 24

CONTINUE WORKING ⟶

26 How many children like all of Porsche, Audi and Peugeot cars?

    A   3   **B**   32   **C**   7   **D**   2   **E**   6

27 How many children like Audi and Peugeot cars, but not Porsche cars?

    A   1   **B**   3   **C**   2   **D**   5   **E**   12

28 Complete the following magic square by choosing the five numbers to go in the place of a, b, c, d and e in the correct order.

Each row, column and diagonal adds up to the same number.

a	b	c
d	e	5
7	1	7

  A   3, 9, 3, 5, 3
  B   2, 9, 3, 5, 5
  C   3, 9, 2, 5, 5
  D   3, 9, 3, 3, 5
  E   3, 9, 3, 5, 5

29 A mystery number, p is divided by 10. The result is subtracted from 99. The answer is 89.

Solve the mystery to find the value of p.

    A   10   **B**   100   **C**   109   **D**   1   **E**   0

30 Mike has five times as many marbles as Julia. Julia has the same number of marbles as Mark. There are 91 marbles in total. How many marbles does Mike have?

    A   39   **B**   13   **C**   26   **D**   65   **E**   60

31 Look at the triangle below, which shows the lengths of each side in cm.

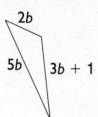

$2b$

$5b$ $3b + 1$

The perimeter = 101 cm. Calculate the value of b.

    A   20   **B**   8   **C**   10   **D**   15   **E**   21

CONTINUE WOKING

(32) Calculate 17 ÷ 0.15

(Include three digits after the decimal point in your answer.)

A   113.333   B   112.344   C   111.785
D   113.345   E   113.453

(33) A gymnastics club has 43 people inside. There are 14 adults. There are 35 men and children.

Use the information above to calculate the number of men, women and children.

A   Men 6, women 8, children 29
B   Men 6, women 6, children 31
C   Men 6, women 8, children 27
D   Men 5, women 9, children 29
E   Men 8, women 5, children 29

(34) How many days are there between the following two dates (including the two dates given).

25th April to 14th June

A   50   B   416   C   51   D   415   E   49

(35) The 16.29 coach takes three hours and 45 minutes to arrive at its destination. What time does the coach arrive at its destination?

A   20.04   B   19.29   C   19.14   D   21.11   E   20.14

(36) Look at the quadrilateral below and calculate the size of angle *a*.

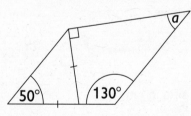

A   65°   B   30°   C   55°   D   80°   E   40°

CONTINUE WORKING

37 Look at the quadrilateral below and calculate the size of angle e (not drawn to scale).

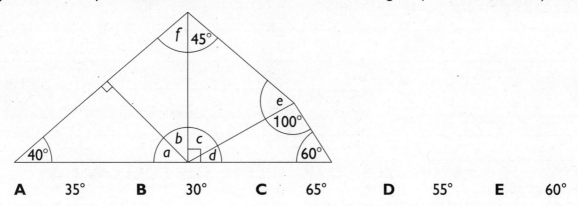

| A | 35° | B | 30° | C | 65° | D | 55° | E | 60° |

38 Look at the following table showing the rate of exchange between the three currencies. Calculate the number that should go in the place of the ?

GB Pounds	Euros	US Dollars
150	165	225
600	660	900
?	1210	1650

A	1,150	B	1,500	C	1,010
D	1,100	E	1,350		

39 I am trying to work out the dimensions of a rectangle. The length is 12 times the width. The perimeter is 104 cm. Calculate the length and width of the rectangle.

A   length 48 cm, width 4 cm
B   length 28 cm, width 24 cm
C   length 20 cm, width 32 cm
D   length 12 cm, width 1 cm
E   length 36 cm, width 3 cm

STOP AND WAIT FOR FURTHER INSTRUCTIONS ⬡✕

Synonyms

 INSTRUCTIONS

 YOU HAVE 5 MINUTES TO COMPLETE THE FOLLOWING SECTION.

YOU HAVE 20 QUESTIONS TO COMPLETE WITHIN THE TIME GIVEN.

EXAMPLES

Example 1

Select the word that is most similar in meaning to the following word:

cold

A	B	C	D	E
collect	fence	foggy	windy	chilly

The correct answer is E. This has already been marked in Example 1 in the Synonyms section of your answer sheet.

Practice Question 1

Select the word that is most similar in meaning to the following word:

start

A	B	C	D	E
cramped	begin	free	without	change

The correct answer is B. Please mark this in Practice Question 1 in the Synonyms section of your answer sheet.

STOP AND WAIT FOR FURTHER INSTRUCTIONS

In each question, identify the word in the table that is most similar in meaning to the given word.

1. assure

A	B	C	D	E
strike	verbose	prohibited	detract	guarantee

2. gracious

A	B	C	D	E
hamlet	pardon	frustration	courteous	stasis

3. frantic

A	B	C	D	E
frenzied	kingdom	arctic	fleeting	confident

4. flourish

A	B	C	D	E
glory	perpetuity	illusion	thrive	alliance

5. fringe

A	B	C	D	E
border	patrol	carousel	amenable	arctic

6. agility

A	B	C	D	E
contend	impertinent	swathe	pious	nimbleness

CONTINUE WORKING ▷

7 uncontrollable

A	B	C	D	E
belief	encounter	unruly	pioneer	rant

8 synthetic

A	B	C	D	E
artificial	fearful	drab	convalescence	drawback

9 royal

A	B	C	D	E
imperial	cartographer	vow	fool	penetrate

10 disguise

A	B	C	D	E
extend	liberal	inconspicuous	masquerade	behaviour

11 flexible

A	B	C	D	E
elude	prosperous	undeniable	supple	deliberate

12 twist

A	B	C	D	E
wring	role	terminus	reposition	assortment

13 impartial

A	B	C	D	E
acclimatise	neutral	guile	celebrated	idler

CONTINUE WORKING

14 overhear

A	B	C	D	E
eavesdrop	correct	understandable	desert	haul

15 understand

A	B	C	D	E
leading	pace	comprehend	gratuity	firm

16 attire

A	B	C	D	E
clothing	disorder	apt	psychiatrist	handicap

17 contest

A	B	C	D	E
erratic	oppose	wail	novice	picture

18 enemy

A	B	C	D	E
coast	pompous	enquire	bustling	foe

19 dishonest

A	B	C	D	E
deceitful	unsanitary	persist	arrogant	yield

20 solve

A	B	C	D	E
flaw	phoney	admission	unravel	persist

STOP AND WAIT FOR FURTHER INSTRUCTIONS

Non-Verbal Reasoning

INSTRUCTIONS

 YOU HAVE 8 MINUTES TO COMPLETE THE FOLLOWING SECTION.

YOU HAVE 9 QUESTIONS TO COMPLETE WITHIN THE TIME GIVEN.

EXAMPLES

COMPLETE THE SEQUENCE Example 1

Select the picture from below that will complete the sequence in place of the ?

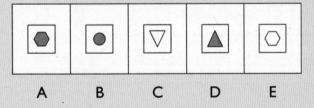

A   B   C   D   E

The correct answer is C. This has already been marked in Example 1 in the Non-Verbal Reasoning section of your answer sheet.

CONTINUE WORKING

COMPLETE THE SEQUENCE Practice Question 1

Select the picture from below that will complete the sequence in place of the ?

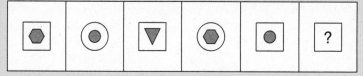

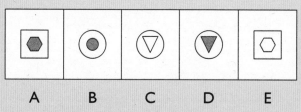

   A   B   C   D   E

The correct answer is D. Please mark this in Practice Question 1 in the Non-Verbal Reasoning section of your answer sheet.

ROTATION Example 2

Select one of the images below that is a rotation of the image on the left.

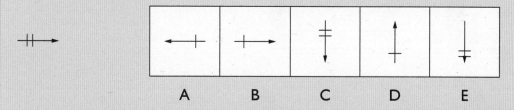

    A   B   C   D   E

The correct answer is C. This has already been marked in Example 2 in the Non-Verbal Reasoning section of your answer sheet.

ROTATION Practice Question 2

Select one of the images below that is a rotation of the image on the left.

 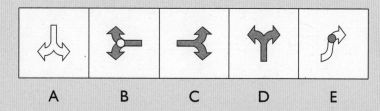

    A   B   C   D   E

The correct answer is B. Please mark this in Practice Question 2 in the Non-Verbal Reasoning section of your answer sheet.

STOP AND WAIT FOR FURTHER INSTRUCTIONS ⊗

Select the pictures which will complete the following sequence:

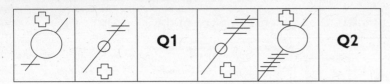

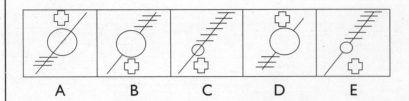

A   B   C   D   E

(1) Select the picture you think should go in place of Q1 here.

(2) Select the picture you think should go in place of Q2 here.

(3) Which pattern completes the sequence in place of the blank grid below?

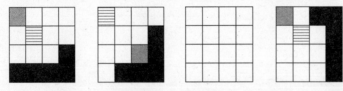

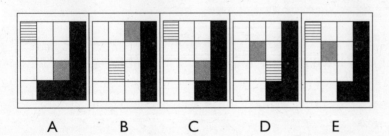

A   B   C   D   E

(4) Which pattern completes the sequence in place of the blank grid below?

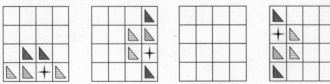

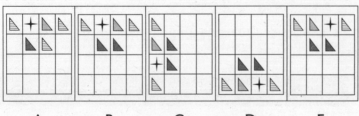

A   B   C   D   E

CONTINUE WORKING

5 Which shape or pattern completes the larger square?

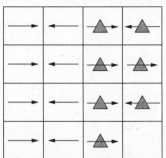

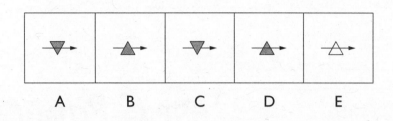

A   B   C   D   E

6 Which shape or pattern completes the larger square?

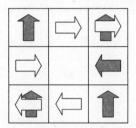

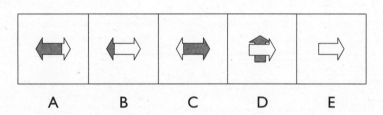

A   B   C   D   E

7 Which shape or pattern completes the larger square?

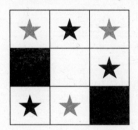

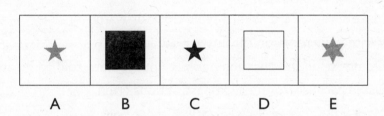

A   B   C   D   E

8 Select one of the images below that is a rotation of the image on the left.

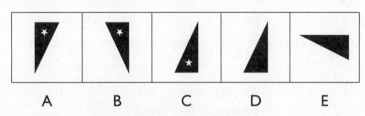

A   B   C   D   E

9 Select one of the images below that is a rotation of the image on the left.

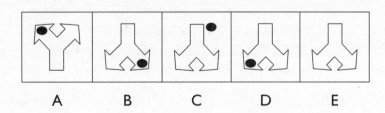

A   B   C   D   E

END OF PAPER

Test C Paper 2

Instructions

1. Ensure you have pencils and an eraser with you.

2. Make sure you are able to see a clock or watch.

3. Write your name on the answer sheet.

4. Do not open the question booklet until you are told to do so by the audio instructions.

5. Listen carefully to the audio instructions given.

6. Mark your answers on the answer sheet only.

7. All workings must be completed on a separate piece of paper.

8. You should not use a calculator, dictionary or thesaurus at any point in this paper.

9. Move through the papers as quickly as possible and with care.

10. Follow the instructions at the foot of each page.

11. You should mark your answers with a horizontal strike, as shown on the answer sheet.

12. If you want to change your answer, ensure that you rub out your first answer and that your second answer is clearly more visible.

13. You can go back and review any questions that are within the section you are working on only. You must await further instructions before moving onto another section.

Symbols and Phrases used in the Tests

 Instructions  Time allowed for this section Stop and wait for further instructions Continue working

Cloze Sentences

 INSTRUCTIONS

 YOU HAVE 7 MINUTES TO COMPLETE THE FOLLOWING SECTION.

YOU HAVE 17 QUESTIONS TO COMPLETE WITHIN THE TIME GIVEN.

EXAMPLES

Example 1

Complete the sentence in the most sensible way by selecting the appropriate word from each set of brackets.

The (dog, big, gate) sat on the (mat, open, great).

A   big, open
B   dog, great
C   gate, mat
D   dog, mat
E   dog, open

The correct answer is D. This has already been marked in Example 1 of the Cloze Sentences section of your answer sheet.

Practice Question 1

Complete the sentence in the most sensible way by selecting the appropriate word from each set of brackets.

My name is (Helen, high, sand) and I am (ten, dig, land) years old.

A   Helen, dig
B   high, land
C   sand, land
D   Helen, land
E   Helen, ten

The correct answer is E. Please mark the answer E in Practice Question 1 in the Cloze Sentences section of your answer sheet.

CONTINUE WORKING

Example 2

One word in the following sentence has had three letters removed from it. Keeping the letters in the same order, identify the three-letter word that is made from these missing letters.

The pupil could not pay attion.

The correct answer is 'ten'. This is shown in Example 2 in the Cloze Sentences section of your answer sheet.

Practice Question 2

One word in the following sentence has had three letters removed from it. Keeping the letters in the same order, identify the three-letter word that is made from these missing letters.

She treasu her mother's bracelet.

The correct answer is 'red'. Please write this in Practice Question 2 in the Cloze Sentences section of your answer sheet.

STOP AND WAIT FOR FURTHER INSTRUCTIONS

Complete the most sensible sentence by selecting the appropriate combination of words from within the brackets. Use one word from each set of brackets.

1. The (plumber, dentist, butcher) took time to reassure me before starting work on my (garden, teeth, hair).

   A   plumber, teeth
   B   butcher, hair
   C   butcher, garden
   D   dentist, teeth
   E   dentist, garden

2. (Despite, Hence, During) the shortfall in numbers, a good (time, weather, seasonal) was had by all (art, rent, guests).

   A   Hence, time, rent
   B   During, time, art
   C   Despite, time, guests
   D   Despite, weather, guests
   E   During, time, rent

CONTINUE WORKING

3. They were hoping the (sympathetic, weather, yesterday) would be better than it had been (recently, tomorrow, treasured).

    A   yesterday, treasured
    B   weather, recently
    C   yesterday, tomorrow
    D   sympathetic, recently
    E   weather, treasured

4. The (support, troubles, health) of the (airport, dream, nation) was behind the athletes.

    A   troubles, nation
    B   troubles, airport
    C   support, nation
    D   health, dream
    E   troubles, dream

5. The (depth, puppy, temperature) of (sympathy, pool, horses) was very much appreciated by the mourners.

    A   depth, pool
    B   temperature, pool
    C   puppy, horses
    D   depth, sympathy
    E   depth, horses

6. The (internet, tortoise, ambulance) rushed to the (scene, clouds, music).

    A   internet, music
    B   tortoise, scene
    C   ambulance, scene
    D   internet, clouds
    E   ambulance, clouds

7. (Where, When, Who) would arrive first was anybody's (dress, guess, blessed).

    A   Where, blessed
    B   Who, dress
    C   When, dress
    D   Who, guess
    E   Where, guess

CONTINUE WORKING ▶

8 The (underneath, ultimate, outcome) of the court case was due (imminently, window, grass).

    A   underneath, imminently
    B   ultimate, grass
    C   outcome, imminently
    D   underneath, grass
    E   ultimate, window

9 The (monkey, bungalow, empathy) perched on her shoulder and (rug, hastened, smiled) for the (chair, camera, sun).

    A   empathy, smiled, camera
    B   bungalow, hastened, sun
    C   empathy, rug, chair
    D   monkey, smiled, camera
    E   monkey, rug, sun

10 How the (direction, completeness, magician) managed to do that, I will (endeavour, never, have) know!

    A   direction, have
    B   completeness, have
    C   magician, never
    D   magician, have
    E   completeness, endeavour

One word in the following sentence has had three letters removed from it. Keeping the letters in the same order, identify the three-letter word that is made from these three missing letters.

11 The flowers were attracg the butterflies.

12 The instabiy of the suspension bridge meant closure was the only option.

13 The pocopier had run out of paper.

14 They were feeling confit as they set out on their expedition.

15 They enjoyed dling their feet in the sea on the hot summer's day.

16 They decided to meet up the foling month.

17 ry little detail had been considered.

STOP AND WAIT FOR FURTHER INSTRUCTIONS

Problem Solving

INSTRUCTIONS

 YOU HAVE 12 MINUTES TO COMPLETE THE FOLLOWING SECTION.

YOU HAVE 10 QUESTIONS TO COMPLETE WITHIN THE TIME GIVEN.

EXAMPLES

A £2.60	B £3.40	C £2.40	D 25	E £1.35
F £3.60	G 14	H 31	I 28	J 34

Example 1

Calculate the following:

If I buy five apples at 20p each, and four bananas at 35p each, how much change will I receive if I pay with a £5 note.

The correct answer is A. This has already been marked in Example 1 in the Problem Solving section of your answer sheet.

Practice Question 1

Calculate the following:

There are 17 people on a bus when it arrives at a bus stop. Eleven people get on the bus, and three get off. How many people are then left on the bus?

The correct answer is D. Please mark this in Practice Question 1 in the Problem Solving section of your answer sheet.

STOP AND WAIT FOR FURTHER INSTRUCTIONS

A 53	B 12	C £527	D £52	E £41.40
F 5	G 9	H 10	I 27	J £35.00

Read the passage below, then select an answer to each question from the 10 different possible answers in the table above. You may use an answer for more than one question.

Sarah is a pupil at Woodbridge Middle School. There are four girls to every five boys in her class. There are 15 boys in Sarah's class.

Sarah's brother Sam attends the same school and Sam is 4 now. In two years' time, Sarah will be twice as old as her brother Sam.

The number of children that attend the school has grown over the last few years, as a new development of houses was recently built in the area. There are now around 150 pupils in the school. There are 76 children in years 4, 5 and 6 combined.

Every year the school raises money for a charity. Sarah is collecting money for the charity from her class, and has completed a sponsored walk. All of the pupils in her class donated £1, except two children who gave £2 each, and six children who donated £5 each. Sarah did not donate any money.

As the number of pupils attending Woodbridge Middle School is growing, the school governors have decided to improve the school by building new classrooms, and refreshing the current classrooms. Sarah's classroom requires a new floor. The dimensions of the floor are 8 m by 4 m. Most of the improvements to the school are being completed at the weekends when the school is always closed.

Part of the money to improve the school is being raised from an increase in the cost of school lunches for the children. These increased by 20p on Wednesday 1st March to £1.80.

Also, in order to raise money, the class organised a raffle for the school fete. A number of prizes were donated, and there was also a special cash prize of £100. The £100 was allocated from the money raised from selling raffle tickets. Ticket sales were as follows:

123 books of tickets were sold at £5 per book.

60 individual tickets were also sold at 20p per ticket.

(1) How many children are there in Sarah's class?

(2) How old is Sarah now?

(3) If there are 23 children in Year 5, how many children are there in years 4 and 6 combined?

CONTINUE WORKING

(4) How much did Sarah raise for charity from her class?

(5) If the tiles used to cover the floor in Sarah's classroom are 50 cm by 50 cm, and come in boxes of 15, how many boxes of tiles are required to cover the entire floor?

(6) Sarah has added up all of the girls' shoe sizes, and they total 60. What is the mean shoe size of the girls in Sarah's class?

(7) How much does Sarah spend on her lunch in March, if she is not absent for any of the school days?

(8) The school buys plastic cups in tubes of 200. If 10 cups cost 3.5p, how much do 50 tubes of plastic cups cost?

(9) In school assembly one morning, there are 174 people in the room. Of these people:

- boys and teachers make up 99 people

- girls and teachers make up 87 people.

How many teachers are in the room?

(10) How much was raised by the raffle after all the prizes were claimed?

STOP AND WAIT FOR FURTHER INSTRUCTIONS

Antonyms

INSTRUCTIONS

 YOU HAVE 10 MINUTES TO COMPLETE THE FOLLOWING SECTION.

YOU HAVE 25 QUESTIONS TO COMPLETE WITHIN THE TIME GIVEN.

EXAMPLES

Example 1

Which word is least similar to the following word:

light

A	B	C	D	E
dark	water	feather	bright	hill

The correct answer is A. This has already been marked in Example 1 in the Antonyms section of your answer sheet.

Practice Question 1

Which word is least similar to the following word:

smooth

A	B	C	D	E
allow	beneath	rough	whilst	shade

The correct answer is C. Please mark the answer C in Practice Question 1 in the Antonyms section of your answer sheet.

STOP AND WAIT FOR FURTHER INSTRUCTIONS

Which word is least similar to the following word:

1 fresh

A	B	C	D	E
board	stale	silence	increase	indeed

2 stationary

A	B	C	D	E
unsurprised	phone	perilous	mobile	paper

3 steep

A	B	C	D	E
home	reject	bold	separate	gradual

4 straight

A	B	C	D	E
crooked	merry	bright	gentle	success

5 superior

A	B	C	D	E
contaminated	silence	dull	inferior	shrink

6 tame

A	B	C	D	E
prohibit	sweet	wild	preserve	modest

CONTINUE WORKING

7 tiny

A	B	C	D	E
fade	incompetent	decrease	enormous	advance

8 unite

A	B	C	D	E
separate	imprudent	selfish	absurd	follower

9 vacant

A	B	C	D	E
height	relaxed	unfriendly	occupied	disperse

10 clear

A	B	C	D	E
reduce	valour	sober	fondness	vague

11 better

A	B	C	D	E
fade	generous	genuine	reaction	worse

12 combine

A	B	C	D	E
contract	separate	fertile	loose	crooked

13 encourage

A	B	C	D	E
courage	impolite	guilty	discourage	mild

CONTINUE WORKING

(14) import

A	B	C	D	E
strict	cavity	indirect	legal	export

(15) brighten

A	B	C	D	E
fade	trick	delight	stale	disobedient

(16) boundless

A	B	C	D	E
limited	gradual	admit	increase	occupied

(17) decrease

A	B	C	D	E
admiration	separate	increase	abundant	genuine

(18) admit

A	B	C	D	E
fail	mobile	legal	immigration	deny

(19) action

A	B	C	D	E
displeasure	constant	inaction	loose	often

CONTINUE WORKING

20 enigmatic

A	B	C	D	E
clear	graceful	innocent	minute	ally

21 changeable

A	B	C	D	E
allay	separate	constant	imprudent	smart

22 pleasure

A	B	C	D	E
fail	encouraged	simple	disperse	displeasure

23 order

A	B	C	D	E
hinder	bright	stale	singular	disorder

24 amateur

A	B	C	D	E
modern	professional	usual	disloyal	cramped

25 domestic

A	B	C	D	E
foreign	mobile	introvert	mild	shrink

STOP AND WAIT FOR FURTHER INSTRUCTIONS ✕

Non-Verbal Reasoning

INSTRUCTIONS

YOU HAVE 8 MINUTES TO COMPLETE THE FOLLOWING SECTION.

YOU HAVE 15 QUESTIONS TO COMPLETE WITHIN THE TIME GIVEN.

EXAMPLES

CODES Example 1

Look at the codes for the following patterns and identify the missing code for the pattern on the far right.

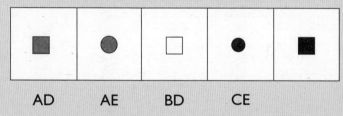

AD   AE   BD   CE

A	BE
B	AD
C	BC
D	BD
E	CD

The correct answer is E. This has already been marked in Example 1 in the Non-Verbal Reasoning section of your answer sheet.

CODES Practice Question 1

Look at the codes for the following patterns and identify the missing code for the pattern on the far right.

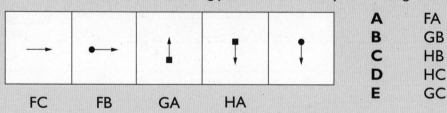

FC   FB   GA   HA

A	FA
B	GB
C	HB
D	HC
E	GC

The correct answer is C. Please mark this in Practice Question 1 in the Non-Verbal Reasoning section of your answer sheet.

CONTINUE WORKING

COMPLETE THE SQUARE Example 2

Which shape or pattern completes the square?

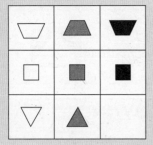 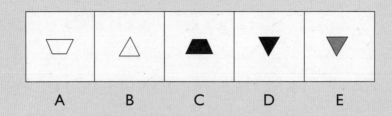

A   B   C   D   E

The correct answer is D. This has already been marked in Example 2 in the Non-Verbal Reasoning section of your answer sheet.

COMPLETE THE SQUARE Practice Question 2

Which shape or pattern completes the square?

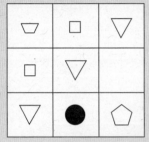 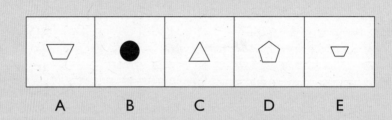

A   B   C   D   E

The correct answer is B. Please mark this in Practice Question 2 in the Non-Verbal Reasoning section of your answer sheet.

STOP AND WAIT FOR FURTHER INSTRUCTIONS

(1) Look at the codes for the following patterns and identify the missing code for the pattern on the far right.

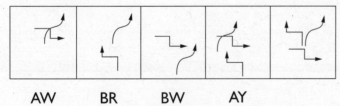

AW   BR   BW   AY

A	BY
B	AR
C	AY
D	BW
E	BR

CONTINUE WORKING

(2) Look at the codes for the following patterns and identify the missing code for the pattern on the far right.

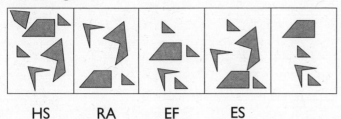

HS RA EF ES

A	EF
B	RF
C	RA
D	RS
E	EA

(3) Look at the codes for the following patterns and identify the missing code for the pattern on the far right.

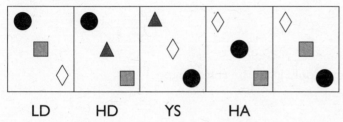

LD HD YS HA

A	LH
B	HD
C	LB
D	YS
E	YA

(4) Look at the codes for the following patterns and identify the missing code for the pattern on the far right.

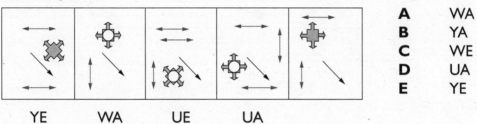

YE WA UE UA

A	WA
B	YA
C	WE
D	UA
E	YE

(5) Look at the two shapes on the left immediately below.
Find the connection between them and apply it to the third shape.

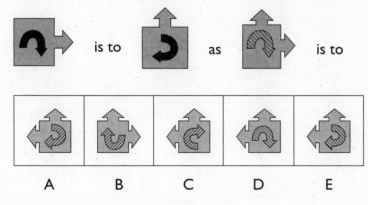

is to   as   is to

A   B   C   D   E

CONTINUE WORKING

6 Look at the two shapes on the left immediately below.
Find the connection between them and apply it to the third shape.

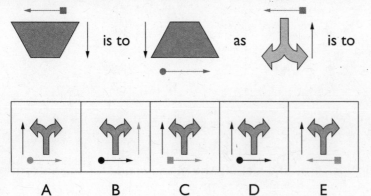

| A | B | C | D | E |

7 Look at the two shapes on the left immediately below.
Find the connection between them and apply it to the third shape.

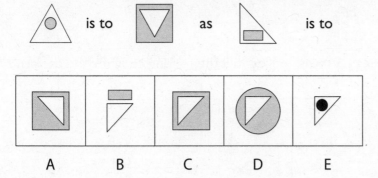

| A | B | C | D | E |

8 Look at the two shapes on the left immediately below.
Find the connection between them and apply it to the third shape.

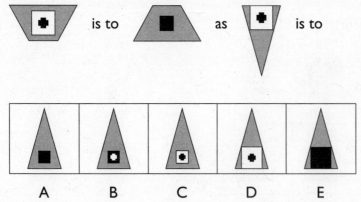

| A | B | C | D | E |

CONTINUE WORKING ⇨

9 Select the correct picture from the bottom row in order to finish the incomplete sequence on the top row.

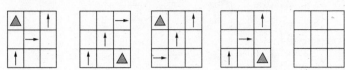

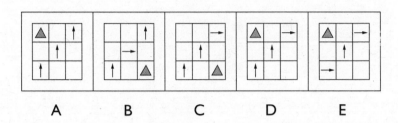

A B C D E

10 Select the picture from below that will complete the sequence in place of the?

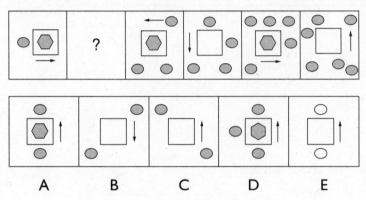

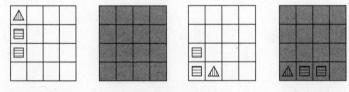

A B C D E

11 Which pattern completes the sequence in place of the blank grid below?

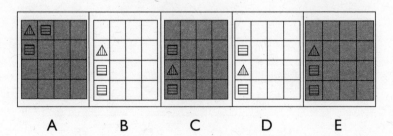

A B C D E

CONTINUE WORKING

(12) Which pattern completes the sequence in place of the blank grid below?

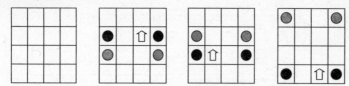

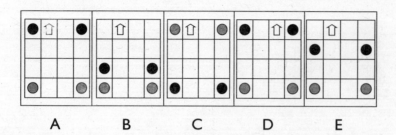

    A   B   C   D   E

(13) Which shape or pattern completes the larger square?

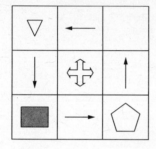

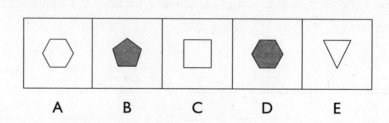

    A   B   C   D   E

(14) Which shape or pattern completes the larger square?

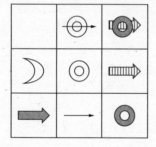

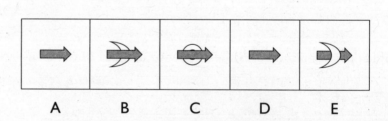

    A   B   C   D   E

(15) Which shape or pattern completes the larger square?

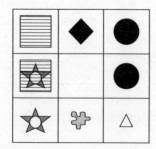

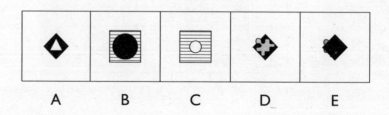

    A   B   C   D   E

STOP AND WAIT FOR FURTHER INSTRUCTIONS

Shuffled Sentences

INSTRUCTIONS

 YOU HAVE 8 MINUTES TO COMPLETE THE FOLLOWING SECTION.

YOU HAVE 15 QUESTIONS TO COMPLETE WITHIN THE TIME GIVEN.

EXAMPLES

Example 1

The following sentence is shuffled and also contains one unnecessary word. Rearrange the sentence correctly, in order to identify the unnecessary word.

dog the ran fetch the to stick gluing.

A	B	C	D	E
gluing	dog	ran	the	stick

The correct answer is A. This has already been marked in Example 1 in the Shuffled Sentences section of your answer sheet.

Practice Question 1

The following sentence is shuffled and also contains one unnecessary word. Rearrange the sentence correctly, in order to identify the unnecessary word.

pushed Emma stood up and closed the table under the chairs.

A	B	C	D	E
chairs	stood	under	closed	Emma

The correct answer is D. Please mark this in Practice Question 1 in the Shuffled Sentences section of your answer sheet.

STOP AND WAIT FOR FURTHER INSTRUCTIONS

The following sentence is shuffled and also contains one unnecessary word. Rearrange the sentence correctly, in order to identify the unnecessary word.

(1) a strewn streets was night's the neighbourhood's across storm of last result debris as an.

A	B	C	D	E
an	night's	result	debris	strewn

(2) airport delays caused the bad weather to severe whether flights at the.

A	B	C	D	E
whether	bad	flights	airport	severe

(3) this big difference is likely to make those a.

A	B	C	D	E
difference	likely	big	those	this

(4) the leaf in the tree decided to she through book bookshop whilst.

A	B	C	D	E
tree	through	whilst	decided	book

(5) although it was now the parents of the responsibility.

A	B	C	D	E
it	now	parents	although	responsibility

(6) checked all the scores there were confirm to their accuracy.

A	B	C	D	E
were	there	accuracy	confirm	scores

CONTINUE WORKING

7 seen she by what was she had scene astounded just.

A	B	C	D	E
she	astounded	scene	what	was

8 the ideal central location was mirrored for them.

A	B	C	D	E
them	central	ideal	mirrored	the

9 was the hallway positioned in the hanging basket.

A	B	C	D	E
hanging	was	in	hallway	the

10 to recover the several attempts were made cargo sunk.

A	B	C	D	E
attempts	sunk	recover	cargo	made

11 the journey taken car hours by three took.

A	B	C	D	E
car	journey	took	taken	hours

12 the ball dress kicked code stipulated for annual formal the attire charity.

A	B	C	D	E
kicked	ball	stipulated	charity	formal

13 provided the storage chest bedroom drawers waist extra of in the.

A	B	C	D	E
waist	drawers	extra	storage	of

CONTINUE WORKING ➡

(14) must use the theatre prohibited of was cameras in.

A	B	C	D	E
prohibited	use	theatre	must	cameras

(15) was in accept a payment return for cash offered discount in.

A	B	C	D	E
discount	accept	cash	in	for

END OF PAPER

Test D Paper 1

Instructions

1. Ensure you have pencils and an eraser with you.
2. Make sure you are able to see a clock or watch.
3. Write your name on the answer sheet.
4. Do not open the question booklet until you are told to do so by the audio instructions.
5. Listen carefully to the audio instructions given.
6. Mark your answers on the answer sheet only.
7. All workings must be completed on a separate piece of paper.
8. You should not use a calculator, dictionary or thesaurus at any point in this paper.
9. Move through the papers as quickly as possible and with care.
10. Follow the instructions at the foot of each page.
11. You should mark your answers with a horizontal strike, as shown on the answer sheet.
12. If you want to change your answer, ensure that you rub out your first answer and that your second answer is clearly more visible.
13. You can go back and review any questions that are within the section you are working on only. You must await further instructions before moving onto another section.

Symbols and Phrases used in the Tests

 Instructions   Time allowed for this section   Stop and wait for further instructions   Continue working

Comprehension

 YOU HAVE 10 MINUTES TO COMPLETE THE FOLLOWING SECTION.

YOU HAVE 10 QUESTIONS TO COMPLETE WITHIN THE TIME GIVEN.

EXAMPLES

Comprehension Example

Some people choose to start their Christmas shopping early in October. It has been reported that some people even buy their Christmas presents in the sales in August. In recent years, people have the option of purchasing their Christmas presents online.

Example 1

According to the passage, what is the earliest that people start their Christmas shopping?

A   In the preceding summer
B   In the preceding October
C   In the preceding November
D   Christmas Eve
E   In early December

The correct answer is A. This has already been marked in Example 1 in the Comprehension section of your answer sheet.

Practice Question 1

In recent years, what has caused a change in how people shop?

A   There are more shops
B   Shops are more crowded
C   You can easily organise your journey to the shops
D   New products are available
E   There has been a rise in use of the Internet

The correct answer is E. Please mark this in Practice Question 1 in the Comprehension section of your answer sheet.

STOP AND WAIT FOR FURTHER INSTRUCTIONS

Read the following passage, then answer the questions below.

A Perspective on the Changing World of Communication

Communication has developed over the millennia at a phenomenal rate. It continues to develop and, as a result, the world has become unrecognisable for many older people.

Communication is made up of verbal communication (spoken), non-verbal communication (body language) and the written word.

Face-to-face communication is complex and subtle messages are often conveyed through body language and eye movements. Many people now study these signs to learn how to read the signals that the person is unintentionally giving away, rather than just listening to the words which are being spoken. People wish to master these signals to enhance their business skills and to assist their career path. People also study this for interpersonal relations outside of the business environment.

Interpreting signals from body language seems quite the opposite of communication via emails and texts, which do not have the benefit of facial expressions and body language to help convey the right message. The tone of emails can easily be misconstrued. When writing an email, it is very important to choose words carefully and read the whole email to check how the email will be interpreted by the recipient. To reintroduce some sort of human emotion, many people also include icons or 'emoticons' in their texts and emails, such as a 'smiley face'. Instantly, the recipient is given the message that this email or text has happy and informal content.

In the context of the business world, emails have drastically reduced the time it takes to communicate to large numbers of people within an organisation, or between organisations. Teams of people can easily be brought together for a meeting via video calls, often saving a huge amount of time and money on travel. The decisions and actions which are a result of these meetings, the 'Minutes', can be communicated easily, cheaply and quickly. In the business environment, icons are inappropriate and should be avoided.

Many people now receive so many emails that it is unmanageable to read and respond to the vast majority of them. As people receive so many emails, many remain unread and are simply deleted. As people become aware that the detail in emails is often skimmed over, people's communication styles have changed. It is advised that lengthy emails should be avoided, unless it is absolutely necessary to write more.

People are now almost always contactable by phone and it is hard to think that just over thirty years ago the first commercially available mobile phones were the size of a household brick and limited to phone calls only. Since then, the size of mobile phones has reduced and the tasks which can be performed on them have broadened. People are able to run their social lives as well as their business lives via 'apps', which is the shortened word for 'applications'. It could be said that people now communicate less by phone, as many would prefer to text or communicate via social media.

CONTINUE WORKING

How different the world is now. A person born in the early to mid-20th century has seen so many fundamental changes in the world, that it has become unrecognisable. Many elderly people find that communicating using today's technology is out of this world and incomprehensible; whereas technology is the norm to most young people. There are now many initiatives which seek to assist elderly people to understand how to use the Internet. Subsequently, elderly people can then learn how to use social media to keep them in touch with their families. In addition, they can complete tasks such as online shopping, online banking and memory games.

(1) What signals are important in face-to-face communication?

    A   The spoken word only
    B   The written word
    C   Body language and eye movements
    D   Signals written on the wall
    E   Emails only

(2) Why do people study body language for business purposes?

    A   To be able to understand what people are saying
    B   To make their emails more coherent
    C   To understand foreign languages
    D   To enhance interpersonal relationships
    E   To further their career and to bring them success

(3) What is the meaning of 'misconstrued'?

    A   Miscalculated
    B   Misdial
    C   Misunderstood
    D   Mislead
    E   Misbehaved

(4) According to the passage, what are the benefits of email communication regarding meetings?

    A   The meetings have to be attended by many people
    B   The meetings are shorter
    C   The details from the meetings are instantly recorded
    D   The details from the meetings can be easily sent to a significant amount of people
    E   The details from the meetings can be typed up easily

CONTINUE WORKING

5 According to the passage, which phrase below best describes how mobile phones have developed?

A   Mobiles phones are now often used in business meetings
B   The size of mobile phones has reduced and their capabilities have increased
C   Mobile phones have not dramatically changed or developed
D   Mobile phones have replaced verbal communication
E   The size of mobile phones has reduced and the use of them is limited

6 According to the passage, what often happens to emails which are received?

A   A large number of emails are unread or deleted
B   Almost all emails are read and responded to
C   Very few emails are deleted
D   Many emails are forwarded to large amounts of people
E   Many emails are lengthy and are always read

7 In the context of the passage, what type of word is 'household'?

A   Noun
B   Adjective
C   Verb
D   Pronoun
E   Adverb

8 What is the meaning of 'commonplace'?

A   A place that everyone knows
B   An item that is low in quality
C   An item that people use in their everyday life
D   An item that is rarely used
E   An item that is easy to understand

9 In the context of the passage, which of the words below is the opposite of 'incomprehensible'?

A   User-friendly
B   Unfriendly
C   Unintelligible
D   Compatible
E   Sensible

10 Which phrase best describes the final paragraph in the passage?

A   Elderly people understand the changes in technology
B   Most elderly people use social media daily
C   Elderly people are being taught how to communicate via social media
D   Many young people are teaching elderly people how to use the Internet
E   Elderly people are being taught the dangers of social media

STOP AND WAIT FOR FURTHER INSTRUCTIONS

Numeracy

 INSTRUCTIONS

 YOU HAVE 17 MINUTES TO COMPLETE THE FOLLOWING SECTION.

YOU HAVE 28 QUESTIONS TO COMPLETE WITHIN THE TIME GIVEN.

EXAMPLES

Example 1

Calculate 53 – 42

A 12   **B** 1   **C** 4   **D** 5   **E** 11

The correct answer is E. This has already been marked in Example 1 in the Numeracy section of your answer sheet.

Practice Question 1

Calculate 95 – 75

A 21   **B** 20   **C** 19   **D** 18   **E** 13

The correct answer is B. Please mark this in Practice Question 1 in the Numeracy section of your answer sheet.

STOP AND WAIT FOR FURTHER INSTRUCTIONS

(1) $36,048 \div 12$

  A 3,040   **B** 304   **C** 4,003   **D** 3,004   **E** 34

(2) $12^2 - 11^2$

  A 144   **B** 23   **C** 133   **D** 10   **E** 165

③ $\frac{1}{3}$ of 294

A   102   **B**   97   **C**   96   **D**   9   **E**   98

④ What is the size of each interior angle in a pentagon?

A   72°   **B**   62°   **C**   105°   **D**   108°   **E**   150°

⑤ Find a, if $b = 2a - 4$ and $b = 4$

A   0   **B**   8   **C**   4   **D**   2   **E**   1

⑥ If $b = 8$, find a using the following equation:

$8a - b = 0$

A   8   **B**   2   **C**   0   **D**   1   **E**   4

⑦ Find the missing number marked by?

$5 \times 3 + ? = 20$

A   1   **B**   5   **C**   4   **D**   17   **E**   10

⑧ Find the missing number marked by?

$8 \times ? - 8 = 72$

A   1   **B**   10   **C**   5   **D**   8   **E**   17

⑨ Find the missing number marked by?

$? + 5 \times 3 = 30$

A   1   **B**   5   **C**   2   **D**   4   **E**   15

⑩ If wrapping paper costs £1.50 per metre, how many rolls can I buy for £10? Each roll is 3 m long.

A   6   **B**   3   **C**   2   **D**   15   **E**   30

CONTINUE WORKING ⇨

11 I have just rolled a 4 on a die. The die is a fair die with 6 sides.

What is the probability that the next time I roll the die, I will roll a 4?

A 1 in 4	**B** 1 in 3	**C** 1 in 16
D 1 in 36	**E** 1 in 6	

12 Calculate the answer to the following:

(25 ÷ 5) + 22 − 11 = ?

A 16   **B** 38   **C** 27   **D** 6   **E** 15

13 I am sharing out a large pizza between guests at a party. There are 20 guests. A quarter of the guests have said they would not like any pizza. The pizza is cut into equal sized slices. A third of the guests who wanted pizza did not have time to eat their pizza. How many pieces of pizza are remaining?

A 4   **B** 5   **C** 7   **D** 6   **E** 10

14 What is the first number in this sequence marked by ?

? , 29, 24, 20, 17, 15

A 34   **B** 33   **C** 35   **D** 28   **E** 31

15 What is half of 52?

A 25   **B** 24   **C** 26   **D** 31   **E** 35

16 I have 56 sweets that I am sharing out equally amongst my 6 friends and myself. How many 7s can I take away from 56?

A 7   **B** 8   **C** 6   **D** 5   **E** 10

17 The news headlines are repeated on a television channel precisely every 15 minutes. How many times are the headlines shown on the television channel each day?

A 144   **B** 95   **C** 40   **D** 96   **E** 48

CONTINUE WORKING ⇨

18 What is the next number in the sequence?

0.1, 0.2, 0.4, 0.8, ?

A   1.6   B   0.16   C   0.10   D   0.12   E   0.18

19 Which amount is largest?

A   one-quarter of 124
B   one-fifth of 160
C   one-tenth of 315
D   half of 62
E   one-third of 94

20 There are five people in a room. After a while, three of the people leave the room and a further seven people enter the room. How many people are now in the room?

A   5   B   3   C   4   D   7   E   9

The following three questions relate to the chart shown below:

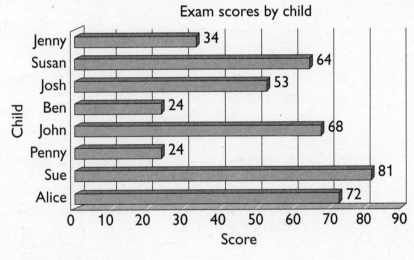

Exam scores by child

21 What is the range?

A   24   B   52   C   35   D   57   E   81

22 What is the mean exam score?

A   52.5   B   55   C   50   D   24   E   81

CONTINUE WORKING

(23) What is the median exam score?

  A   56   **B**   81   **C**   58.5   **D**   54   **E**   35

The following five questions relate to the chart shown below:

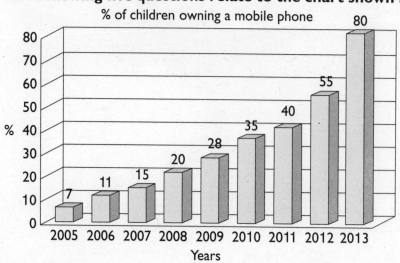

% of children owning a mobile phone

(24) What percentage of children owned a mobile phone in the year 2011?

  A   25   **B**   35   **C**   40   **D**   20   **E**   15

(25) Between which two years did the percentage of children owning a mobile phone increase by five times exactly?

  A   2006–2012   **B**   2005–2009   **C**   2011–2013
  D   2008–2013   **E**   2000–2007

(26) Between which two consecutive years did the percentage of children owning a mobile phone increase the most?

  A   2004–2005   **B**   2001–2002   **C**   2007–2008
  D   2009–2010   **E**   2012–2013

(27) Calculate the mean percentage of children owning a mobile phone over the period shown.

  A   31   **B**   34   **C** 32 and $\frac{1}{3}$
  D 23 and $\frac{1}{4}$ **E** 25 and $\frac{1}{5}$

(28) If the mean percentage of children owning a mobile phone increases to 38 over the period to 2014 (from 2005), what is the percentage of children who owned a mobile phone in 2014?

  A   65   **B**   60   **C**   75   **D**   89   **E**   100

STOP AND WAIT FOR FURTHER INSTRUCTIONS

Synonyms

 YOU HAVE 9 MINUTES TO COMPLETE THE FOLLOWING SECTION.

YOU HAVE 20 QUESTIONS TO COMPLETE WITHIN THE TIME GIVEN.

EXAMPLES

Example 1

Select the word that is most similar in meaning to the following word:

cold

A	B	C	D	E
collect	fence	foggy	windy	chilly

The correct answer is E. This has already been marked in Example 1 in the Synonyms section of your answer sheet.

Practice Question 1

Select the word that is most similar in meaning to the following word:

start

A	B	C	D	E
cramped	begin	free	without	change

The correct answer is B. Please mark this in Practice Question 1 in the Synonyms section of your answer sheet.

STOP AND WAIT FOR FURTHER INSTRUCTIONS

In each row, identify the word in the table that is most similar in meaning to the word above the table.

(1) daily

A	B	C	D	E
irregularly	routinely	seldom	momentous	calmly

(2) falsify

A	B	C	D	E
verify	rectify	easily	distort	validate

(3) vigour

A	B	C	D	E
vitality	lethargy	apathy	balanced	caged

(4) blossom

A	B	C	D	E
notion	infer	fritter	crazed	unfold

(5) recollect

A	B	C	D	E
dial	remember	perverse	despise	recourse

(6) organisation

A	B	C	D	E
intermittent	company	alcove	consensus	arrested

CONTINUE WORKING

7 vintage

A	B	C	D	E
misshapen	advantageous	classic	inopportune	contemporary

8 disclosure

A	B	C	D	E
hone	tumbler	pious	shifting	admission

9 energetic

A	B	C	D	E
multitude	spirited	passive	insolent	motionless

10 thanks

A	B	C	D	E
restless	denial	emptiness	gratitude	anomaly

11 hasten

A	B	C	D	E
hurry	improvement	dawdle	periodic	beautiful

12 quantity

A	B	C	D	E
thoughtless	conviction	delightful	averse	amount

13 ravage

A	B	C	D	E
entail	devour	sustenance	revelry	triumph

CONTINUE WORKING ➡

14 sophisticated

A	B	C	D	E
squalid	derogatory	deplorable	reluctant	civilised

15 genial

A	B	C	D	E
genius	detract	unhappy	detestable	happy

16 radiate

A	B	C	D	E
bard	emanate	aligned	deduce	foolish

17 courteous

A	B	C	D	E
enshroud	affray	polite	pliable	suggest

18 serene

A	B	C	D	E
rounded	glaring	pomp	tranquil	honour

19 diminish

A	B	C	D	E
nifty	lessen	increase	equality	lesson

20 course

A	B	C	D	E
glut	attentive	series	sterile	affectionate

STOP AND WAIT FOR FURTHER INSTRUCTIONS

Non-Verbal Reasoning

 YOU HAVE 9 MINUTES TO COMPLETE THE FOLLOWING SECTION.

YOU HAVE 15 QUESTIONS TO COMPLETE WITHIN THE TIME GIVEN.

EXAMPLES

REFLECTION Example 1

Select an image from the row below that shows how the following shape or pattern will appear when reflected.

The correct answer is E. This has already been marked in Example 1 in the Non-Verbal Reasoning section of your answer sheet.

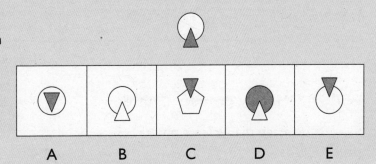

REFLECTION Practice Question 1

Select an image from the row below that shows how the following shape or pattern will appear when reflected.

The correct answer is C. Please mark this in Practice Question 1 in the Non-Verbal Reasoning section of your answer sheet.

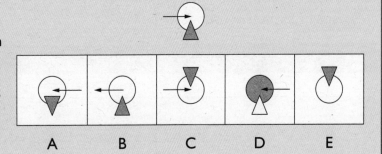

ROTATION Example 2

Select an image from the row below that is a rotation of the following image.

The correct answer is C. This has already been marked in Example 2 in the Non-Verbal Reasoning section of your answer sheet.

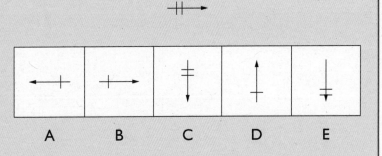

CONTINUE WORKING

ROTATION Practice Question 2

Select an image from the row below that is a rotation of the following image.

The correct answer is B. Please mark this in Practice Question 2 in the Non-Verbal Reasoning section of your answer sheet.

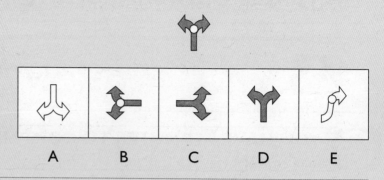

LEAST SIMILAR Example 3

Select the image that is least similar to the other images.

The correct answer is B. This has already been marked in Example 3 in the Non-Verbal Reasoning section of your answer sheet.

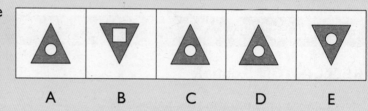

LEAST SIMILAR Practice Question 3

Select the image that is least similar to the other images.

The correct answer is E. Please mark this in Practice Question 3 in the Non-Verbal Reasoning section of your answer sheet.

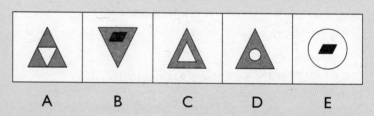

STOP AND WAIT FOR FURTHER INSTRUCTIONS

1 Look at the following image. Select the image in the row below that is a rotation of the image.

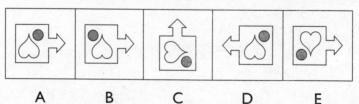

CONTINUE WORKING

② Look at the following image. Select the image in the row below that is a rotation of the image.

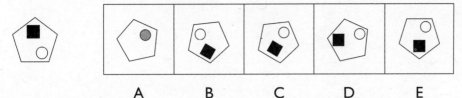

         A   B   C   D   E

③ Select the image that is least similar to the other images in the row.

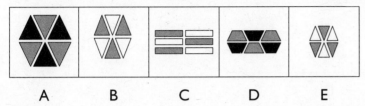

         A   B   C   D   E

④ Select the image that is least similar to the other images in the row.

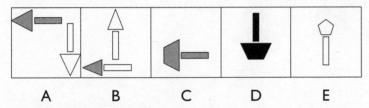

         A   B   C   D   E

⑤ Select the image that is least similar to the other images in the row.

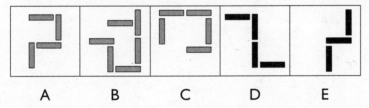

         A   B   C   D   E

⑥ Select the image that is least similar to the other images in the row.

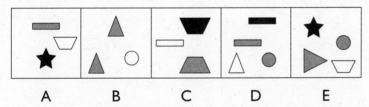

         A   B   C   D   E

⑦ Select the image that is least similar to the other images in the row.

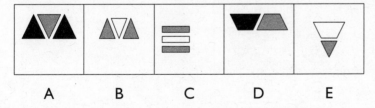

         A   B   C   D   E

CONTINUE WORKING ⇨

8 Select the image that is least similar to the other images in the row.

A	B	C	D	E

9 Select the image that is least similar to the other images in the row.

A	B	C	D	E

10 Select the image that is least similar to the other images in the row.

A	B	C	D	E

11 Select the image that is least similar to the other images in the row.

A	B	C	D	E

12 Select the image that is least similar to the other images the row.

A	B	C	D	E

13 Select an image from the row below that shows how the following image will appear when reflected in the dashed line.

A	B	C	D	E

CONTINUE WORKING ➡

(14) Select an image from the row below that shows how the following image will appear when reflected in the dashed line.

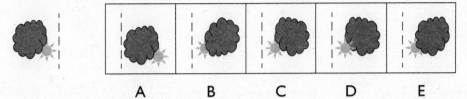

A   B   C   D   E

(15) Select an image from the row below that shows how the following image will appear when reflected in the dashed line.

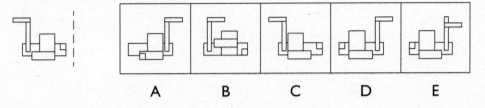

A   B   C   D   E

END OF PAPER

Test D Paper 2

Instructions

1. Ensure you have pencils and an eraser with you.
2. Make sure you are able to see a clock or watch.
3. Write your name on the answer sheet.
4. Do not open the question booklet until you are told to do so by the audio instructions.
5. Listen carefully to the audio instructions given.
6. Mark your answers on the answer sheet only.
7. All workings must be completed on a separate piece of paper.
8. You should not use a calculator, dictionary or thesaurus at any point in this paper.
9. Move through the papers as quickly as possible and with care.
10. Follow the instructions at the foot of each page.
11. You should mark your answers with a horizontal strike, as shown on the answer sheet.
12. If you want to change your answer, ensure that you rub out your first answer and that your second answer is clearly more visible.
13. You can go back and review any questions that are within the section you are working on only. You must await further instructions before moving onto another section.

Symbols and Phrases used in the Tests

 Instructions  Time allowed for this section Stop and wait for further instructions Continue working

Cloze Sentences

 YOU HAVE 7 MINUTES TO COMPLETE THE FOLLOWING SECTION.

YOU HAVE 17 QUESTIONS TO COMPLETE WITHIN THE TIME GIVEN.

EXAMPLES

A	B	C	D	E	F	G	H	I	J
dog	small	tiny	huge	minute	free	big	enormous	gigantic	penguin

Example 1

Complete the sentence in the most sensible way by selecting an appropriate word from the table above.

The _____ sat by the fire.

The correct answer is A. This has already been marked in Example 1 in the Cloze Sentences section of your answer sheet.

Practice Question 1

Complete the sentence in the most sensible way by selecting an appropriate word from the table above.

The _____ laid an egg.

The correct answer is J. Please mark the answer J in Practice Question 1 in the Cloze Sentences section of your answer sheet.

Example 2

One word in the following sentence has had three letters removed from it. Keeping the letters in the same order, identify the three-letter word that is made from the missing letters.

The pupil could not pay attion.

The correct answer is 'ten'. This has been marked in Example 2 in the Cloze Sentences section of your answer sheet.

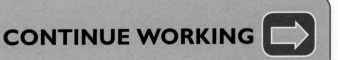 **CONTINUE WORKING**

Practice Question 2

One word in the following sentence has had three letters removed from it. Keeping the letters in the same order, identify the three-letter word that is made from the missing letters.

She treasu her mother's bracelet.

The correct answer is 'red'. Please mark this in Practice Question 2 in the Cloze Sentences section of your answer sheet.

STOP AND WAIT FOR FURTHER INSTRUCTIONS

Complete the most sensible sentence by selecting an appropriate word from the table below.

A fantastical	B dehydrated	C laborious	D fractured	E subterranean
F extracted	G ruling	H standard	I ample	J adventure

(1) The blood was _____ from the ancient specimen.

(2) The judge's _____ was final.

(3) The _____ cave was dark and cold.

(4) The parking signs gave the residents _____ warning that the road would close at midnight.

(5) The work was painstaking and _____.

(6) The animal's limb was _____ in several places.

(7) The journey came to an end and the _____ was over.

CONTINUE WORKING

(8) The film was a ＿＿＿＿＿＿ story, set in space.

(9) The athlete's dedication to her training had set a high ＿＿＿＿＿＿.

(10) After a day of walking in the mountains, the boy felt ＿＿＿＿＿＿.

One word in the following sentence has had three letters removed from it. Keeping the letters in the same order, identify the three-letter word that is made from the three missing letters.

(11) The hairdresser tmed the girl's hair.

(12) The landse was rugged.

(13) The project failed for one rea.

(14) The boy hed in the glorious sunshine.

(15) The girl's clothes were sped when she splashed in the mud.

(16) Does this car have a sp tyre?

(17) The se of the book had broken and all the pages had fallen out.

STOP AND WAIT FOR FURTHER INSTRUCTIONS ⊗

Problem Solving

 INSTRUCTIONS

 YOU HAVE 12 MINUTES TO COMPLETE THE FOLLOWING SECTION.

YOU HAVE 10 QUESTIONS TO COMPLETE WITHIN THE TIME GIVEN.

EXAMPLES

A £2.60	B £3.40	C £2.40	D 25	E £1.35
F £3.60	G 14	H 31	I 28	J 34

Example 1

Calculate the following:

If I buy five apples at 20p each, and four bananas at 35p each, how much change will I receive if I pay with a £5 note.

The correct answer is A. This has already been marked in Example 1 in the Problem Solving section of your answer sheet.

Practice Question 1

Calculate the following:

There are 17 people on a bus when it arrives at a bus stop. Eleven people get on the bus, and three get off. How many people are then left on the bus?

The correct answer is D. Please mark this in Practice Question 1 in the Problem Solving section of your answer sheet.

STOP AND WAIT FOR FURTHER INSTRUCTIONS

Several questions will follow for you to answer.

A 35	B £104	C 8	D 10	E 95
F 7	G 85	H £84	I £94	J 4

Select an answer to each question from the 10 different possible answers in the table above.
You may use an answer for more than one question.

(1) Edward is planning a birthday party at the local zoo. He invites eight boys and four girls. If $\frac{3}{4}$ of the children invited attend the party, and there are two girls at the party, how many boys are at the party (including Edward himself)?

(2) How many children are at the party in total?

(3) At the entrance to the zoo, the following entry prices are displayed:
    Adults £12 each
    Children £8 each
    For groups of 11 or more, £7 (per adult or child)
If two adults also go to the zoo to supervise the children, what is the total entry cost for the party?

(4) Edward receives some gifts and money from his friends and family for his birthday. He receives a £10 note from each of four friends, £20 from one family member, and a £5 note from each of six other people. Finally, he receives a birthday card with four £1 coins taped inside. How much money did Edward receive for his birthday?

(5) At lunchtime, there is a birthday party lunch at the zoo for everyone in the party group. The zoo provides a set party lunch for each of the adults and children. The cost is £8.50 per child and £9.50 per adult. What is the total cost of the party lunch?

(6) Everyone sits down for lunch at 13:05 and the lunch finishes at 14:40. How long did the lunch last in minutes?

(7) Following lunch, the group decide to go on the zoo train that carries visitors around the zoo. The train stops at various places around the zoo. When the entire party boarded the train, there were already 68 people on board. At the next stop, 13 other zoo visitors alight from the train, and a further 18 visitors board the train. How many people are on the train at that point?

CONTINUE WORKING

(8) The next stop for the train is the tiger and lion enclosures, which are very popular. 78 of the passengers alight from the train at this point. Nobody is able to board the train at this stop. How many people are on the train after the 78 people have alighted?

(9) The party get off the train at the final destination which is the aquarium. The time at this point is 15:25. How many minutes were they on board the train if they first boarded the train at 14:50?

(10) The group left the aquarium quite late in the day. The train had stopped running for the day at this point. The group had only 15 minutes to reach the exit of the zoo before it was locked at 5 p.m. If the zoo exit was 1 km from the aquarium, at what speed in km/h did they have to walk in order to reach the exit at closing time, at the latest?

STOP AND WAIT FOR FURTHER INSTRUCTIONS

Antonyms

 YOU HAVE 10 MINUTES TO COMPLETE THE FOLLOWING SECTION.

YOU HAVE 25 QUESTIONS TO COMPLETE WITHIN THE TIME GIVEN.

Examples

Example 1

Select the word that is least similar to the following word:

light

A	B	C	D	E
dark	water	feather	bright	hill

The correct answer is A. This has already been marked in Example 1 in the Antonyms section of your answer sheet.

Practice Question 1

Select the word that is least similar to the following word:

smooth

A	B	C	D	E
allow	beneath	rough	whilst	shade

The correct answer is C. Please mark the answer C in Practice Question 1 in the Antonyms section of your answer sheet.

STOP AND WAIT FOR FURTHER INSTRUCTIONS

In each row, select the word from the table that is least similar to the word above the table.

(1) educated

A	B	C	D	E
familiar	uninformed	mourning	forgiveness	unusual

(2) implausible

A	B	C	D	E
nimble	vulgar	frenetic	logical	impossible

(3) pensioner

A	B	C	D	E
proficient	impressionable	draft	infant	inept

(4) bald

A	B	C	D	E
sulk	restriction	flair	custom	hairy

(5) customer

A	B	C	D	E
modest	tradesman	sense	retreat	direct

(6) neglect

A	B	C	D	E
nourish	congeal	outgoing	urgency	refinement

CONTINUE WORKING ⇨

7 glistening

A	B	C	D	E
dull	friendship	gleaming	timely	tangle

8 casual

A	B	C	D	E
digress	slovenly	interior	planned	result

9 occupy

A	B	C	D	E
fickle	vacate	agitated	resort	retrieve

10 invigorated

A	B	C	D	E
receptacle	jovial	tired	slender	vivid

11 compress

A	B	C	D	E
superlative	restrain	mirth	determine	expand

12 debt

A	B	C	D	E
profit	fad	fiscal	verdict	spectre

CONTINUE WORKING

(13) glamorous

A	B	C	D	E
immaterial	plain	commode	majestic	attractive

(14) auxiliary

A	B	C	D	E
prudent	harrowing	main	apprehend	gaunt

(15) uneven

A	B	C	D	E
detested	predictive	merriment	level	revelation

(16) truth

A	B	C	D	E
beg	rumour	parameter	unkempt	gumption

(17) concentrate

A	B	C	D	E
earnest	profanity	dilute	solitude	tendency

(18) subdue

A	B	C	D	E
aggravate	forecast	typical	quell	subtlety

CONTINUE WORKING

19 minute

A	B	C	D	E
estimate	inhibit	timely	colossal	immature

20 demolish

A	B	C	D	E
rotund	destruct	resent	undulation	assemble

21 stable

A	B	C	D	E
equilibrium	imbalanced	jovial	reveal	august

22 love

A	B	C	D	E
fondness	beloved	enamoured	animosity	devotion

23 finale

A	B	C	D	E
elitist	opening	jaunt	conclusion	supreme

24 leader

A	B	C	D	E
tireless	consume	follower	guide	shaded

25 mundane

A	B	C	D	E
recapitulate	severe	drowsy	exciting	innate

STOP AND WAIT FOR FURTHER INSTRUCTIONS ⊗

Non-Verbal Reasoning

 YOU HAVE 8 MINUTES TO COMPLETE THE FOLLOWING SECTION.

YOU HAVE 15 QUESTIONS TO COMPLETE WITHIN THE TIME GIVEN.

EXAMPLES

CUBES Example 1

Look at the cube net.

Select the only cube that could be formed from the net.

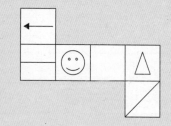

The correct answer is E. This has already been marked in Example 1 in the Non-Verbal Reasoning section of your answer sheet.

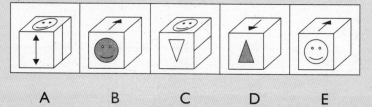

A   B   C   D   E

CUBES Practice Question 1

Look at the cube net.

Select the only cube that could be formed from the net.

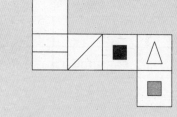

The correct answer is A. Please mark this in Practice Question 1 in the Non-Verbal Reasoning section of your answer sheet.

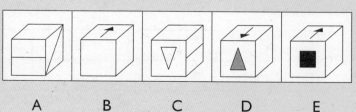

A   B   C   D   E

CONTINUE WORKING

REFLECTION Example 2

Select an image from the row below that shows how the following shape or pattern will appear when reflected.

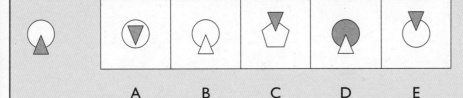

The correct answer is E. This has already been marked in Example 2 in the Non-Verbal Reasoning section of your answer sheet.

REFLECTION Practice Question 2

Select an image from the row below that shows how the following shape or pattern will appear when reflected.

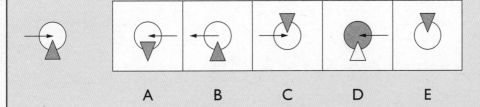

The correct answer is C. Please mark this in Practice Question 2 in the Non-Verbal Reasoning section of your answer sheet.

STOP AND WAIT FOR FURTHER INSTRUCTIONS

(1) Look at the cube net. Select the only cube that could be formed from the net below.

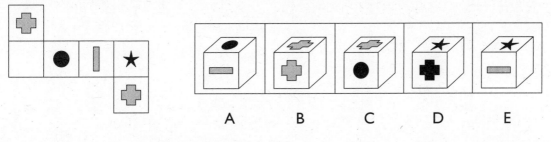

CONTINUE WORKING

(2) Look at the cube net. Select the only cube that could be formed from the net below.

(3) Look at the cube net. Select the only cube that could be formed from the net below.

(4) Look at the cube net. Select the only cube that could be formed from the net below.

(5) Look at the cube net. Select the only cube that could be formed from the net below.

(6) Look at the codes for the following patterns and identify the missing code for the pattern on the far right.

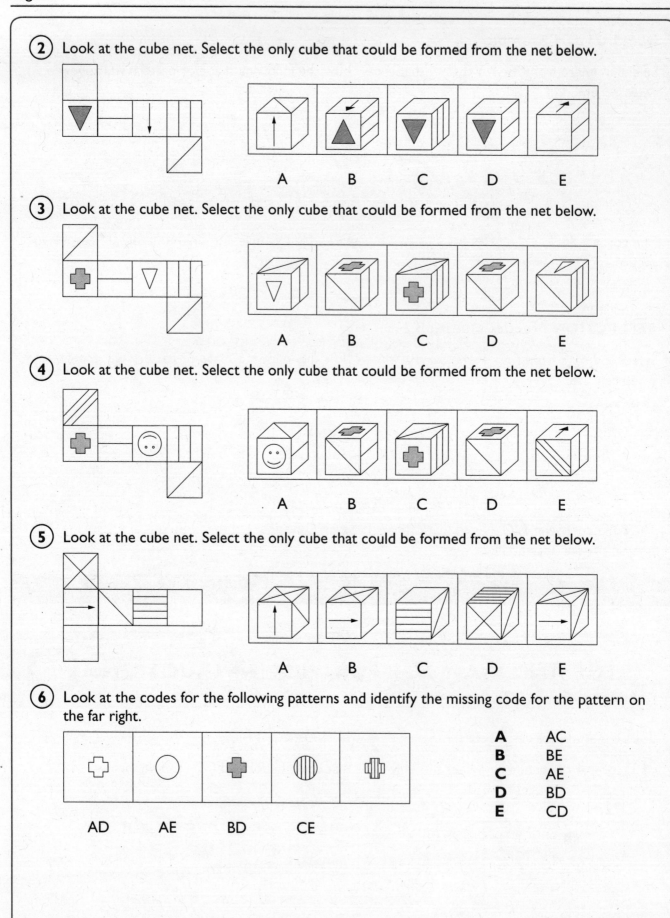

CONTINUE WORKING

(7) Look at the codes for the following patterns and identify the missing code for the pattern on the far right.

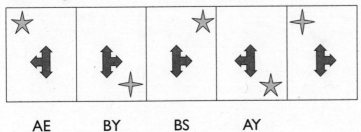

AE   BY   BS   AY

A   BS
B   AS
C   BE
D   AE
E   BY

(8) Look at the codes for the following patterns and identify the missing code for the pattern on the far right.

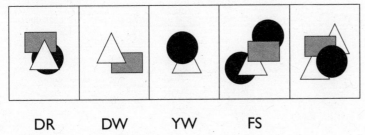

DR   DW   YW   FS

A   YS
B   FS
C   DS
D   DY
E   YR

(9) Look at the codes for the following patterns and identify the missing code for the pattern on the far right.

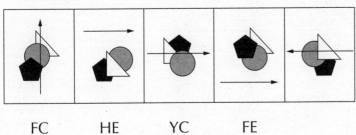

FC   HE   YC   FE

A   HE
B   YC
C   HC
D   FE
E   FY

(10) Look at the codes for the following patterns and identify the missing code for the pattern on the far right.

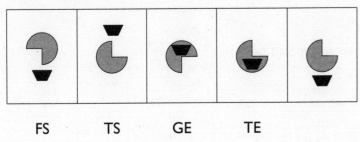

FS   TS   GE   TE

A   TS
B   GE
C   GS
D   FE
E   FS

CONTINUE WORKING ➡

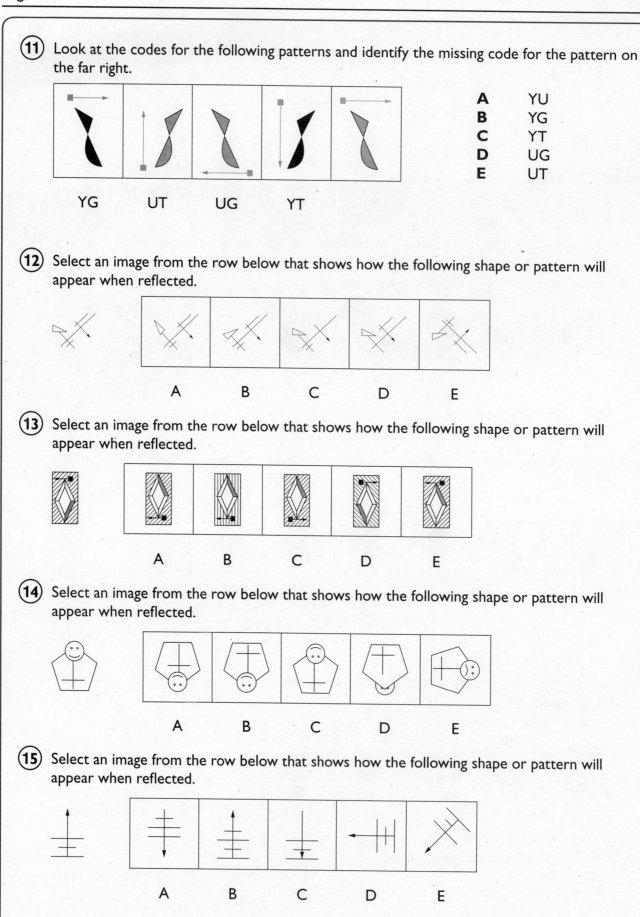

Shuffled Sentences

INSTRUCTIONS

 YOU HAVE 8 MINUTES TO COMPLETE THE FOLLOWING SECTION.

YOU HAVE 15 QUESTIONS TO COMPLETE WITHIN THE TIME GIVEN.

EXAMPLES

Example 1

The following sentence is shuffled and also contains one unnecessary word. Rearrange the sentence correctly, in order to identify the unnecessary word.

dog the ran fetch the to stick gluing.

A	B	C	D	E
gluing	dog	ran	the	stick

The correct answer is A. This has already been marked in Example 1 in the Shuffled Sentences section of your answer sheet.

Practice Question 1

The following sentence is shuffled and also contains one unnecessary word. Rearrange the sentence correctly, in order to identify the unnecessary word.

pushed Emma stood up and closed the table under the chairs.

A	B	C	D	E
chairs	stood	under	closed	Emma

The correct answer is D. Please mark this in Practice Question 1 in the Shuffled Sentences section of your answer sheet.

STOP AND WAIT FOR FURTHER INSTRUCTIONS

Each of the following sentences is shuffled and also contains one unnecessary word.
Rearrange the sentence correctly, in order to identify the unnecessary word.

(1) beautiful sea shelled house overlooking live we but the small a in.

A	B	C	D	E
shelled	a	house	overlooking	the

(2) chimney misty moonlit the stars in twinkled the sky was and air the.

A	B	C	D	E
and	chimney	misty	was	the

(3) unbeatable shop noisy overpriced discounts was advert the stated but the.

A	B	C	D	E
but	was	the	stated	noisy

(4) entrance van site candidly the the of the at parked was.

A	B	C	D	E
the	site	candidly	was	van

(5) hand by mine ancient dug digger was the subterranean

A	B	C	D	E
digger	dug	the	by	hand

(6) sunrise sight stirred emotions tears the of my the.

A	B	C	D	E
the	tears	of	my	sight

(7) in test marks tables achieved boy the full achievement times his.

A	B	C	D	E
to	achieved	achievement	went	tables

CONTINUE WORKING

8 stabilised enforced steel tunnel the with was.

A	B	C	D	E
the	was	tunnel	enforced	with

9 unemployment many problem countries in is a high there.

A	B	C	D	E
there	countries	in	problem	a

10 shone the dazzling sunlight in the packet diamond.

A	B	C	D	E
diamond	shone	in	the	packet

11 bag landed collected he school son as missing was his noticed he that from his.

A	B	C	D	E
his	was	landed	that	from

12 talking questions the the carefully listen have you elongated answer to people to to.

A	B	C	D	E
talking	to	you	the	elongated

13 rounded bag evidence a in the placed he.

A	B	C	D	E
in	placed	a	rounded	he

14 up for let's view hill go the run a.

A	B	C	D	E
let's	view	a	the	for

CONTINUE WORKING ⏵

(15) looked looking plant strange at this look.

A	B	C	D	E
look	at	this	looking	looked

END OF PAPER

Answers to Test C Paper 1

Comprehension

1 C
Verb

2 A
Allotments are very popular

3 E
Allotments require people to spend time and effort.

4 D
Nothing happens

5 B
A busy place

6 A
A large quantity

7 D
Envelop

8 E
Every seven days

9 D
Repel

10 B
Noun

Grammar

1 E
No errors

2 C
she

3 C
got

4 D
is wore out,"

5 E
No errors

6 C
she hurted her leg

7 C
emily realised

8 A
"Lets run

9 D
no further

Numeracy

Q1 E
14, as 7 (a third of 21) is half the number

Q2 C
37, +1 +2 +3 +4 are the differences between consecutive numbers in the sequence

Q3 A
4,1,1,1 as 4 − 1 = 3 in the units column, then in the tens column, the original number must have been 1 which when 1 hundred is borrowed and converted into tens makes the original 1 into 11, and 11 − 8 = 3. The 9 in the hundreds column has now become an 8, so 8 − 7 = 1, and 4 − 0 = 4 in the thousands column.

Q4 E
12 minutes, 8 miles per hour (or 60 minutes) means 1.6 miles will be travelled in 1.6 ÷ 8 × 60 = 12 minutes.

Q5 D
£6, as £24 is the price paid after the discount i.e. 80% of the original price. So 20% must be £24 ÷ 4 = £6.

Q6 B
11, Emily and William are twins, so are the same age (7). Mohammed is 4 years older, 7 + 4 = 11 years old.

Q7 A
$\frac{1}{10}$ m, 101 mm, 10.11 cm, 11 cm, 10 km, as there are 100 cm in 1 m and 1,000 mm in 1 m. Converting all options to cm gives: 10 cm, 10.1 cm, 10.11 cm, 11 cm, 1,000,000 cm

Q8 A
453 − 2 = 452 − 0, as 451 is not the same as 452, and the other answer options are all equal on left and right sides of the equation.

Q9 E
676, as 26 × 20 = 520, and 6 × 26 = 156, 520 + 156 = 676

Q10 D
8.75 midway between 8.5 and 9

Q11 B
1 : 20 p.m. (add 4 hours to get 1 : 25 pm, and then deduct 5 minutes)

Q12 C
$\frac{1}{9}$, as to make the fraction 3 times smaller requires multiplying the denominator by 3.

Q13 *A*

15, 23 + 7 = 30 and half of 30 is 15

Q14 *E*

2,500 m, converted to cm in real life the churches are 0.5 × 500,000 = 250,000 cm apart = 2,500 m (by dividing by 100)

Q15 *D*

520 as there are 1,000 g in 1 kg, so it is necessary to multiply by 1,000.

Q16 *A*

0.77, 1% of 70 is $\frac{1}{100}$ of 70 = 0.7. So 1.1% of 70 is 1.1 times 0.7, or 0.7 + 0.07 = 0.77

Q17 *A*

5, as 5 × 15 = 75

Q18 *D*

basketball, identified by the smallest segment of the chart with the lowest number of children choosing this hobby.

Q19 *A*

3 as the mode is the most frequently occurring piece of data.

Q20 *B*

Australia, which has the second highest number of medals after the UK.

Q21 *A*

3.5, arranging the 10 pieces of data in order of size gives 1,2,3,3,3,4,5,5,7,8 and the median is the middle of this data (in this case the middle of 2 numbers as there is an even number of pieces of data). Halfway between the 5th and 6th pieces of data is 3.5.

Q22 *D*

4.1 as the sum of all of the data is 41. The mean is calculated by dividing this by the number of pieces of data, which gives an answer of 4.1.

Q23 *B*

3 as this is the overlapping section of the data sets.

Q24 *C*

25, i.e. 8 + 5 + 11 + 1 = 25 which is the sum of all numbers outside of the Peugeot set.

Q25 *A*

12, which is 8 + 4, this is represented by the area within the Porsche set but excluding any numbers that may be within the Audi set (so exclude the 5 + 2).

Q26 *D*

2 because they are represented by the overlapping part of all 3 sets.

Q27 *A*

1 represented by the overlapping Audi and Peugeot set which is not within the Porsche set (so need to exclude the 2).

Q28 *E*

3, 9, 3, 5, 5

The sum of the bottom row is 15, so all rows columns and diagonals sum to 15 (as noted in the question). Next calculate c is 3, then e is 5, so d is 5. Then a must be 3, and finally b is 9.

Q29 *B*

100, $99 - \frac{p}{10} = 89$, so $\frac{p}{10}$ must be 10, and so p must be 100.

Q30 *D*

65, dividing the marbles up in the ratio 5:1:1 gives both Julia and Mark 91 divided by 7 (5 + 1 + 1) = 13 marbles each. Mike has 91 ÷ 7 × 5 = 65 marbles.

Q31 *C*

10, as the perimeter is 10b + 1 = 101, so 10b = 100, and b is therefore 10.

Q32 *A*

113.333 (make question easier by multiplying both numbers by 100 to eliminate the decimal point to give 1,700 divided by 15)

Q33 *A*

men 6, women 8, children 29

Women = 43 − 35 = 8, and this means of the 14 adults, 6 must be men, which in turn means that 29 of the 35 men and children are actually children.

Q34 *C*

51 (1 + 5 + 31 + 14 = 51) The 1 must be added in as the dates are inclusive in the question.

Q35 *E*

20.14 as 16.29 add 3 hours and 45 minutes gives 20.14 (could add on 4 hours then subtract 15 minutes).

Q36 *E*

40°

The left triangle is isosceles in which 2 of the angles are 50°, and the other angle is 80°

which is at the bottom right of the triangle. Using the fact that all of the interior angles in the quadrilateral (4 sided shape) sum to 360°, the missing angle is calculated as 360° − 130° − 50° − 50° − 90° = 40°

Q37 C

65°

Angle d is 180° − 100° − 60° = 20°.

So angle c is 70°. So angle e must be 180° − 70° − 45° = 65°

Q38 D

1100

Can work out either the Euro to Pounds exchange rate of 660 ÷ 600 = 1.1 or Dollar to Pound exchange rate of 900 ÷ 600 = 1.5 from the data given in the table.

Use either of these to calculate the number of pounds. 1,210 ÷ 1.1 = 1,100 or 1,650 ÷ 1.5 = 1,100

Q39 A

length 48 cm, width 4 cm

Write length (l) in terms of width (w) to establish perimeter in terms of width,

Perimeter = w + 12w + w + 12w = 26w

Perimeter from question is 104 cm

So 26w = 104

w = 4, so l = 48 (12 × 4)

Alternatively the same method could be followed by writing the width in terms of length, but this may be more challenging.

Synonyms

Q1	E *guarantee*	**Q11**	D *supple*
Q2	D *courteous*	**Q12**	A *wring*
Q3	A *frenzied*	**Q13**	B *neutral*
Q4	D *thrive*	**Q14**	A *eavesdrop*
Q5	A *border*	**Q15**	C *comprehend*
Q6	E *nimbleness*	**Q16**	A *clothing*
Q7	C *unruly*	**Q17**	B *oppose*
Q8	A *artificial*	**Q18**	E *foe*
Q9	A *imperial*	**Q19**	A *deceitful*
Q10	D *masquerade*	**Q20**	D *unravel*

Non-Verbal Reasoning

Q1 D

Alternating circle size, increasing count on horizontal lines, background is diagonal line, foreground circle.

Q2 C

Alternating circle size, increasing count on horizontal lines, small circle should be in the background, with diagonal line in the foreground.

Q3 D

Outer line of five black squares are moving around the outside of the overall grid in an anti-clockwise direction, grey squares moving diagonally towards top left, and striped square always follows grey.

Q4 B

Five triangles and the star are moving anti-clockwise around the overall grid. Alternating outer and inner are solid black triangles and striped triangles. Within triangles are star and grey triangle, again alternating position.

Q5 D

The arrows switch between pointing left and right, as well as alternating between being in the background and foreground in relation to the triangle.

Q6 B

Each row has one grey and one white arrow. These are combined in the other square on each row, with the white always in the foreground and grey in the background. Diagonal from bottom left to top right is sum of other 2 in row, with white in the foreground.

Q7 B

Each column has one of each of the three images featured in the overall grid. The black square is the missing square in the middle column.

Q8 B

Others are reflections or do not include all of the image.

Q9 D

A is a reflection of the image on the left. Must ensure that the dot remains in the same relative position to the arrow when the overall image is rotated.

Answers to Test C Paper 2

Cloze Sentences

Q1 D
dentist, teeth
The dentist took time to reassure me before starting work on my teeth.

Q2 C
Despite, time, guests
Despite the shortfall in numbers, a good time was had by all guests.

Q3 B
weather, recently
They were hoping the weather would be better than it had been recently.

Q4 C
support, nation
The support of the nation was behind the athletes.

Q5 D
depth, sympathy
The depth of sympathy was very much appreciated by the mourners.

Q6 C
ambulance, scene
The ambulance rushed to the scene.

Q7 D
Who, guess
Who would arrive first was anybody's guess.

Q8 C
outcome, imminently
The outcome of the court case was due imminently.

Q9 D
monkey, smiled, camera
The monkey perched on her shoulder and smiled for the camera.

Q10 C
magician, never
How the magician managed to do that, I will never know!

Q11 tin
The flowers were attracting the butterflies.

Q12 lit
The instability of the suspension bridge meant closure was the only option.

Q13 hot
The photocopier had run out of paper.

Q14 den
They were feeling confident as they set out on their expedition.

Q15 pad
They enjoyed paddling their feet in the sea on the hot summer's day.

Q16 low
They decided to meet up the following month.

Q17 Eve
Every little detail had been considered.

Problem Solving

Q1 I
27
There are 15 ÷ 5 × 4 girls = 12 girls and 15 boys = 27 children in the class.

Q2 H
10
Sam is 6 in two years' time, so Sarah will then be 12. Now (two years earlier), Sarah is 10.

Q3 A
53
76 − 23 = 53 children.

Q4 D
£52
27 − 1 = 26 children (excluding Sarah);
6 × £5 + 2 × £2 + (26 − 8) × £1 = £52

Q5 G
9
Floor area = 8 × 4 = 32 square metres. 4 tiles (2 × 2) will fit exactly into each square metre. So 4 × 32 = 128 tiles are required to cover the floor. 128 ÷ 15 = 8 remainder 8, so 9 boxes will be required.

Q6 F
5
60 divided by 12

Q7 E
£41.40
23 × 1.80 = £41.40

Q8 J
£35
Each tube costs 20 × 3.5 = 70p, so 50 tubes cost £35

Q9 B
12
Girls = 174 − 99 = 75, so teachers
= 87 − 75 = 12

Q10 C
£527
Money raised = 123 × £5 = £615 from the
books of tickets. Individual tickets raised a
further 60 × 20p = £12. Total is £615 + £12
= £627. £100 special prize is deducted from
the £627 to leave £527.

Antonyms

Q1	B stale	Q14	E export
Q2	D mobile	Q15	A fade
Q3	E gradual	Q16	A limited
Q4	A crooked	Q17	C increase
Q5	D inferior	Q18	E deny
Q6	C wild	Q19	C inaction
Q7	D enormous	Q20	A clear
Q8	A separate	Q21	C constant
Q9	D occupied	Q22	E displeasure
Q10	E vague	Q23	E disorder
Q11	E worse	Q24	B professional
Q12	B separate	Q25	A foreign
Q13	D discourage		

Non-Verbal Reasoning

Q1 A
BY
First letter relates to whether arrows cross or not, second letter relates to the appearance of the non curved arrow(s).

Q2 D
RS
First letter relates to number of shapes, second letter relates to the number of triangles.

Q3 E
YA
First letter relates to shape at the bottom, second letter relates to the shape at the top.

Q4 B
YA
First letter relates to number of double ended arrows, second letter relates to orientation of the square shape with the arrows coming from it.

Q5 A
Connection is outer arrow is rotated a quarter turn anti-clockwise. Also inner arrow is rotated clockwise.

Q6 A
Large shape turns upside down, dark arrow switches from the right hand side of the large shape to left hand side. Light arrow changes from the top to the bottom, also changes direction from pointing left to pointing right and changes the arrow base from a square to circle.

Q7 C
Outer shape is inverted (reflected in a horizontal line), inner grey shape transforms into a large grey square.

Q8 A
The outer shape is inverted, the middle square has become black and smaller. The cross disappears.

Q9 D
The triangle alternates from top left to bottom right corners, the horizontal arrow moves up the diagonal from bottom left to top right. The other arrows remain vertical.

Q10 C
The arrows rotate anti-clockwise around the perimeter of the square. The number of circles increases and the inner hexagon appears in alternate squares as the sequence progresses.

Q11 C
The triangle moves through the sequence of three shapes, from back to front as the sequence progresses. The triangle will be in the middle of the three shapes in the blank grid. The three shapes are moving around the perimeter of the grid in an anti-clockwise direction.

Q12 A
The arrow moves down the grids as the sequence progresses, alternating between the middle two columns. The pairs of black and grey dots move down and up the grids.

Q13 *D*

The number of sides on the shapes increase in an anti-clockwise direction around the corners of the grid. The sides increase from 3 to 4, to 5 therefore the shape in the top right should have six sides. The shapes in the corners of the diagonals are the same colour, ie the hexagon should be grey.

Q14 *B*

The bottom row and middle row are combined in the top row, with the bottom row being in the foreground and the middle row being in the background.

Q15 *E*

The top and bottom rows combine to make the middle row with the top row in the foreground and bottom row in the background.

Shuffled Sentences

Q1 *A*

an

Debris was strewn across the neighbourhood's streets as a result of last night's storm.

Q2 *A*

whether

The bad weather caused severe delays to flights at the airport.

Q3 *D*

those

This is likely to make a big difference.

Q4 *A*

tree

She decided to leaf through the book whilst in the bookshop

Q5 *D*

although

It was now the responsibility of the parents.

Q6 *B*

there

The scores were all checked to confirm their accuracy.

Q7 *C*

scene

She was astounded by what she had just seen.

Q8 *D*

mirrored

The central location was ideal for them.

Q9 *A*

hanging

The basket was positioned in the hallway.

Q10 *B*

sunk

Several attempts were made to recover the cargo.

Q11 *D*

taken

The journey took three hours by car.

Q12 *A*

kicked

The dress code stipulated formal attire for the annual charity ball.

Q13 *A*

waist

The chest of drawers provided extra storage in the bedroom.

Q14 *D*

must

Use of cameras was prohibited in the theatre.

Q15 *B*

accept

A discount was offered in return for payment in cash.

Answers to Test D Paper 1

Comprehension

1. *C*

Body language and eye movements

2. *E*

To further their career and to bring them success

3. *C*

Misunderstood

4. *D*

The details from the meetings can be easily sent to a significant amount of people.

5. B
The size of mobile phones has reduced and their capabilities have increased.
6. A
A large number of emails are unread or deleted.
7. B
Adjective
8. C
An item that people use in their everyday life
9. A
User-friendly
10. C
Elderly people are being taught how to communicate via social media.

Numeracy

1. D
3004
2. B
23
$144 - 121 = 23$
3. E
98
$294 \div 3 = 98$
4. D
108°
interior + exterior $= 180°$
exterior $= 360 \div 5$ (number of sides) $= 72°$
interior $= 180 - 72 = 108°$
5. C
4
Substitute information in the question:
$4 = 2a - 4$
so rearranged,
$8 = 2a$, and $a = 4$
6. D
1
Substitute information in the question:
$8a - 8 = 0$, so $8a = 8$, and $a = 1$
7. B
5
$15 + ? = 20$, so $? = 5$
8. B
10
$8 \times ? = 72 + 8$
$8 \times ? = 80$
$? = 10$

9. E
15
$? + 15 = 30$
$? = 15$
10. C
2
1 roll costs $£1.50 \times 3 = £4.50$
For £10, I can buy 2 rolls costing £9 and I will have £1 left over.
11. E
1 in 6
The number the die lands on does not depend on the previous throws, and there are 6 faces which are equally likely for the die to land on.
12. A
16
$5 + 22 - 11 = 16$
13. B
5
15 would like pizza. Of the 15 pizza slices, one-third were not eaten, so 5 remain.
14. C
35
From right to left, the sequence increases by an increasing amount, with each difference being 1 higher than the last. Differences are 2, 3, 4, 5 so next is a difference of 6 (added onto 29 to give 35).
15. C
26
16. B
8
56 divided by 7 = 8
17. D
96
Headlines are shown 4 times per hour,
4×24 (hours in a day) $= 96$
18. A
1.6
Difference is doubling between each consecutive pair of numbers in the sequence. Next difference is 0.8.
19. B
one-fifth of 160
In order of answers: 31, 32, 31.5, 31, 31.33
20. E
9
$5 - 3 + 7 = 9$
21. D
57
Range is highest less the lowest $= 81 - 24 = 57$

22. A

52.5

Mean is the sum of the data, divided by the number of pieces of data = 420 ÷ 8 = 52.5

23. C

58.5

Find middle data value when arranged in size order:

24, 24, 34, 53, 64, 68, 72, 81 so halfway between 53 and 64, which is 117 ÷ 2 = 58.5

24. C

40

25. A

2006–2012

Need to find the only 2 years listed in the answers between which the % of the higher value is 5 times that of the lower.

26. E

2012–2013

27. C

32 and $\frac{1}{3}$

Divide the sum of the data by 9 (the number of pieces of data).

291 ÷ 9 = 32.333

28. D

89

One additional year means there are now 10 years. This means that as the mean is 38, the total of all 10 years data must be 10 x 38 = 380. After 9 years, the sum was 291, so the 10th year (2014) must be 380 − 291 = 89% of children.

Synonyms

1. **B** routinely	11. **A** hurry
2. **D** distort	12. **E** amount
3. **A** vitality	13. **B** devour
4. **E** unfold	14. **E** civilised
5. **B** remember	15. **E** happy
6. **B** company	16. **B** emanate
7. **C** classic	17. **C** polite
8. **E** admission	18. **D** tranquil
9. **B** spirited	19. **B** lessen
10. **D** gratitude	20. **C** series

Non-Verbal Reasoning

1. B

This is a half turn of the original image.

2. D

This is a quarter turn anticlockwise of the original image.

3. C

The only answer where closing the shapes together does not make a hexagon.

4. B

The only answer where the rectangle and the shape it leads into are not the same shade. (There is shading on one of the triangles, but not on the rectangle.)

5. B

The only answer where the rectangles do not join at the ends – one joins another rectangle in the middle.

6. B

The only answer where there are not black, grey and white shapes.

7. E

The only answer where closing the shapes together makes a 3-sided shape, rather than a quadrilateral. E is also the only image made up of different-sized shapes.

8. E

The only answer where there is not a white shape inside.

9. A

The only answer where there is not a grey triangle in the background.

10. B

The only answer where the arrow does not point to the left.

11. D

The only answer where the stem is in background, and flower in foreground.

12. B

The only answer where the arrow is rotating anticlockwise.

13. B

14. C

15. D

Answers to Test D Paper 2

Cloze Sentences

1. **F**
   The blood was **extracted** from the ancient specimen.
2. **G**
   The judge's **ruling** was final.
3. **E**
   The **subterranean** cave was dark and cold.
4. **I**
   The parking signs gave the residents **ample** warning that the road would close at midnight.
5. **C**
   The work was painstaking and **laborious.**
6. **D**
   The animal's limb was **fractured** in several places.
7. **J**
   The journey came to an end and the **adventure** was over.
8. **A**
   The film was a **fantastical** story, set in space.
9. **H**
   The athlete's dedication to her training had set a high **standard.**
10. **B**
    After a day of walking in the mountains, the boy felt **dehydrated.**
11. **rim**
    The hairdresser **trim**med the girl's hair.
12. **cap**
    The lands**cap**e was rugged.
13. **son**
    The project failed for one rea**son.**
14. **bat**
    The boy **bat**hed in the glorious sunshine.
15. **oil**
    The girl's clothes were sp**oil**ed when she splashed in the mud.
16. **are**
    Does this car have a sp**are** tyre?
17. **pin**
    The s**pin**e of the book had broken and all the pages had fallen out.

Problem Solving

1. **C**
   8
   $\frac{3}{4}$ of 12 = 9, 9 − 2 = 7, plus Edward equals 8
2. **D**
   10
   $\left(\frac{3}{4} \text{ of } 12 + 1\right)$
3. **H**
   £84
   10 + 2 = 12 × 7 = £84
4. **I**
   £94
5. **B**
   £104
   (8.50 × 10) + (9.50 × 2)
6. **E**
   1 hour and 35 minutes = 95 minutes
7. **G**
   85
   68 + 12 − 13 + 18 = 85
8. **F**
   7
   85 from previous question less 78 = 7
9. **A**
   35
10. **J**
    4
    1 km in 15 minutes is the same as walking at 4 km/h as 1 hour is 60 minutes, and in 60 minutes they would cover 4 km.

Antonyms

1. **B** uninformed
2. **D** logical
3. **D** infant
4. **E** hairy
5. **B** tradesman
6. **A** nourish
7. **A** dull
8. **D** planned
9. **B** vacate
10. **C** tired
11. **E** expand
12. **A** profit
13. **B** plain
14. **C** main
15. **D** level
16. **B** rumour
17. **C** dilute
18. **A** aggravate

19. **D** *colossal*
20. **E** *assemble*
21. **B** *imbalanced*
22. **D** *animosity*

23. **B** *opening*
24. **C** *follower*
25. **D** *exciting*

Non-Verbal Reasoning

1. **C**
   Net requires half-turn rotation, use the cross that will then be on top.
2. **D**
   No rotation of net required.
3. **B**
   No rotation of net required.
4. **A**
   Net requires half-turn rotation.
5. **D**
   Net requires half-turn rotation.
6. **E**
   CD The first letter relates to the shading. The second letter relates to the shape.
7. **C**
   BE The first letter relates to the position of the arrows. The second letter relates to the position of the star.
8. **A**
   YS The first letter relates to the shape in the foreground. The second letter relates to the number of shapes.
9. **C**
   HC The first letter relates to the shape in the foreground. The second letter relates to whether the arrow crosses the shapes.
10. **A**
    TS The first letter relates to the position of the $\frac{3}{4}$ circle. The second letter relates to whether the trapezium overlaps the $\frac{3}{4}$ circle.
11. **D**
    UG The first letter relates to the shading of the shape. The second letter relates to the position of the shape. The arrows are irrelevant.
12. **E**
    Reflection in a horizontal line.
13. **D**
    Reflection in a vertical line.
14. **B**
    Reflection in a horizontal line.
15. **D**
    Reflection in a diagonal line to the top right or bottom left of the image.

Shuffled Sentences

1. **A**
   shelled
   We live in a small but beautiful house overlooking the sea.
2. **B**
   chimney
   The stars twinkled in the moonlit sky and the air was misty.
3. **E**
   noisy
   The advert stated unbeatable discounts but the shop was overpriced.
4. **C**
   candidly
   The van was parked at the entrance of the site.
5. **A**
   digger
   The ancient subterranean mine was dug by hand.
6. **B**
   tears
   The sight of the sunrise stirred my emotions.
7. **C**
   achievement
   The boy achieved full marks in his times tables test.
   The words 'to' and 'went' do not appear in the shuffled sentence and can be eliminated immediately.
8. **D**
   enforced
   The tunnel was stabilised with steel.
9. **A**
   there
   High unemployment is a problem in many countries.

10. E
packet
The diamond shone in the dazzling sunlight.

11. C
landed
As he collected his son from school he noticed that his bag was missing.

12. E
elongated
You have to listen carefully to the people talking to answer the questions.

13. D
rounded
He placed the evidence in a bag.

14. B
view
Let's go for a run up the hill.

15. E
looked
Look at this strange looking plant.

THIS PAGE HAS DELIBERATELY BEEN LEFT BLANK

Pupil's Full Name:

Instructions:
Mark the boxes correctly like this ⬛

Please sign your name here:

Comprehension

Example 1

| A̶ | B | C | D | E |

Practice Question 1

| A | B | C | D | E |

	A	B	C	D	E
1	A	B	C	D	E
2	A	B	C	D	E
3	A	B	C	D	E
4	A	B	C	D	E
5	A	B	C	D	E
6	A	B	C	D	E
7	A	B	C	D	E
8	A	B	C	D	E
9	A	B	C	D	E
10	A	B	C	D	E

Grammar

Example 1

| A | B | C | D | E̶ |

Practice Question 1

| A | B | C | D | E |

	A	B	C	D	E
1	A	B	C	D	E
2	A	B	C	D	E
3	A	B	C	D	E
4	A	B	C	D	E
5	A	B	C	D	E
6	A	B	C	D	E
7	A	B	C	D	E
8	A	B	C	D	E
9	A	B	C	D	E

Numeracy

Example 1

| A | B | C | D | E̶ |

Practice Question 1

| A | B | C | D | E |

	A	B	C	D	E
1	A	B	C	D	E
2	A	B	C	D	E
3	A	B	C	D	E
4	A	B	C	D	E
5	A	B	C	D	E
6	A	B	C	D	E
7	A	B	C	D	E
8	A	B	C	D	E
9	A	B	C	D	E
10	A	B	C	D	E
11	A	B	C	D	E
12	A	B	C	D	E
13	A	B	C	D	E
14	A	B	C	D	E
15	A	B	C	D	E
16	A	B	C	D	E
17	A	B	C	D	E
18	A	B	C	D	E
19	A	B	C	D	E
20	A	B	C	D	E
21	A	B	C	D	E
22	A	B	C	D	E
23	A	B	C	D	E
24	A	B	C	D	E
25	A	B	C	D	E
26	A	B	C	D	E
27	A	B	C	D	E
28	A	B	C	D	E
29	A	B	C	D	E
30	A	B	C	D	E
31	A	B	C	D	E
32	A	B	C	D	E

33	Ⓐ	Ⓑ	Ⓒ	Ⓓ	Ⓔ
34	Ⓐ	Ⓑ	Ⓒ	Ⓓ	Ⓔ
35	Ⓐ	Ⓑ	Ⓒ	Ⓓ	Ⓔ
36	Ⓐ	Ⓑ	Ⓒ	Ⓓ	Ⓔ
37	Ⓐ	Ⓑ	Ⓒ	Ⓓ	Ⓔ
38	Ⓐ	Ⓑ	Ⓒ	Ⓓ	Ⓔ
39	Ⓐ	Ⓑ	Ⓒ	Ⓓ	Ⓔ

Synonyms

Example 1

| | Ⓐ | Ⓑ | Ⓒ | Ⓓ | Ⓔ |

Practice Question 1

	Ⓐ	Ⓑ	Ⓒ	Ⓓ	Ⓔ
1	Ⓐ	Ⓑ	Ⓒ	Ⓓ	Ⓔ
2	Ⓐ	Ⓑ	Ⓒ	Ⓓ	Ⓔ
3	Ⓐ	Ⓑ	Ⓒ	Ⓓ	Ⓔ
4	Ⓐ	Ⓑ	Ⓒ	Ⓓ	Ⓔ
5	Ⓐ	Ⓑ	Ⓒ	Ⓓ	Ⓔ
6	Ⓐ	Ⓑ	Ⓒ	Ⓓ	Ⓔ
7	Ⓐ	Ⓑ	Ⓒ	Ⓓ	Ⓔ
8	Ⓐ	Ⓑ	Ⓒ	Ⓓ	Ⓔ
9	Ⓐ	Ⓑ	Ⓒ	Ⓓ	Ⓔ
10	Ⓐ	Ⓑ	Ⓒ	Ⓓ	Ⓔ
11	Ⓐ	Ⓑ	Ⓒ	Ⓓ	Ⓔ
12	Ⓐ	Ⓑ	Ⓒ	Ⓓ	Ⓔ
13	Ⓐ	Ⓑ	Ⓒ	Ⓓ	Ⓔ
14	Ⓐ	Ⓑ	Ⓒ	Ⓓ	Ⓔ
15	Ⓐ	Ⓑ	Ⓒ	Ⓓ	Ⓔ
16	Ⓐ	Ⓑ	Ⓒ	Ⓓ	Ⓔ
17	Ⓐ	Ⓑ	Ⓒ	Ⓓ	Ⓔ
18	Ⓐ	Ⓑ	Ⓒ	Ⓓ	Ⓔ
19	Ⓐ	Ⓑ	Ⓒ	Ⓓ	Ⓔ
20	Ⓐ	Ⓑ	Ⓒ	Ⓓ	Ⓔ

Non-Verbal Reasoning

COMPLETE THE SEQUENCE
Example 1

| | Ⓐ | Ⓑ | Ⓒ | Ⓓ | Ⓔ |

COMPLETE THE SEQUENCE
Practice Question 1

| | Ⓐ | Ⓑ | Ⓒ | Ⓓ | Ⓔ |

ROTATION Example 2

| | Ⓐ | Ⓑ | Ⓒ | Ⓓ | Ⓔ |

ROTATION Practice Question 2

	Ⓐ	Ⓑ	Ⓒ	Ⓓ	Ⓔ
1	Ⓐ	Ⓑ	Ⓒ	Ⓓ	Ⓔ
2	Ⓐ	Ⓑ	Ⓒ	Ⓓ	Ⓔ
3	Ⓐ	Ⓑ	Ⓒ	Ⓓ	Ⓔ
4	Ⓐ	Ⓑ	Ⓒ	Ⓓ	Ⓔ
5	Ⓐ	Ⓑ	Ⓒ	Ⓓ	Ⓔ
6	Ⓐ	Ⓑ	Ⓒ	Ⓓ	Ⓔ
7	Ⓐ	Ⓑ	Ⓒ	Ⓓ	Ⓔ
8	Ⓐ	Ⓑ	Ⓒ	Ⓓ	Ⓔ
9	Ⓐ	Ⓑ	Ⓒ	Ⓓ	Ⓔ

Test C Paper 2

Pupil's Full Name:

2

Instructions:
Mark the boxes correctly like this ➵

Please sign your name here:

Cloze Sentences

Example 1

Ⓐ   Ⓑ   Ⓒ   ~~D~~   Ⓔ

Practice Question 1

Ⓐ   Ⓑ   Ⓒ   Ⓓ   Ⓔ

Example 2 _____ *ten* _____

Practice Question 2 _____

1	Ⓐ	Ⓑ	Ⓒ	Ⓓ	Ⓔ
2	Ⓐ	Ⓑ	Ⓒ	Ⓓ	Ⓔ
3	Ⓐ	Ⓑ	Ⓒ	Ⓓ	Ⓔ
4	Ⓐ	Ⓑ	Ⓒ	Ⓓ	Ⓔ
5	Ⓐ	Ⓑ	Ⓒ	Ⓓ	Ⓔ
6	Ⓐ	Ⓑ	Ⓒ	Ⓓ	Ⓔ
7	Ⓐ	Ⓑ	Ⓒ	Ⓓ	Ⓔ
8	Ⓐ	Ⓑ	Ⓒ	Ⓓ	Ⓔ
9	Ⓐ	Ⓑ	Ⓒ	Ⓓ	Ⓔ
10	Ⓐ	Ⓑ	Ⓒ	Ⓓ	Ⓔ

11 _____
12 _____
13 _____
14 _____
15 _____
16 _____
17 _____

Problem Solving

Example 1

★ Ⓑ Ⓒ Ⓓ Ⓔ Ⓕ Ⓖ Ⓗ Ⓘ Ⓙ

Practice Question 1

Ⓐ Ⓑ Ⓒ Ⓓ Ⓔ Ⓕ Ⓖ Ⓗ Ⓘ Ⓙ

1	Ⓐ	Ⓑ	Ⓒ	Ⓓ	Ⓔ	Ⓕ	Ⓖ	Ⓗ	Ⓘ	Ⓙ
2	Ⓐ	Ⓑ	Ⓒ	Ⓓ	Ⓔ	Ⓕ	Ⓖ	Ⓗ	Ⓘ	Ⓙ
3	Ⓐ	Ⓑ	Ⓒ	Ⓓ	Ⓔ	Ⓕ	Ⓖ	Ⓗ	Ⓘ	Ⓙ
4	Ⓐ	Ⓑ	Ⓒ	Ⓓ	Ⓔ	Ⓕ	Ⓖ	Ⓗ	Ⓘ	Ⓙ
5	Ⓐ	Ⓑ	Ⓒ	Ⓓ	Ⓔ	Ⓕ	Ⓖ	Ⓗ	Ⓘ	Ⓙ
6	Ⓐ	Ⓑ	Ⓒ	Ⓓ	Ⓔ	Ⓕ	Ⓖ	Ⓗ	Ⓘ	Ⓙ
7	Ⓐ	Ⓑ	Ⓒ	Ⓓ	Ⓔ	Ⓕ	Ⓖ	Ⓗ	Ⓘ	Ⓙ
8	Ⓐ	Ⓑ	Ⓒ	Ⓓ	Ⓔ	Ⓕ	Ⓖ	Ⓗ	Ⓘ	Ⓙ
9	Ⓐ	Ⓑ	Ⓒ	Ⓓ	Ⓔ	Ⓕ	Ⓖ	Ⓗ	Ⓘ	Ⓙ
10	Ⓐ	Ⓑ	Ⓒ	Ⓓ	Ⓔ	Ⓕ	Ⓖ	Ⓗ	Ⓘ	Ⓙ

© 2015 The 11 Plus Tutoring Academy

Antonyms

Example 1

	A	B	C	D	E
	~~A~~	B	C	D	E

Practice Question 1

	A	B	C	D	E
1	A	B	C	D	E
2	A	B	C	D	E
3	A	B	C	D	E
4	A	B	C	D	E
5	A	B	C	D	E
6	A	B	C	D	E
7	A	B	C	D	E
8	A	B	C	D	E
9	A	B	C	D	E
10	A	B	C	D	E
11	A	B	C	D	E
12	A	B	C	D	E
13	A	B	C	D	E
14	A	B	C	D	E
15	A	B	C	D	E
16	A	B	C	D	E
17	A	B	C	D	E
18	A	B	C	D	E
19	A	B	C	D	E
20	A	B	C	D	E
21	A	B	C	D	E
22	A	B	C	D	E
23	A	B	C	D	E
24	A	B	C	D	E
25	A	B	C	D	E

Non – Verbal Reasoning

CODES Example 1

	A	B	C	D	E
	A	B	C	D	~~E~~

CODES Practice Question 1

	A	B	C	D	E

COMPLETE THE SQUARE Example 2

	A	B	C	D	E
	A	B	C	~~D~~	E

COMPLETE THE SQUARE Practice Question 2

	A	B	C	D	E
1	A	B	C	D	E
2	A	B	C	D	E

	A	B	C	D	E
3	A	B	C	D	E
4	A	B	C	D	E
5	A	B	C	D	E
6	A	B	C	D	E
7	A	B	C	D	E
8	A	B	C	D	E
9	A	B	C	D	E
10	A	B	C	D	E
11	A	B	C	D	E
12	A	B	C	D	E
13	A	B	C	D	E
14	A	B	C	D	E
15	A	B	C	D	E

Shuffled Sentences

Example 1

	A	B	C	D	E
	~~A~~	B	C	D	E

Practice Questions 1

	A	B	C	D	E
1	A	B	C	D	E
2	A	B	C	D	E
3	A	B	C	D	E
4	A	B	C	D	E
5	A	B	C	D	E
6	A	B	C	D	E
7	A	B	C	D	E
8	A	B	C	D	E
9	A	B	C	D	E
10	A	B	C	D	E
11	A	B	C	D	E
12	A	B	C	D	E
13	A	B	C	D	E
14	A	B	C	D	E
15	A	B	C	D	E

Pupil's Full Name:

Instructions:
Mark the boxes correctly like this ━

Please sign your name here:

Comprehension

Example 1

| A | B | C | D | E |

Practice Question 1

| A | B | C | D | E |

	A	B	C	D	E
1	A	B	C	D	E
2	A	B	C	D	E
3	A	B	C	D	E
4	A	B	C	D	E
5	A	B	C	D	E
6	A	B	C	D	E
7	A	B	C	D	E
8	A	B	C	D	E
9	A	B	C	D	E
10	A	B	C	D	E

Numeracy

Example 1

| A | B | C | D | E |

Practice Question 1

| A | B | C | D | E |

	A	B	C	D	E
1	A	B	C	D	E
2	A	B	C	D	E
3	A	B	C	D	E
4	A	B	C	D	E
5	A	B	C	D	E
6	A	B	C	D	E
7	A	B	C	D	E
8	A	B	C	D	E
9	A	B	C	D	E
10	A	B	C	D	E

	A	B	C	D	E
11	A	B	C	D	E
12	A	B	C	D	E
13	A	B	C	D	E
14	A	B	C	D	E
15	A	B	C	D	E
16	A	B	C	D	E
17	A	B	C	D	E
18	A	B	C	D	E
19	A	B	C	D	E
20	A	B	C	D	E
21	A	B	C	D	E
22	A	B	C	D	E
23	A	B	C	D	E
24	A	B	C	D	E
25	A	B	C	D	E
26	A	B	C	D	E
27	A	B	C	D	E
28	A	B	C	D	E

Synonyms

Example 1

	A	B	C	D	E

Practice Question 1

	A	B	C	D	E
1	A	B	C	D	E
2	A	B	C	D	E
3	A	B	C	D	E
4	A	B	C	D	E
5	A	B	C	D	E
6	A	B	C	D	E
7	A	B	C	D	E
8	A	B	C	D	E
9	A	B	C	D	E
10	A	B	C	D	E
11	A	B	C	D	E
12	A	B	C	D	E
13	A	B	C	D	E
14	A	B	C	D	E
15	A	B	C	D	E
16	A	B	C	D	E
17	A	B	C	D	E
18	A	B	C	D	E
19	A	B	C	D	E
20	A	B	C	D	E

Non-Verbal Reasoning

REFLECTION Example 1

	A	B	C	D	E

REFLECTION Practice Question 1

	A	B	C	D	E

ROTATION Example 2

	A	B	C	D	E

ROTATION Practice Question 2

	A	B	C	D	E

LEAST SIMILAR Example 3

	A	B	C	D	E

LEAST SIMILAR Practice Question 3

	A	B	C	D	E
1	A	B	C	D	E
2	A	B	C	D	E
3	A	B	C	D	E
4	A	B	C	D	E
5	A	B	C	D	E
6	A	B	C	D	E
7	A	B	C	D	E
8	A	B	C	D	E
9	A	B	C	D	E
10	A	B	C	D	E
11	A	B	C	D	E
12	A	B	C	D	E
13	A	B	C	D	E
14	A	B	C	D	E
15	A	B	C	D	E

Pupil's Full Name:

2

Instructions:
Mark the boxes correctly like this ⬛

Please sign your name here:

Cloze Sentences

Example 1

Ⓐ B C D E F G H I J

Practice Question 1

A B C D E F G H I J

Example 2 _____ ten _____

Practice Question 2 _____

1	A	B	C	D	E	F	G	H	I	J
2	A	B	C	D	E	F	G	H	I	J
3	A	B	C	D	E	F	G	H	I	J
4	A	B	C	D	E	F	G	H	I	J
5	A	B	C	D	E	F	G	H	I	J
6	A	B	C	D	E	F	G	H	I	J
7	A	B	C	D	E	F	G	H	I	J
8	A	B	C	D	E	F	G	H	I	J
9	A	B	C	D	E	F	G	H	I	J
10	A	B	C	D	E	F	G	H	I	J

11 _____
12 _____
13 _____
14 _____
15 _____
16 _____
17 _____

Problem Solving

Example 1

Ⓐ B C D E F G H I J

Practice Question 1

A B C D E F G H I J

1	A	B	C	D	E	F	G	H	I	J
2	A	B	C	D	E	F	G	H	I	J
3	A	B	C	D	E	F	G	H	I	J
4	A	B	C	D	E	F	G	H	I	J
5	A	B	C	D	E	F	G	H	I	J
6	A	B	C	D	E	F	G	H	I	J
7	A	B	C	D	E	F	G	H	I	J
8	A	B	C	D	E	F	G	H	I	J
9	A	B	C	D	E	F	G	H	I	J
10	A	B	C	D	E	F	G	H	I	J

Antonyms

Example 1

	A	B	C	D	E
	~~A~~	B	C	D	E

Practice Question 1

	A	B	C	D	E
	A	B	C	D	E
1	A	B	C	D	E
2	A	B	C	D	E
3	A	B	C	D	E
4	A	B	C	D	E
5	A	B	C	D	E
6	A	B	C	D	E
7	A	B	C	D	E
8	A	B	C	D	E
9	A	B	C	D	E
10	A	B	C	D	E
11	A	B	C	D	E
12	A	B	C	D	E
13	A	B	C	D	E
14	A	B	C	D	E
15	A	B	C	D	E
16	A	B	C	D	E
17	A	B	C	D	E
18	A	B	C	D	E
19	A	B	C	D	E
20	A	B	C	D	E
21	A	B	C	D	E
22	A	B	C	D	E
23	A	B	C	D	E
24	A	B	C	D	E
25	A	B	C	D	E

Non – Verbal Reasoning

CUBES Example 1

	A	B	C	D	E
	A	B	C	D	~~E~~

CUBES Practice Question 1

	A	B	C	D	E
	A	B	C	D	E

REFLECTION Example 2

	A	B	C	D	E
	A	B	C	D	~~E~~

REFLECTION Practice Question 2

	A	B	C	D	E
	A	B	C	D	E
1	A	B	C	D	E
2	A	B	C	D	E
3	A	B	C	D	E

4	A	B	C	D	E
5	A	B	C	D	E
6	A	B	C	D	E
7	A	B	C	D	E
8	A	B	C	D	E
9	A	B	C	D	E
10	A	B	C	D	E
11	A	B	C	D	E
12	A	B	C	D	E
13	A	B	C	D	E
14	A	B	C	D	E
15	A	B	C	D	E

Shuffled Sentences

Example 1

	A	B	C	D	E
	~~A~~	B	C	D	E

Practice Questions 1

	A	B	C	D	E
	A	B	C	D	E
1	A	B	C	D	E
2	A	B	C	D	E
3	A	B	C	D	E
4	A	B	C	D	E
5	A	B	C	D	E
6	A	B	C	D	E
7	A	B	C	D	E
8	A	B	C	D	E
9	A	B	C	D	E
10	A	B	C	D	E
11	A	B	C	D	E
12	A	B	C	D	E
13	A	B	C	D	E
14	A	B	C	D	E
15	A	B	C	D	E